Handbook of Fashion Design and Technology

Handbook of Fashion Design and Technology

Parul Gupta

MD Publications Pvt Ltd
New Delhi

Published by
MD Publications Pvt Ltd
"MD House", 11, Darya Ganj
New Delhi-110002
Tel. : +91-11-41563325, 41562846
E-mail : contact@mdppl.com
Website : www.mdppl.com

ISBN: 978-81-7533-123-5

PRICE: Rs. 995.00

Published and Printed by **MD Publications Pvt Ltd** at Times Press,
910, Jatwara Street, Darya Ganj, New Delhi.

Contents

PREFACE

Fashion has a very strong influence on the attitudes and actions of people. This is particularly so with regard to diet and exercise. The predominant fashion in Western cultures is for women to have slim, almost boyish looks. Being slim has not always been fashionable. One has only to look at a Rubens painting to realize that his feminine ideal was a plump, curvaceous woman. It is unclear whether the fashion industry originally created the trend for slimness or merely followed it. Fashion designers have been accused of creating the cult of the super-thin model, reinforcing the desire for thinness. In order to follow the fashions worn by models, many women have needlessly subjected themselves to weight-loss diets and exercise regimes, not to keep fit and healthy, but to look acceptable. Not surprisingly, this has led to many impressionable young women going to extreme lengths to achieve their goal. An increase in the incidence of the eating disorders, anorexia and bulimia, have followed this fashion for thinness.

Until recently, apart from a few advertisements for body building, men were not under the same pressure as women to achieve a particular body shape. However, this has changed with the advent of mass parties where it is fashionable for young men to display their naked upper torsos. Consequently, there is an increasing trend for men to use artificial aids, especially anabolic steroids, to build bodies with well defined muscles.

The 1970s and 80s saw the beginning of more divergent trends in fashion. This was the result of the increasing popularity of ready-to-wear collections by major designers, which made fashionable label-conscious dressing possible for the middle class. Ethnic-inspired looks and the punk style enjoyed a period of popularity. The look of luxuriance that emerged in the 1980s was countered in the 1990s with the production of classic understated clothes.

Fashion designers, especially in the period from the 1920s onwards, diversified into ranges of ready-to-wear garments, scent, and cosmetics. Specialist suppliers of accessories became equally aware of the possibilities inherent in designer footwear; jewellery, luggage and much more. Ultimately, as both compliment and curse, talented copyists ignored patent law to produce cheap facsimiles of the most luxurious labels, and, within the law, chain stores 'imitated' the latest suit, dress, shoe, or scarf, to offer affordable fashion to mass markets.

And, to a degree, alternative fashion is about men reasserting their right to attention through the adoption of unusual, exotic, or bizarre forms of dress. Ironically, these so-called street fashions have in turn, influenced the expensive, handmade creations of the powerful fashion designers.

Today, so we are led to believe, we can create our own fashion statements by buying across the spectrum from charity shops to couture houses. Fashion is fun, it is adventurous, it defines us and our approach to life. In fact, the majority prefer to conform to the dress codes of their social group, accepting or rejecting the dictates of fashion according to their circumstances and means.

I express my gratitude and thanks to all my colleagues and scholars whose works I have consulted in compilation of this book. I would also like to thanks Mr. Pranav Gupta of **MD Publications Pvt. Ltd.**, New Delhi for the elegant and timely production of this book.

Parul Gupta

1

Fashion Design: Definition and Meaning

Introduction

It struck me at the time that very little, if anything, was known about the working lives or careers of this kind of worker. In addition, I was slightly puzzled by the immediate equation Murray made between being a designer and designing for capitalism. The designers I knew personally, including the fashion designers, rarely saw themselves in this way. The extent to which notions of art, creativity and culture intruded upon and defined their practices as designers produced, at the very least, a sense of tension between themselves and the world of business. Clearly there are many different types of 'designer', from the art directors of the big advertising agencies for whom designing is indeed about selling commodities, to the small scale fashion designer for whom design work often seems to be at odds with what the market wants, to people like the graphic designer, Neville Brody, whose work throughout the 1980s could be seen in magazines like The Face and the left wing New Socialist. Figures like Brody and designers like, for example, Pam Hogg, seemed to me to be more ambivalently poised in relation to working for capitalism and it was this tension which I wanted to explore in greater depth.

There was also an underlying political motive in pursuing a study of fashion designers, as a case study of the 'new cultural worker'. Left-wing thinking at the time was only able to interpret this kind of work in one of two ways. The first argued that these were 'Thatcher's children', prime examples of the 'enterprise culture', who would fufil the Tory dreams of rebuilding British society along highly individualist lines. These would be self-reliant young men and women who would literally embody the virtues of 'going it alone' and 'fending for yourself without the support of the 'Nanny State'. For the left, people like these could only be seen as Tory supporters, new anti-union 'Yuppies', deeply intertwined and committed to the consumer culture for whom they provided the fancy wrapping paper. In contrast, the second approach suggested instead that they were simply fodder. They had been fed the jargon of enterprise and the joys of 'being your own boss' and then shoved into the cold and left to fend for themselves and, as a result, were working longer hours than even a nineteenth century employer could expect of his workforce. More fool them! These would be the middle class or professional equivalent of the newly casual and flexible workers described by Anna Pollert as being encouraged repeatedly during this period to 'live with insecurity and learn to love it'. Neither of these characterisations seemed to me to be convincing or adequate as accounts of the 'cultural intermediaries' who were entering, or rather, creating their own labour market throughout this decade.

My interest in providing a fuller account of these kinds of careers was motivated by both a sociological and a political concern. The absence of documentation of this kind of work in sociology or in cultural studies meant that political commentary was inevitably speculative. My reservations about consigning such workers to the camp of the new right, and thus ignoring them as potential allies, were based on a commitment on my part to attempting to build political bridges and draw different kinds of workers into the political processes, something that seemed all the more urgent in the face of the strong right wing government of the time, and the dwindling impact of the left. But the experience of teaching students who would become part of this creative workforce also led me to rather different conclusions from the mainstream left. In practice they showed few signs of embracing the language of Thatcherism. Although their education and social identities did, by and large, give them a more individualist outlook (not unusual for arts or media students) than their 1960s or 1970s counterparts who were more thoroughly 'subjectivised' by the statist discourses of 'the social' and by the prospect of careers in the public sector, this did not turn them into rampant That cherites. Many came from disadvantaged social backgrounds, some were gay or lesbian. There was also an increasing flow of young people from different ethnic backgrounds into higher education, particularly into the new universities and the art colleges throughout the 1980s.

All the experiences we now associate with the social dislocation of Britain in the late 1970s and 1980s had also made some impact upon these young people. They grew up in different types of families, and were certainly not going to be party to the demonisation of single mothers conducted by the Tory press during this time. Many had parents who were unemployed and were unlikely to work again, others were struggling with the difficulties of coming out as gay or lesbian. In every respect, the old structures of support which in the past determined many of the patterns of people's lives had faded away and so self-reliance was more of a survival strategy than a political statement. Most significant, in retrospect, was the sheer determination on the part of the young women whom I taught during this period to make careers for themselves and find ways of being economically independent, without having to depend in the future upon a male breadwinner. Indeed, many of the careers charted in this book are the fruits of this kind of effort, and are indicative of a labour market being produced from virtually nothing by young women designers who were part of a first generation of full-time female workers for whom a career of whatever sort would now be for life. The great irony is that just as this process comes underway, jobs for life are becoming a thing of the past. The various attempts at self-employment on the part of the designers I interviewed were therefore doubly significant in so far as they brought together these changing dynamics of both gender and employment.

Even amongst my own generation of women, educated in the 1960s, the idea of working and earning a living becoming an absolute necessity did not exist (but now in the 1990s, with so many marriages ending in divorce with dire financial consequences for women, I am regularly surprised to discover how many of my old schoolmates are, in fact, full-time housewives, and this idea now seems like such an anachronism). So, in debate with some of the old Marxist Left, for whom the dreams and aspirations of their design and media studies students to be successful and to have rewarding careers were so much self-illusion, I wanted to introduce a gender dimension as well as a note of political realism.

'We are just sending out cannon fodder', said one academic, 'it s like the battle of the Somme. They leave with big ideas of being film directors, or fashion designers, and they get mown down within a couple of years!'. This, of course, emphasises the old notion of 'false consciousness', that students are seduced in this case, by the ideological offensive of Thatcherism, have no real understanding of their position as workers, eschew trade unionism, and then come to grief. This kind of comment poured scorn upon the enthusiasm and hard work of the exstudents I knew who were struggling to make a living for themselves in a way in which they found rewarding. And, if this was laced by glamour or fantasy, I wanted to argue with the old, puritan Left that these were hardly crimes, nor did they make these young workers automatically enemies of the Left. Much of the work in this book is aimed at producing a more complex and informed account of the new creative workforce.

The *New Times* collection was refreshing in its suggestion of moving beyond these old positions. It asked how the Left should respond to the enormous changes which had taken place in British society over the previous decade and under the political leadership of Mrs Thatcher. There was a clear sense that familiar theories needed to be revised. The Left had to shake itself up and plug in more successfully to what people wanted and to what it was that made Mrs Thatcher so popular. More specifically, there was the recognition that Britain had become a more fluid society. It seemed as if various different social groups had become unanchored from their traditional moorings in the class structure. Class still provided an overall map of opportunities, expectations and outcomes, it still worked as a macro-structure of lifechances, but it was also a moving macro-structure, as were the other positionings of gender, generation, ethnicity and sexuality. These shifts were most vividly charted in changes in the economy and in work and patterns of employment, and the writers of the New Times acknowledged how these changes 'collided' with the growth of popular consumption and the rise of the service sector as a place of work.

The 1980s saw the retail revolution transform the British high street. This was symbolised, as several writers since then have noted, by the success of the Next chain, which brought fashion with a higher design input within the reach of average income consumers, male and female. The availability of more differentiated goods, together with what appeared to be a more carefully designed appearance, reinforced the process of social fragmentation as tastes proliferated, and people strove to be different through the access they appeared to have to a wider range of goods. Even low income groups began participating more noticeably in this leisure field where individuals were invited or prevailed upon to 'invent themselves' in different ways as a mark of individuality, a sign of identity. As Stuart Hall very recently noted, young black people, 'with hardly a penny in their pockets', paraded the streets in demonstrations of spectacular consumption. As Baudrillard argued, consumption had achieved a new prominence simultaneously with the way that culture and the media were now focal points in people's lives. Suddenly everything seemed to become more cultural. This was as true for the single mum who would deprive herself in order to be able to buy some of the goods seen by her children on television, as it was for the more affluent working classes. For young people themselves, in the poorest areas, consumption was often accomplished through illicit means. The 1980s gave rise to new forms of hidden economy, from weekend street markets, to working 'off the cards', to handling stolen goods, drug dealing and, increasingly, working in and around the emergent club scene.

The *New Times*' writers attributed the availability of designer goods to the growth of Post-Fordism (in response to global competition and saturated markets) and the application of new technology to the production of more differentiated goods. Flexible specialisation in production boosted flagging consumption by bringing niche marketed goods made in short runs to more discerning consumers. The people who were responsible for the higher input of quality and symbolic content in the new products were the designers and, while the traditional manufacturing workforce was slimmed down, there was a growth in this new branch of the service sector, the creative professionals. This, in turn, fed directly into the new kind of society in which we now live, where we are more likely to consume images of things than the actual objects or products to which they refer. The expanded market for images has created the need for a new workforce of image makers and, once again, the cultural intermediaries step in to play this role. The New Times, however, stops short of asking the question of who the cultural intermediaries actually are, what precisely they do, and what the conditions of their labour are?

By taking fashion designers as a case study, this book goes some way towards answering these questions but it also, in two respects, follows the lead set by Nixon. In his account of the growth of the market for male products during this same period he comments upon the ambivalent position occupied by the editor and founder of The Face magazine, Nick Logan. He is, argues Nixon, a 'committed entrepreneur', not the kind of 'gung-ho' capitalist championed by Mrs Thatcher but rather a product of the British working-class youth cultures of the late 1960s for whom values, other than simply profit and the market, influenced how he set himself up in the magazine business. In the case of The Face magazine, now very successful but still run on a shcestring, as we will see in chapter 10, this meant spurning the revenue from advertising in favour of retaining editorial independence and freedom in order to develop a new kind of magazine. Nixon does not pursue further the particular qualities of being a 'committed entrepreneur' though the term does suggest some social, cultural or even ethical dimension.

The socio-cultural dynamics of the particular brand of enterprise culture pursued by the fashion designers forms one strand in the current study, though it does remain uncertain how exactly they are positioned in relation to labour and capital. There is a sense in which they represent both and neither of these poles, so fluid and precarious are their careers in the enterprise culture. They share with Nick Logan a commitment to artistic or cultural integrity over the values of the market-place but, trained in the fine art tradition, they do not have the same entrepreneurial vision. Their enterprise comes more from necessity and the experience of unemployment. There were few 'proper' jobs in fashion design in the mid- and late 1980s and so the newly emerging fashion designers created their own jobs on the strength of dole payments, then the Enterprise Allowance Scheme (EAS), and with the help of a sewing machine, a few stretches of fabric and access to a stall or unit at Camden Lock or one of the other city centre markets. I was interested in how these small scale cultural entrepreneurs fitted into the occupational map of the Left (and indeed of contemporary sociology). How do we allocate them a class position? What does the future of work hold for them? I have already alluded to the role of youth culture and will return to it shortly, but a second feature of Nixon's work, his explorations of movements in the new economy of culture, also shapes the present inquiry. This was broached by Stuart Hall when he wrote 'Culture has ceased to be a decorative addendum to the "hard world" of production and things, the icing on the cake of material culture the material world of commodities and technologies is profoundly cultural'.

Hall's comment indicates a realignment of relations between the cult ural and the economic. No longer can the economic be understood as existing in some pure state, untainted by the cultural and the symbolic and providing a kind of bottom line from which all cultural phenomena develop. Nixon argues that economic decisions are, in fact, increasingly rendered in cultural discourse, that cultural knowledge wielded by the creative professionals actively produces new economies. The account of these realignments which are quite fundamental to contemporary society, is directed in Nixon's work ultimately towards the new products, the launching of the new man as a potential market and also as a dynamic feature of consumer culture. As we will see, in the field of fashion design economic issues are continually subordinated to creative or cultural priorities, producing what Bourdieu has called a kind of 'anti-economy'. But this does not mean that designers do not think about cash-flows and earning a living. Far from it, it is rather that they rationalise their own economic fragility by seeing their market failure as a sign of artistic success, or at least artistic integrity.

Bourdieu argues that this display of economic 'disinterest' is actually a strategy for longer term success as an artist which requires short term sacrifice in the name of 'no sell out' to commercial opportunities. But the model Bourdieu proposes depends upon the 'rarity of the producer'. What happens, I ask, when so many young people are being trained in art schools and pursue artistic careers of some description after graduation? The designers whom I interviewed all perceived themselves as artists. But Bourdieu's model of artists spurning the market and disavowing the need to earn a living, as a kind of symbolic investment, a testimony to the purity of their motives, does not quite tally with the enormous expansion of the cultural economy which is full of 'struggling artists' who are becoming simply another part of the low pay, casual economy. This points to another, rather different, relation between culture and economy, one which I hope at least to unravel in the following pages.

Various other writers have called either for renewed emphasis to be paid to the complex economies of culture and to the 'interplay between the symbolic and the economic' or they have commented on the way in which 'the connections among the political, the social and the cultural are in movement both in society and in our heads'. In fact, its origin predates the 1989 appearance of the New Times and draws extensively upon what might be called the Hall tradition. By this I mean the particular convergence of themes and issues which have characterised the work of Stuart Hall, and the cultural studies tradition which has developed around these interests. Inevitably there is a lot more to Hall's work than those elements on which I choose to focus here. However, the general frame provided by Hall is characterised precisely by its continuing attempt to connect sociological and cultural analysis with the political transformation of British society in the post-war years. From the Gramscian-inspired analysis of working-class youth cultures in the mid-1970s, through the account of the ideological groundwork carried out by the popular press and media in the years running up to the Tory victory of 1979, there has been a persistent attempt in Hall's work to draw upon 'theory' with a view to making full use of it in political analysis, or as Grossberg puts it, to 'allow you to re-describe the context that poses the political challenge'.

The political challenge underlying this book was posed by Britain ten years after the election to power of the Tories in 1979, when there seemed to be no end in sight to the successes of Thatcherism. Writing about the emergence of a new occupational strata, in this case the young fashion designers who had graduated from art school in the mid-1980s, it was tempting to pursue a pathway which depicted these young workers as merely the product of the inexorable logic of capital, a version of the 'nation of shopkeepers' which Mrs Thatcher herself was keen to promote through her commitment to 'enterprise culture'. Hall's influence can be seen, I suggest, in the way I have argued that these 'disciplinary regimes' cannot completely dictate their own outcomes. The young workers who emerge from the other side of 'enterprise' are, in this book, as much positioned by other previous or accompanying formations such as that provided by virtue of their race, or sexuality or family background or even by their working class identities, as they are by the apparently dominant discourse of the 'enterprising self. These jostle with each other, producing something other than a group of young cultural workers who could simply be described as 'Thatcher's children'. Yet the political challenge is that they do not fit, either in their occupational positioning as self-employed, or indeed as cultural entrepreneurs and small employers, with existing Left vocabularies. Hall's influence resides, I suggest, in the way he tends to stop short at fully endorsing the determinist version of history whereby all social and political phenomena are the outcome of the workings of the ideological apparatus or the products of the power of the 'subjectivising discourses'. As he puts it, the system is always more 'leaky' than these models permit. It produces its own failures as well as successes.

I have chosen to interpret this particular kind of workforce through the history and development of youth culture and popular culture in post-war Britain, not in isolation but rather as they intersect with education, in particular the art school, and with the commercial mass media, and also more dramatically with the growth of what Schwengell has called the *Kulturgesellschaft* Culture Society. Added to this, there is also in the focus on fashion a more specific attention to gender within these various intersections. The work I describe is broadly women's work and the young women who play a key role in the study hope to find the space to work independently by opting for self-employment. Although very few of them had children (none of the younger designers), there was a sense that this way of working could, at some point in the future, more easily accommodate family life. In fact, as we shall see, the work involved in being a one-woman business forces many women to postpone motherhood indefinitely.

But why does the youth culture tradition analysed at length by Hall and others in the mid-1970s offer a useful path towards considering the working practices of fashion designers in Britain in the 1980s and 1990s? I have already sketched out an answer to this question in two fairly recent articles. In the first, I argue that whilst the youth culture work, best exemplified in the work of Cohen, Hall and Jefferson and Hebdige offered a rich analysis of the history and meaning of these formations and their symbolic worlds, it overlooked the fact that these phenomena also generated opportunities for young people to make a living. The clothes and other items of youth cultural style had to be purchased somewhere and, I argue, many of those who provided for this market were in fact recruited from within. They found ways of making a living for themselves by servicing the youth subcultures in the form of record stalls and small shops, fashion outlets and again market stalls. Later, the whole dance club scene saw an enormous rise in what at the time I called 'subcultural entrepreneurialism'. This self-generated, self-employment demonstrated the existence of a sprawling network of micro-economies initially inside the youth cultures, and then extending far beyond them.

It was here in the street markets, where new fashion ideas mingled with the second-hand dresses, that a good deal of the groundwork in creating British fashion design was carried out. I also argued at the time that the subcultural field in which new styles were so rapidly displayed and then replaced with new ones, meant that the origins of these fashions could never really be attributed to any one individual. Even though Vivienne Westwood and Malcolm McLaren are recognised as the inventors of punk fashion, it is more the case that they provided a basic set of symbols, ideas and meanings (such as binliners, safety pins, bondage trousers). It was not so much the specific styles, more the combination of elements, the garish colours, the artificial fabrics, the aggressively do-it-yourself ethos which encouraged so many young people to create their own version. This, together with the idea of raiding the second-hand clothes shops, and poring through old magazines for a new 'old' look, is once again more reflective of British fashion than any straightforward history of its designers can demonstrate. It is also far removed from the *haute couture* tradition of European fashion design. Indeed, it is precisely because British fashion has followed this particular pop culture course, that no history of the designers can recount the whole story accurately.

It does not make sense to tell the story of British fashion by leaping from people such as Hardy Amies to Mary Quant to Ossie Clark, to the designers of the early 1980s, such as Bodymap, because these names alone tell us very little about fashion as a participative practice, a form of popular culture. This is recognised in most accounts, including the feminist accounts of British fashion, which all make connections with popular culture, women's magazines, shopping and consumption and youth cultures. But if fashion design as a highly creative practice appears to take shape in the youth subcultures, and if in the United Kingdom it is inextricably connected with the growth of pop music and popular culture, if it is a 'popular' thing, rather than an 'élite' thing, it does not stop there deed I will argue that this is, in fact, merely a starting point. Much of this book is concerned with the key role of British art schools in shaping fashion design. As large institutions they are 'legitimating agencies'. By the end of the 1980s, as a direct result of the expansion of this sector and as the fashion departments in art schools gain confidence in promoting their own products, what emerged was a relatively new phenomenon, the fashion designer as *auteur*, as an artist in his or her own right. It is at this point that British fashion began to be associated with a series of names, from the 'genius' of John Galliano to those following in his footsteps, including Alexander McQueen and, more recently, Antonio Berardi. This still does not mean that British fashion is model- ling itself on its European counterparts far from it. It is more a matter of fashion finally gaining status as a kind of fine art practice in the way it has sought for so long. As long as the puzzled observer asks when a series of unlikely shapes and colours make their way down the catwalk, 'but is it art, and what does it mean?' then fashion has indeed fulfilled the conditions of its own existence.

I wish, however, to hold onto and signal strongly the earlier and more nebulous beginnings of British fashion which were inside the sweaty spaces of the raves and night clubs, and in the bedrooms of the groups of girls who designed and made their own outfits for these events, and then sometimes made them for their friends and ended up selling them at a market or to small shops. I want to stress the social context of this cultural activity because, in the conclusion to this book, I suggest the need for a return to a more socialised field of cultural production the designers need to be able to collaborate and share their resources. The art ethos which they have been taught to embody is limited in its individualising focus. If art work is becoming more commonplace in the cultural economy of Britain in the late 1990s, this ethos needs to be revised and updated especially when, as we shall see in this book, it simply does not make economic sense for designers to work in isolation from each other and from the people who do their manufacturing. They can make a better living and produce cheaper clothes if they are able to pool their talents and abandon the ethos of working like an artist, alone in his or her studio.

The second and related theme I developed out of the youth culture studies was that subcultures could conceivably be seen as informal, unofficial job creation schemes, more popular and successful than the Youth Training Schemes set up by the Government at the time. There was a degree of fluidity in the youth cultures where consumers often crossed over to be producers, and although this is more widely recognised in music, it has also been true for fashion. Being a participant in a youth culture could result in learning various skills, from poster production, to fanzine journalism, to mixing music and learning sound production, to designing and selling clothes. It is a fairly short route from these leisure activities into a BTEC or HND course at the local college and from there into art school. This kind of pathway was undreamt of by policy makers and government ministers when they expanded places in fashion design or sound production courses at and below degree level. But my research, as well as the history of British pop music, shows there to be an established link between youth culture as leisure activity, art school education, and then work in cultural production. However, as I will show in the first three chapters of this book, art school imposes its own disciplinary vocabulary upon its subjects and, perhaps not surprisingly, this involves negating or at least dislodging the importance of these informal cultural practices associated with the street.

A final question which must be raised by my locating this work within the Hall tradition is the issue of Britishness and, connected with this, the value of such a localised study as the one I pursue here. In a world of global culture, it might seem strangely old-fashioned, indeed redundant, to document a local form of cultural activity and to dwell on its apparently national characteristics. Grossberg, for example, recently disputed the claims to political connectedness made by those who study the local on the grounds that it gives them some access to public representativeness, that is, by being local they are somehow in touch with real people in a way that those who do theory are not. My justification for the kind of study that I have undertaken here is not that it retreats to the easily recognisable contours of nation as a way of holding at bay the more threatening forces of globalisation, but rather that the history it documents also tells us something about the formation of nation, the 'peculiarities of the British'. This is a story of class and gender antagonism and the struggle over culture waged inside the art school. It is also a story about how women from different social backgrounds created a labour market for themselves in the field of fashion, and about how they modified 'government rationalities' as they developed in the 1980s to suit their own needs, in this case making use of enterprise culture to allow them to pursue their careers as creative fashion designers.

The question of the Britishness of these phenomena is more intractable. Are these various forms of cultural production (notably fashion, music and magazines) a kind of last ditch attempt at cultural imperialism, with Britfrocks following Britpop in the attempt to rule the waves, as they might put it in the tabloid press? Or am I merely avoiding the challenge posed by thinking through the role of fashion design as part of the new international division of labour, where the art work is done in the privileged post-industrial metropolitan centres, while the preindustrial work of fashion manufacture and production is outsourced to wherever there is a regular supply of cheap female labour? It is true that I have drawn a series of boundaries around this investigation. It remains beyond the scope of this book to consider in more depth and in a way which is more deeply informed by recent questions about the nature of 'culture' itself by a number of authors including Stratton and Ang and Grossberg, the extent to which it can be said that the fashion design I describe here is somehow the product of British post-war cultural history. However, if there is a close relation between fashion and 'pop', as I suggest, then fashion might also be seen as one of those features of symbolic disruption produced by the deep, indeed seismic ruptures of class, sex and ethnicity in British society which were first felt in the late 1950s.

Pop music bears the traces more evidently of the cultural journeys made by diasporic peoples and the way these have been adopted and commercialised for use by white audiences than does the field of fashion design, and for this reason it has been the subject of extensive analysis. The cleavages of class, race and sex can also be read in and through the parades of fashion and style of the post-war years, but these particular narratives remain less thoroughly documented than the story of pop. Feminist scholars have made substantial contributions in this respect but a good deal more work remains to be done. Fashion education, for example (and fashion designers themselves) sometimes display a remarkably imperialistic attitude in their uncritical plundering and exoticisation of other cultures in search of new fashion ideas. Geography is as rich a resource in this respect as history, and fashion photography as a genre is steeped in notions of 'exotic locations'. But the significance of fashion orientalism requires much more work than a simple reference can do justice to in this context.

To those who query the value of local studies, and dispute the claims to political relevance, I argue that, as Murdock recently reminded us, the case study (in this case, geographically 'local') performs a knowledge-generating function. It allows us the opportunity to see how things actually work in practice and how more general social, and even global, trends like those described by social theorists including Beck, Giddens and Lash as well as Lash and Urry and also by cultural theorists like Jameson and Harvey are translated or modified when they become grounded. The local study of the sort carried out here also provides the opportunity to witness how the people who are the subjects of these social changes respond to the changes in their daily practice and, in this case, in their working lives. There is also a sense in this study that I am attempting to fulfil an objective which Laclau has described as honouring 'the dignity of the specific'. That is, it is my intention to fill out the spaces left behind by more abstract writing about, for example, processes of class realignment and the growth of identity politics which both Laclau and Mouffe have so fruitfully considered, but at an entirely theoretical level.

Finally, my defence of the Britishness of such an undertaking does not mean that studies of the same type in other locations are not of equal value. Just as I would like to have moved away from London with this investigation, including other cities with revitalised cultural sectors, so also it is important to know how new forms of work in the cultural industries are developing in different cities across the world. While there is doubtless much that is specific to London and to Britain which has spawned this focus among some sectors of young people, in producing cultural phenomena on a seemingly do-it-yourself basis, the same may well be true of other large cities as they shift into a post-industrial mode. In addition, culture travels as Tricia Rose has demonstrated so well hip hop music began as a localised innovation and is now the most influential current in the global music industry. On a much smaller scale, Nick Logan, who is from a working-class Mod background and who brought that experience to bear on the look of a tiny circulation, independendy-funded style magazine, could not have anticipated that several years later the magazine would be looked at monthly by art directors in advertising agencies across the world, so that the magazine operates more or less as a mobile job centre for the photographers and stylists as well as the fashion designers whose work it features. It hardly matters that Logan can still not afford to pay them!

Two other theorists, Pierre Bourdieu and Michel Foucault, have, alongside Hall, played a major role in shaping this study. Bourdieu in particular not only demonstrates empirically how the acquisition of cultural goods including food, fashion and other domestic commodities, plays a practical role in actively reproducing as well as confirming social inequalities, but also turns his attention to the cultural intermediaries who create such symbolic goods. However, as will be apparent later in this book, I part company with Bourdieu in his relegation of this strata of workers to the conservative 'rump' of the lower middle classes, and I concur with Lash in his suggestion that Bourdieu is overwhelmingly concerned with social and cultural reproduction, rather than with the dynamics of social change. Nonetheless Bourdieu's work on the whole field of cultural production offers a most useful way in to conceptualising the work of fashion designers. In his short essay entitled '*Haute Couture* and Haute Culture' he focuses upon what is a recurrent theme in his work on cultural production the way in which it is the job of the critics and reviewers, the journalists and specialist writers to produce the belief in the object, to create and sustain the aura and the special, even sacred, status of art works. Fashion journalism plays this role for the charismatic designers of French haute couture, but by extension the same could be said of the role of the fashion media in contemporary Britain, as we see in chapter 10. However, and this is the point at which this book departs somewhat from a Bourdieusian framework, Bourdieu suggests that a sociological analysis of a field such as fashion must inevitably act as a force of destruction upon the field: 'If any Tom, Dick or Harriet...can make dresses, then the specialist field is destroyed' which raises the question, is there life or fashion after sociology?

The status of the analysis presented here is less of a clearing operation. I would like this sociological account to contribute to the improvement or betterment of fashion as a place of livelihoods. I envisage this investigation feeding into a field already comprising of various competing accounts, of which, however, there are relatively few sociological studies of this type. I do not want fashion, under attack from sociology or cultural studies, to fade away, and anyway this is hardly a realistic scenario, as though sociology has ever had such an impact. Bourdieu implies that if it can be shown that there is really nothing special about fashion, and that more or less anybody can do it, then it ceases to occupy that special, sacred place in the public's estimation, and thus in a sense it ceases to exist, as it is this system of belief (i.e. words) which creates the thing. The aim of this book is to combine the sociological work of demystification with one of reconstitution so that fashion is better able to attend to its own business, particularly in the area of manufacture and production. I want these elements to be brought back into the field rather than seeing the field somehow disappearing. My aim is then unequivocally reformist, in that there is an attempt to connect sociological and cultural analysis with a concern for policy.

The other feature of Bourdieu's work which also informs this book is one briefly referred to earlier, that is his account of how a field such as fashion will attempt to gain a place for itself in the cultural hierarchy by developing a strategy for gaining autonomy, part and parcel of which will involve a kind of disavowal or spurning of commerce and of the need to earn a living. This repudiation of money is, in reality, playing a double role. It protects young artists against feelings of failure. If they can console themselves that their work is misunderstood by the public which in turn accounts for their difficulties in scraping together a living, then they can at least be assured of their own artistic integrity. Bourdieu once again reveals this to be a strategy or a rule of the game which in fact benefits only those who are in a position to 'be poor' for some period of time. The history of painting and of literature shows that living on a shoestring is usually a long-term investment, on the expectation that eventually the writer or artist will gain recognition. Since only those who have access to some other financial means (a small private income, for example) can pursue such a threadbare existence, most cultural producers sooner or later have to compromise their art for the sake of earning a living. In this way economic capital, hidden away somewhere in the family vaults, ensures the reproduction of cultural capital in the hands of the already privileged social classes.

Bourdieu's account, rich as it is in explaining the disdain for money on the part of many of the designers I interviewed, requires some modification on the basis of the material context in which the designers were working. They most certainly were not from family backgrounds which could support them through years of poverty. But more significantly, these young designers were no longer a tiny, privileged few. They were educated and trained in the art school system which expanded its intake quite dramatically throughout the 1980s. More generally, art work no longer has the exclusive identity which Bourdieu attributes to it and instead it is a very crowded field. In addition, it is a field which attracts government funding in the form of publicly administered grants or unemployment schemes such as the EAS. These provide, at least in the early days. Therefore, instead of describing the strategies of a privileged élite set on playing the game of cultural production, I explore the career pathways of a group of young cultural workers who are creating for themselves a series of micro-economies based on their own self-employment strategies.

The later work of Michel Foucault, and more particularly that of his followers, also provides a useful frame for understanding the power relations which produce creative work like fashion design as a field of pleasure and reward. In his essay 'What is an Author?' Foucault describes the way in which the figure of the author is created as a certain type of person. The author is produced from the 'individualising' and 'subjectivising' techniques which are also the normative means through which we come to recognise the existence of creativity, or artistry. This could quite easily be extended to the fashion designer, whose distinctive characteristics and biographical snippets so frequently repeated in journalism impinge upon and influence how we make sense of the work. However, in this book I have concentrated instead on the significance of the growth of new kinds of creative labour as a disciplinary technique. These current incitements to make work a source of intense personal satisfaction (independent of financial reward in this case) can be understood in Foucauldian terms as a regulatory practice, an example of how governmental rationality is finely tuned to the construction of 'new ways for people to be at work'.

However, if people today are virtually 'forced to be free' in a deregulated, privatised economy and are forced to seek work which promises them the satisfaction of creativity, this is not a fixed state, a kind of final destiny for the workforce of the western world, as I argue later. Not only is there movement and contest within these positionings, there is also the strong likelihood that many of these 'rationalities' will fail. This makes the whole field of cultural work more open and less certain in its focus and direction than an application of Donzelots model of 'pleasure in work' would allow. There is no reason why the organisation of cultural work should not, in these circumstances, be more open to accounts which like this current one, will make a stronger case for the resocialisation of creative labour and for new kinds of association between designers and producers in the field of fashion. This final note goes some way towards answering the criticism of the theorists who dispute the apparently privileged access of 'local' studies to political centres of gravity. What I have also taken from the work of Stuart Hall is the idea that politics cannot be suspended until such time as theory gets it right.

The image of the fashion design sector which has acted as a central motif throughout this research, is of a skimpy, silky dress, carelessly tossed between two pillars of support, but always threatening to slide to the ground into a crumpled heap. The dress itself is the underfunded, underrated design industry, a fragile, flimsy thing of some beauty and importance. One pillar represents the world of the art school, and the other the commercial world of women's magazines. These also provide the structural supports (or the corsetry) for this book. First, I look at the history of fashion in the art schools, then I consider the practices of the fashion designers and the fate of their skimpy, silky dresses and, finally, I consider the magazine industry as the other pillar of support. I have concentrated exclusively upon women's fashion and on the work of a group of young, female, British fashion designers who share much the same background in both training and in their London location. I define fashion design as the application of creative thought to the conceptualisation and execution of items of clothing so that they can be said to display a formal and distinctive aesthetic coherence which takes precedence over function, and which is recognised as such by those whose expertise allows them to categorise and evaluate work according to criteria established as part of a professional repertoire of meaning and judgement. In this sense, fashion is inevitably a fiction, and what follows is a narrative, a sociological story about fashion design, whose value or relevance will also be judged accordingly.

Finally, there are a number of brief points I should make about this book. First, it is based upon the assumption that fashion, despite its trivialised status, is a subject worthy of study. As part of the industrial society, it has been a place of livelihoods for over a century. Despite great variations in wealth and poverty, with all that implies for the meaning of pleasure, fashion has nonetheless given pleasure to women as a form of personal and practical aesthetics based on the bringing together of shape, colour and textures against the body to intersect with the body s own shapes, colours and textures. So my intent is a serious one; to give fashion the attention it deserves, in this case as a key part of the expanding culture industries. Second, I want to emphasise that this is, of course, also a partial account. As a non-specialist entering a specialist field, carrying the baggage of a cultural studies and a sociological vocabulary, I will inevitably tread on some more fashionable feet during the course of this book. In particular, my own academic language is both close to, but very different from, the fashion academics interviewed. I could not have carried out the study without them and for this I am especially grateful, but I hope that the different inflection I bring to an analysis of the fashion field is seen not as a critique of their practice, but rather as an additional voice in a field of cultural importance. Third, it may be appropriate to point out that some might argue that the historical moment described is already one that has passed. This was the moment of setting up alone as a fully-fledged fashion designer just after leaving college, a moment which for the sake of convenience we could take as 1987, exactly ten years before this book was concluded. Many experts will say that the recklessness of such an endeavour has been replaced by a much more carefully planned set of career strategies on the part of fashion designers graduating a decade later. They have all, it is claimed, learned from the mistakes of their elders. While it is indeed most likely that a degree of realism has crept into the working practices of young designers, it remains open to debate whether or not the moment of this study has been completely eclipsed.

There is also an assumption that although the focus is entirely on fashion, this study has wider repercussions for the future of work in the culture industries. While it is difficult to prove this conclusively, in the absence of a comparative analysis with another sector (e.g. graphic design, independent film production) there is some attempt in the pages that follow to emphasise the absolute distinctiveness, indeed the sheer peculiarity of the British fashion design sector, without completely losing sight of how and where it intersects with other practices. For example, the chapter on fashion journalism shows editors, journalists and writers to be working within similar 'artistic' principles as the designers themselves. As one editor says, 'the page is art'. While the rationale for carrying out such a study has been to suggest this as a field which is somehow exemplary and perhaps prefigurative of future work in the creative industries, there is inevitably a tension between the specific and the general. Is fashion seen by its practitioners as a highly creative field, like being an artist, for the simple reason that it lacks the traditional career pathways of the established professions? If so, then we can see parallels between fashion and film making, advertising, television and video production and, of course, the popular music industry. Is work in fashion, described in this book as highly fluid, constantly changing and requiring a multiskilled, flexible and increasingly freelance workforce, a sign of things to come, or of things which have already come in other similar fields, for example, television journalism? Is fashion like these other fields, yet distinct from them in its gendered identity? Or, alternatively (and thinking more historically) is it fashion's feminine status which has marked it out as different from both a fully fledged fine art tradition and also from those craft traditions which generated their own training hierarchies based first on guilds and then on apprenticeships? This would certainly begin to provide us with an account of the historical distinctiveness of fashion as a culture industry.

The final assumption which underpins this book is that it provides a useful opportunity for developing and putting into practice a methodology for researching the new or emergent culture industries (in this case, fashion design). The necessity of an individualising focus, the need to simply pursue a whole range of individuals in isolation from each other, to find out how fashion works, tells us something about the desocialisation of work in the cultural sector. And although it is tempting to explain this by taking seriously the image of the designers as practising artists (who have always worked in an isolated way) this favoured selfimage only takes us (and the designers themselves) so far. Like it or not, the designers are usually small scale employers who need the services of pattern cutters, machinists and others. So we are confronted with the reality of a post-industrial system based on the practices of a substantial number of designers doing much the same thing, dotted about the cities, rarely liaising with each other, never mind collaborating, yet experiencing exactly the same problems. It is the sheer anomaly of this situation which motivates the study as a whole. My starting point however, is a historical one. It is in the British art schools that the vast majority of fashion designers are trained. But the presence of fashion on the academic syllabus in a set of institutions dominated by the fine arts has not been uncontested and, as we shall see, the opposition to fashion design has been conducted along the lines of both class and gender. It is to these debates that we now turn.

2

HISTORY OF FASHION DESIGNING

Introduction

The American Indian, early settlers, military uniforms, colonists, civil dress, and a section on children's clothing are included. Twentiethcentury material proceeds to 1960, with the table of contents serving as the index. *Mirror, Mirror: A Social History of Fashion*, by Michael and Ariane Batterberry, provides an overview of fashion history from ancient times to the twentieth century, with the United States coming into focus with World War I. Mention of individuals and their contributions add to the volume's usefulness as a social history. Fashions are visually represented in many colored and black and white photographs; there is less emphasis on children. The same time period is covered by Maggie P. Murry in *Changing Styles in Fashion: Who, What, Why*. The major focus of this history is to explain fashion cycles and how clothing evolves and reflects culture. Coverage is from ancient times to the twentieth century. Murry concludes with thoughts on the "slowly merging cohesiveness in the clothing of mankind" as a "reflection of an emerging similarity in us all." *Common Threads: A Parade of American Clothing*, by Lee Hall, also reflects this theme, as her title indicates. This too is a highly visual account, with many black and white photographs covering the period 1492 to the twentieth century. This is the only source in this group that discusses masters and slaves, in a section on the southern hierarchy and clothing. All of these titles, highly visual, have bibliographies and are written for the general public. Diana De Marly covers the period 1492 through 1800 in her *Dress in North America, volume 1: The New World*. Special features include a chronology of major clothing events, such as the start of the homespun business in Boston in 1767; a glossary of textile terms; and two appendixes, "English Cloth and Clothing Exports to the American Colonies and Canada" and the "Commencement of American Cloth Production." One Ph.D. dissertation, by Lydia Wares, concentrates on the "Dress of the African American Woman in Slavery and Freedom: 1500-1935."

1600s

Alice M. Earle 1903 classic work, *Two Centuries of Costume in America*, covering 1620- 1820, was preceded by many earlier works on colonial life. Her book contains documented illustrations of paintings, portraits, and drawings from publications, as well as quotations from many primary sources. Arrangement is by costume subject, with information presented chronologically within two volumes or parts. Separate sections include "Venerable Hood," "Batts and Broags, Boots and Shoes," "Commodes, Mobs and Pinners," and "Bridal Dress." Men, women, and children receive attention, as do fashion dolls and fashion plates, "Masculine Vanities Muffs and Ear-Rings," Quaker dress, the riding habit, mourning dress, and uniforms.

In 1904 Elisabeth McClellan, working in Philadelphia, produced *Historic Dress in America, 1607-1870*, illustrated with black and white drawings by Sophie B. Steel and Cecil W. Trout. The arrangement is in two volumes or parts: volume 1, *The Seventeenth Century*, focuses on English and Dutch colonies, and volume 2, *The Eighteenth Century*, focuses on women's, children's, and men's clothing each from 1700 to 1800. The drawings are meant to reveal hair styles and accessories, and all sources of illustrations are identified. However, the documentation is not precise in linking an illustration to a specific source, as indicated by statements such as "from a print."Authorities Consulted" serves as the bibliography, showing the depth of study and research. The text focuses on the clothing itself and is interspersed with many quotations. The result is somewhat disjointed. Special features include a glossary, lists of European rulers and U.S. presidents, an introduction on Spanish settlements in Florida and California, 1565-1764, and French settlements in the South, 1680-1764. The clothing items with the most entries in the index are, in volume 1, wigs and periwigs, thirteen; hoods, eight; shoes, eight. In volume 2, they are bonnets, sixty; coiffure, thirty-four; sleeves, thirty-one; waistcoats and vests, twenty three ; and hats, thirty-three. Uniforms are featured for the period 1775- 1800, with readers referred to an 1889 U.S. government publication covering the topic, "fully illustrated," from 1800 to 1870, although no actual source is provided.

Twenty-four years later, in 1929, Edward Warwick, dean of the Philadelphia Museum College of Art, and Henry C. Pitz, a period illustrator, published their *Early American Costume* covering the period from about 1607 to the frontier years of Daniel Boone, or about 1790. The work includes black and white photographs, many credited to the collection of Elisabeth McClellan, and drawings by Pitz designed to show the "shape, character, and method of wearing" of the clothes. Chapters emphasize clothing for men and women in Virginia, New England, New York, and Pennsylvania, and also reflect changes in colonial life between 1675 and 1775, the Revolution and New Republic, and life on the frontier. Special sections are "Sources and Authorities" and "Bibliographical Notes," which serve as an excellent guide to the literature. The index reveals several items of clothing receiving more attention than others: the bodice, body garments (the term *underwear* is not used), boots, and breeches. In fact, knickerbockers or knee breeches are mentioned as the type most worn by Puritan/Pilgrim men. This work was reissued in 1965 with modifications to text and illustrations by Alexander Wycoff, an editor and scholar, and Pitz to reflect a more accurate depiction of clothing worn in America. A new chapter is "Children in North America: 1585-1790." The introduction elaborates on American artists, works on early painters are included in the bibliography, and the authors caution on the use of illustrative source materials in making decisions about what people wore. The original foreword from the 1929 volume is not included. Plates and drawings covering the period 1440 to 1790-1800 are grouped chronologically, with their page locations.

The Story of Everyday Things by Arthur Train Jr., provides an overview of American material culture from the 1600s to the early

1900s, with clothes receiving attention, along with houses, furniture, food, agriculture, transportation, industry, and community life. Train looks at this time period and suggests that the material background reveals seventeenth-century "simplicity," eighteenth-century "comfort," nineteenth century "bad taste," and the twentieth-century as the "dawn of a new aestheticism" where machine-made things became "simple" and "functional." Each chronological section discusses the items, with a few black and white drawings included. The clothing covered provides Train's idea of popular clothing items for each century. One particularly interesting chapter, "Our Days: An Age of Transition," mentions the "first American competition in designs for women's wear" in 1916 and the opening the next year of the Metropolitan Museum's "new textile gallery." Also from this section he mentions a t-shirt trend of the early twentieth century, where cartoon characters were used for decoration. The clothes discussion concludes:

> *When men got out and stuck each other through with rapiers, they were not afraid to wear frills on their wrists. But the man who spends the better part of his waking life in a swivel chair avoids any hint of interest in beauty for fear of seeming effeminate. He dresses as much like a sparrow or a mole as he can, and stubbornly resists any efforts to improve his sartorial lot. Athwart his serge or broadcloth bosom falls the shadow of his Puritan forefathers.*

It includes extremely colorful drawings featuring men, women, and children, including slaves. This volume is more of a collectors' item today than a source for historical data.

In 1980 Estelle Worrell wrote and illustrated *Children's Costume in America, 1607-1910*. Arrangement is chronological, with brief sociocultural background information followed by groups of drawings of children in various styles of clothing for that period. Each costume is fully described. Worrell indicates that between 1770 and 1800, children's clothing began to have its own character rather than simply copying adult attire. Many popular trends she brings into focus include the close association of girl's clothing to toys, especially dolls; the popularity of boy's baseball suits designed after the first American baseball team was founded in Cincinnati in 1869; similar development of sailor suits and pea coats from U.S. Navy uniforms and official regulation wear in the early 1880s; overalls or apron overalls originally advertised for work that evolved into modern children's playwear between 1890 and 1900; the middy for girls, which became "almost an American school girl uniform" and the teddy bear, often depicted with a sleeping child wearing night clothes, which appeared between 1900 and 1919. Worrell concludes, "There have been few new concepts in children's clothing design since only variations on and improvements in those already conceived." This high-quality production is a pleasure to read, as are the black and white and some colored drawings to view, although there are no footnotes, bibliography, or index. Acknowledgments are provided for various institutions and people who assisted the author in her research.

Several theses cover these early years. In 1957 Emma Briscoe at Colorado State University researched Spanish colonial embroidery in New Mexico. Sumptuary laws affecting appearance in the seventeenth century were studied by Joana Phillips in 1961. Analyzing childhood using costume as one of several artifacts was researched by Karin Calveri in her 1984 Ph.D. dissertation, and the social and economic mobility of servants and gentlemen in Massachusetts bay as visible in costume was studied by Donna Bartsch in 1988.

1700s

Histories beginning coverage with the eighteenth century range from those where the United States is only mentioned and does not receive major focus to those that concentrate solely on this country. Iris Brooke in 1930, Agnes B. Young in 1937, and Jane Dorner in 1974 provide sources that serve mainly as background. Brooke *Encyclopedia of Children's Costume since 1775* provides a British focus. She states that the earliest record of a distinctly child costume was in 1770 or 1775. The author's drawings accompany text and descriptions by decade. Young *Recurring Cycles of Fashion, 1760-1937* analyzes women's dress with helpful illustrations. Dorner *Fashion: The Changing Shape of Fashion through the Years, 1700-1970s*, is a highly visual treatment emphasizing, for example, "sexual display," "decorative dandyism," "physical freedom," "social equality," and "self expression. "American Influences" provides a cursory discussion from the 1620s to the 1970s. Regional studies include Catherine Fennelly *The Garb of Country New Englanders, 1760-1840* and Ellen J. Gehret *Rural Pennsylvania Clothing*.

The celebration of the U.S. bicentennial in 1975 provided the opportunity to publish materials on historic American costume. The few items examined were cheaply produced but represent a beginning look at a larger body of ephemeral materials. Alan Armstrong and Ken Small *American Costume of 1776* was intended to show how to reproduce basic clothes for working-class and fashionable men, women, and children.

It was printed on newsprint and has deteriorated over the years. *Women's Wear Daily* celebrated with Tobi Nyberg *The Changing American Woman, WWD, 200 Years of American Fashion,* Covering 1776-1976. Text plus advertisements reflecting decades are arranged from the 1970s back to 1900, then conclude with 1850-1900 and 1776-1850. This book too was produced on poor-quality paper; it is in tabloid format. Advertisements, many designed for the occasion, provide much popular interest—for example: Wamsutta's display of fabrics from 1846 to 1976, De Weese swimwear designs from the 1930s through the 1970s, and changing styles of the shirtdress from 1905 to 1976 reflected in an advertisement by David Crystal of New York City.

In 1977 Peter F. Copeland completed *Working Dress in Colonial and Revolutionary America* covering 1710- 1810, the period before mass-produced clothes were available. Arranged by type of occupation (e.g., transportation workers, household servants, criminals), it concludes with a glossary, a bibliography, and an index. Drawings are documented if taken from other sources. Copeland found very little change over the years, especially in clothing for the farmer, waggoner, and sailor. Linda Baumgarten, curator of textiles at Colonial Williamsburg Foundation, wrote *Eighteenth Century Clothing at Williamsburg*. The colored and black and white photographs of documented paintings and clothing of Virginia for men, women, and children complement the excellent text. The volume is the first in a series to introduce subjects to "intelligent lay people." Both formal dress and informal "undress" plus accessories are covered, with clear explanations of clothing terms used during the eighteenth century.

The 1990s has brought to the light one aspect of costume and fashion that previously received little attention: African-American dress. Barbara Starke , Lillian Holloman, and Barbara Nordquist have produced an edited volume of essays, *African American Dress and Adornment: A Cultural Perspective.* Covering the 1700s to the 1980s, it is the first attempt at documenting clothing and adornment of African Americans in the commercial press. Clothing, accessories, hair treatment, jewelry, and cosmetics are included, with chapters written by different scholars and arranged in three subject groupings: *"African Historical Perspectives"* (three essays), *"African American Slave Clothing"* (three essays), and *"20th Century African American Dress and Adornment"* (ten essays). Special features are lists of African-American designers with biographical information, a selected bibliography on African-American dress, and bibliographies for each chapter. In 1990, as Vermont prepared to celebrate its bicentennial the following year, Meredith Wright wrote *Put on Thy Beautiful Garments: Rural New England Clothing 1783-1800*. Illustrated by Nancy Rexford, the volume includes historical background as well as patterns to assist in the reproduction of the garments. The bibliography and a list of costume pieces in museum collections are special features. Also in 1991, Nancy Rexford, herself a costume consultant, completed *Shoes*, the first volume of her own series, *Women's Clothing in America 1795-1930*. Her research is being sponsored by the National Endowment for the Humanities.

Although not specifically focused on the United States, Farid Chenoune's excellent and well-researched *A History of Men's Fashion* provides an enlightening panorama from 1760 to 1990 of world influences and interrelationships that make up the history of men's fashion. The work was sponsored by the *Federation Française des Industries du Vetement Masculin* and has been translated from the French by Deke Dusinberre. Richard Martin, curator of the Costume Institute, Metropolitan Museum of Art, in his preface mentions the "great historical codifications *ancien regime elegance*. Empire austerity. Victorian embellishment rational repression. The modern in dress and the emergence of the body" reflecting changes in men's as well as women's wear and exhibiting "themes of consonance as much as styles of difference. The phenomenon of men's fashions' being adopted by women and the important influence of gay men's clothing styles on men's fashion generally is covered. The volume looks at four periods: "Dress Coat and Frock Coat, 1760-1850"; "Overcoat and Mourning Coat, 1850-1914," on European ready-to-wear; "Lounge Suit and Business Suit, 1914-1940," the "new American elegance"; and "Pin Stripes and Black Leather, 1940-1990," covering topics such as antifashion, unstructured tailoring, "Tribes and Fashion Victims," and "Fashion Winners. Fashion Losers." Notes, a bibliography, an index, and photographic credits conclude the volume. The index is by proper name followed by an "Index of the Male Wardrobe" by clothing type. Most entries refer to coats, jackets, pants, and suits.

Exhibition catalogs include *Of Men Only: A Review of Men's and Boy's Fashions, 1750-1975,* published in 1975 for the Brooklyn Museum exhibition. "Pattern of Male Fashion" by Elizabeth A. Coleman, costume curator, provides the overview; most of the catalog consists of colored photographs of clothing and accessories in the exhibition. The Smithsonian's exhibit *Men and Women: A History of Costume, Gender, and Power* covers the period from 1780 to the 1980s. The printed catalog, written by Barbara C. Smith and Kathy Peiss in 1989, analyzes gender themes and includes the "black is beautiful" movement of the 1960s as an attempt to provide an alternative to the "white" idea of beauty. The exhibit sought to encourage thinking about how fashion and appearance came to be of more concern to women than men and how strength and muscular bodies came to be associated with men. The popular culture aspects of this exhibit are evidenced in the use of early magazines, the theater, movies, and television. The authors admit that their work and that of other costume researchers focuses on middle- and upper-class white Americans at the expense of "working-class immigrants and Black Americans." Although these groups do appear in the exhibit and catalog, the authors write that scholars do not yet know enough about their behaviors and ideals."

Several theses touch on the eighteenth century. Nancy Oberseider in 1966 looked at women's clothing in Westmoreland County, Virginia, 1700- 1775; Eunice Glosson wrote in 1985 on the influence of fashionable dress on American stage costume; and Terri Riggs studied male servant's dress in North Carolina from 1770 to 1794 in 1989.

1800s

Monographs focusing on the nineteenth century include an esoteric source written in 1885 by Mary E. Tillotson, *History of the First Thirty-five Years of the Science Costume Movement in the United*

States of America. It chronicles incidents of repression experienced by dress reformers in the movement to establish a healthy "scientific system of garmenture. In 1974 Stella M. Newton wrote *Health, Art and Reason: Dress Reform of the 19th Century*, covering 1850 to the 1980s, with her focus on the movement in England. Illustrations, a bibliography, and an index are provided.

Kathryn Weibel 1977 *Mirror, Mirror: Images of Women Reflected in Popular Culture* provides a look at various images from 1827 to 1977 as reflected in fashion. These images come from fiction, television, movies, women's magazines, magazine advertisements, and fashionable women themselves. Written during the women's movement of the 1970s, it reflects that interest but pays no specific attention to the minority woman's image (or lack of it) as reflected in the same media forms. Some of her points include that until the turn of the century, fashion was designed for the "idle" woman; that fashion became less complicated as women entered the workforce; and that "suburban housewife" clothing became a fashion of its own in the 1950s. Weibel provides an overview of trends from about 1810 to the 1970s in "Images of the Fashionable Woman." Notes, clear black and white drawings, and an index are provided.

Estelle A. Worrell, a lecturer on Americana and a designer of dolls, doll houses, puppets, and miniature period clothing, wrote and illustrated *American Costume, 1840-1920*. The arrangement is chronological, with text followed by her drawings and their descriptions. Although she states that she tells the "story even when it's shameful because I show what slaves and Indians wore as well as child laborers, minority groups," there are no illustrations of slaves in the volume. The last chapter, "Design and Construction," includes drawings of patterns for men's and women's basic clothing as well as trimmings. The volume is not footnoted but does include acknowledgments and an index.

A very different visual approach is provided in William H. Shaw *American Men's Wear, 1861-1982*. Shaw's illustrations are black and white photographs from his own collection and from clothing industry archives. The chapters center around major historical periods, with each chapter containing historical events, notes on innovation in clothing styles, and specific types of clothing (e.g., coat, vest, trousers), with characteristics, fabrics discussion, and photographs to illustrate the period. Emphasis is on ordinary men and boys from all walks of life; military, sports, and religious clothing is not included. The photographs are documented with date, location, and other descriptive information. There is an index of people in the photographs, as well as a bibliography.

In 1985 and 1986 two works were published focusing on western clothing: Betty J. Mills *Calico Chronicle: Texas Women and Their Fashions, 18301910* and E. L. Reedstrom *Historic Dress of the Old West.* Mills focuses on women's frontier clothing using the collections at the Museum of Texas Tech University. Calico as an important fabric of the time is used to symbolize, as it did then, a "badge of respectability, [a way] to make a decent appearance. Mills used many primary sources in her study and benefited from donations of frontier clothing for the Ranching Heritage Center at Texas Tech University, established in 1967. Special features include the foldout "Capsule Fashion Commentary 1830-1910," which links seven time periods to fabric choices, colors, design, trim, general observations, and silhouette emphasis, and seven line drawings by L. C. Ross. A glossary, a bibliography, and an index are provided. A popular culture connection is that the research completed for the book was first used in 1983-1984 to produce the Amanda series of paper dolls produced by Texas Tech University.

Reedstrom *Historic Dress of the Old West* includes thirty-two colored plates plus many black and white drawings by the author that include the weapons, saddles, and other gear in common use. Clothing for men and women is featured, with arrangement by occupation (e.g., soldiers, hunters, outlaws, cattlemen, hurty-gurty girls, and cowboy) and including historical background, with plates and their descriptions. A western illustrator, Reedstrom's research technique included personal interviews, including those with western outfitters and historians, visits to various institutions and exhibits including gun shows, and use of photographs from libraries and archives from around the country. A bibliography and an index are included.

Caroline R. Milbank, in *New York Fashion: The Evolution of American Style*, emphasizes the history of U.S. design and style. The first chapter, on the nineteenth century, is followed by one for each decade of the twentieth century, to the 1980s. Only women's styles are covered, with black and white and some colored photographs making up a major portion of the presentation. Beginning with the

1950s, brief biographical information is included on selected designers, noting when they worked, for what companies, and special features of their designs. In some cases costs of garments are discussed. Simplicity is mentioned as a major American style element, symbolizing both "self-sufficiency" and "the freedoms inherent in a democracy." This style was reflected at the end of the nineteenth century by the popular "Gibson Girl's shirtwaist and skirt, a fashion that was easily manufactured and appropriate to all classes." This oversized, glossy volume appealing to the general audience has a bibliography, an index, and documentation for all photographs.

Exhibition catalogs are more plentiful for this period. *Costumes and Portraits of Newarkers* by Elizabeth A. Coleman and Robert R. Kerr was published by the Newark Museum, Newark, New Jersey, for an exhibition in 1966. *Flashes of Fashion: 1830-1972* by Betty Mills, curator of historic fashion and textiles, Texas Tech University Museum, was produced by the West Texas Museum Association in 1973 as a follow-up to a fashion show. The show, exhibit, and catalog were produced to promote the costume collection at the museum. The catalog consists of colored photographs of local models wearing costumes from the collection with descriptions of the garments, including provenance. Photographs are arranged by type of costume for example, "unusual" and "traditional" wedding dresses, color on black," "jewels on black," "the pink look," and Duchess Gowns from Fiesta de San Jacinto. This last category represents the recognition in the collection of the local San Antonio celebration of Texas's independence from Mexico. During the celebration a queen is crowned, and elaborate dresses are designed for the occasion. A bibliography including periodicals is provided. Also in 1972, from the Brooklyn Museum came Elizabeth A. Coleman *Changing Fashions, 1800-1970*, accompanying the first exhibition in the "newly designed Costume Galleries." The catalog consists of thirty-four photographs of costumed mannequins with brief descriptions of the costumes. Clothing worn by American women is featured.

A major research effort is exemplified in the classic *Suiting Everyone: The Democratization of Clothing in America* by Claudia B. Kidwell, associate curator, Division of Costume and Furnishings, and Margaret C. Christman. The publication, supported by Sears, Roebuck and Company, Chicago, and complementing the Smithsonian exhibit of the same name, hoped to inspire scholars to explore this area of study. Clothes for men and women made from woven cloth are featured. It became necessary during preparations for the Smithsonian exhibit to appeal to the American public for donations of daytime and sportswear clothing for the period 1920-1970. The public responded with examples from both "our industries' greatest designers" and "clothing worn by the majority of Americans. Black and white and some color photographs illustrate the manufacturing aspects, which are the major focus of the volume, but also show examples of American clothing itself depicted in advertisements, company catalogs, posters, lithographs, brochures, and other primary sources. A bibliography is included. Other catalogs produced in the 1970s include *What She Wore: Fashion in America, 1870-1900* for the 1977 exhibition at the Helen Ward Memorial Costume Room, Allen Memorial Art Museum, Oberlin, Ohio; *Eight Chicago Women and Their Fashions, 18691929* by Elizabeth Jachimowicz for the Chicago Historical Society; and *Women's Clothing and Accessories, 1800-1930* a booklet produced for the Dartmouth College Museum and Galleries exhibition in 1979, with an introduction by Margaret E. Spicer.

A *Stitch in Time: Clothing the Middle Class Family, 1850-1910* published by the Margaret Woodbury Strong Museum, Rochester, New York, was accompanied by transparencies and slides. Also in the 1980s the Crocker Art Museum, Sacramento, California, produced *A Century of Women's Costume, 1814-1914* from its own collections; the catalog was designed by Ardwe Strich with photographs by Hilary F. Marks. Another museum collection was featured in *An Elegant Art; Fashion and Fantasy in the Eighteenth Century* collections of the Los Angeles County Museum of Art are the focus. Museum director Earl A. Powell III mentions costume as a fairly recently recognized art form and costume history as a relatively new area for academic research; the exhibit and catalog required nearly four years of research and planning. Also in 1983 Riverside, California, celebrated its centennial with *A Century of Costume, 1883-1983* by Brenda B. Focht in cooperation with B. Vincent Moses. Many wedding gowns are featured. The Los Angeles County Museum of Art's Edward Maeder with Dale C. Gluckman organized in 1984 *Dressed for the Country, 1860-1900*; an essay by Evelyn Ackerman is provided in the catalog. Sports clothes from the United States and Europe are featured. At the Museum of Art, Rhode Island School of

Design, *American Style: Masterpieces of Fashion, 18801968* accompanied the 1986 exhibit. The introduction is by Susan A. Hay, curator of costumes and textiles, with text by Phyllis Feldkamp. Biographies of fifteen designers conclude the catalog. Otto C. Thieme, curator of costumes and textiles, Cincinnati Art Museum, produced *Simply Stunning: 200 Years of Fashion from the Cincinnati Art Museum* in 1988.

Beate Ziegert *American Clothing. Identity in Mass Culture, 1840 to 1990* was published as part of the special 1991 spring issue of the *Human EcologyForum.*

Forum, devoted to the Cornell University costume exhibit of the same name and the costume collection at Cornell. Clothing as popular culture is emphasized. In 1992 the Mint Museum of Art, Charlotte, North Carolina, produced *The Gilded Cage: Victorian Bustle Fashion 1867* through 1889 to accompany its exhibit. With *Grace and Favor: Victorian and Edwardian Fashion in America* by Otto C. Thieme, Elizabeth A. Colemen, Michelle Oberly, and Patricia Cunningham represented a major traveling exhibition first shown at the Cincinnati Art Museum in 1993. Thieme mentions in his acknowledgments that the "catalogue is the first major publication devoted to our understanding of the dynamics of women's fashion in the United States between 1837 and 1910. It includes color photographs of clothing in the exhibit, as well as a glossary and a bibliography.

In 1994 Richard Martin and Harold Koda collaborated to produce *Orientalism: Visions of the East in Western Dress* for the exhibition "Exoticism in Art" at the Metropolitan Museum of Art. Also in 1994 Barbara A. Schreier wrote *Becoming American Women: Clothing and the Jewish Immigrant Experience, 1880-1920* for the exhibition first shown at the Chicago Historical Society and then at the Ellis Island Immigration Museum and the National Museum of American Jewish History in Philadelphia.

Theses noted for this period include an early 1923 work for the Faculty of Household Arts Education at Columbia University by Anna Wilson, "History of American Dress as Affected by Political, Social, and Economic Conditions." In 1945 at Cornell, Elizabeth Brown wrote "American Woman's Dress as Seen in a Fashion Publication, 1870-1899, the Bustle Era." In 1955 Lois Foreman, at Cornell, and Betty Henshaw, at the University of Colorado, researched urban men's clothing and the dress reform movement of the 1850s, respectively. Marilyn Clifford wrote "The Evolution of American Children's Clothing from 1890 to 1930 while during the next two years, Mississippi plantation clothing practices and dress reform received attention from Lucy Sibley and Jane Purdy, respectively.

The 1960s reveals a thesis by Lorraine Simpson on women's Civil War clothing, Dorothy Smith work on the industrial revolution's effects on nineteenth-century costume, and a doctoral dissertation by Roberta Baker on high fashion as an expression of social and artistic trends, 1870-1900. In 1963 Georgia Parker focused on the clothing of William Henry Harrison and his associates, while two other theses concentrated on women's clothing in specific regions: Suman Shenoi on Minnesota and Barbara Fargo on Kansas.

In 1970 the Sears catalogs were used by Janet Jelen to analyze changes in style and customs. Sally Helvenston related children's costume, 1841-1885, to the child's role in society, and Barbara Ekeland wrote "The Evolution of Women's Fashions in the United States and the Development of the Ready-to-Wear Garment Industry 1890-1900". The other theses noted during this decade focus on regions of the United States: Carmen Abbott studied Knoxville, Tennessee, women's dress, 1895-1910, and relationships to socioeconomic and political factors; Kristine Halleran compared northern and southern women's dress, 1830-1850; Debra Bennett researched Mormon dress in Nebraska, 1840-1860; Joyce Larson studied pioneer women's clothing in the Dakotas, 1861-1889; and Margaret Ordonez completed "A Frontier Reflected in Costume, Tallahassee, Leon County, Florida: 1824-1861".

The 1980s reveal the most numerous theses covering the nineteenth century. Play in American culture using costume, 1890-1930, was studied by Michael Dominque. The male image as reflected in popular humor about dress during the period 1880-1910 was researched by Jo Paoletti. Other theses featuring popular culture and clothing include Hae Kim 1989 look at how *Harper's Bazaar* revealed Eastern influences on dress during the period 1890-1927. Several master's theses concentrate on methods of dating and categorizing clothing. Joyce Shore tested an "Instrument Developed to Categorize Adult Female Clothing 1870 to 1898"; Pamela Rabalais evaluated a "Dating Procedure Applied to Fashion Illustrations in Godey's Lady's Book from 1870 to 1897"; and Julie Renner researched the "Dating Process of a Nineteenth-Century Dress and Bodice." Regional studies include nonIndian clothing of the Sonoran Desert area, Arizona, 1880-1930, by Brenda Brandt; Kansas women's clothing, 1845-1985, by Sally Helvenston and rural North Carolina men's clothing, 1860-1870, by Rebecca Cornwell. Health issues were studied in 1986 by Ernabeth Rey for the period 1860-1910, in 1988 by Nancy Taylor for the period 1851-1897, and in 1989 by Christina Serra for the period 1890-1920s, with a focus on "Health Advice Concerning Children's Clothing." Other works cover the "fashionable silhouette" and the crinoline, 1850- 1870, by Janis Burch "Navajo Women's Dress 1860-1910," by Cynthia Grounds and the "Dress of the James J. Hill Family, 1863-1916" by Carol Colburn.

These noted completed during the first half of the 1990s reflect some new interests, such as: "Clothing Adaptations of Civil War Amputees" by Laurann Figg, "The Influence of Fashion on the Dress of AfricanAmerican Women in Georgia, 1870-1915" by Patricia Hunt, and "preRaphaelite influences" on Victorian women's dress by Pamela Radcliffe, all completed in 1990. Morman clothing, 1840-1850, was researched by Carma de Jung Anderson in 1992. In 1993 "The Role of Dress in Eastern Dakota and White Interaction, 1834-1862" was researched by David Trayte where dress was seen as a "symbol in contending cultures."

1900s

Monographs featuring the twentieth century include the 1940 David L. Cohn publication, *The Good Old Days: A History of American Morals and Manners as Seen through the Sears, Roebuck Catalogs 1905 to the Present*. The foreword by Sinclair Lewis was written on December 22, 1939. Cohn uses the Sears merchandise to show how American products expressed U.S. independence from Europe. Clothing and accessories featured include watches and watch cases, beauty products, hair products, hats, silk stockings, corsets, underwear, bathing suits, and men's sports equipment, underwear, and night shirts. In the section "Clothes Make the Man," the "Staunton suit" is mentioned as winning friends and influencing people, a product so designed by Sears with Dale Carnegie's ideas in mind that one could experience the benefits of wearing the suit while paying only two dollars a month. Part 4 concentrates on the history and influence of the Sears catalogs on Americans. An index and some illustrations by the author are included.

Some British authors provide helpful background on twentieth-century European fashion generally. Jane Dorner has written for the general audience on this period: *Fashion in the Twenties and Thirties* and *Fashion in the Forties and Fifties*. Both are highly visual, using many photographs in black and white and some in color, as well as cartoons. Arrangement is by topic. Each chapter contains a few pages of text followed by the illustrations. Forewords by Prudence Glynn and James Laver, respectively, add further analysis to the presentations. The focus is on everyday clothing. Elizabeth Ewing first edition of *History of Twentieth Century Fashion* was also produced in England in 1974. It provides background as well and generated enough interest for second and third editions in 1986 and 1992. The 1992 edition, revised and updated by Alice Mackrell, is arranged chronologically, with an index and bibliography, and including 307 illustrations. British journalist Ernestine Carter wrote *The Changing World of Fashion, 1900 to the Present*. The volume is dedicated to Doris Langley Moore and states that due to her "perseverence and generosity Britain owes its unique Museum of Costume at Bath." Carter discusses the "best of the best (and the most typical)" styles for women, according to Diana Vreeland's introduction. Vreeland adds that Carter's opinions and theories on how "certain silhouettes evolved" are enlightening and include comparisons between the American and European fashion centers. The chapter "Where America Leads" presents Carter's thoughts on American fashion. Illustrations in color and black and white are documented; notes, a bibliography, and an index are provided. The 1960s are featured again from the British viewpoint in Barbara Bernard's 1978 overview. Mostly photographs, the volume provides background on the Quant phenomenon and the mods as well as Chelsea shops and styles.

In 1981 the Men's Fashion Association produced *Generation of Change: A History of Male Fashion Trends, 1956-1980*. Written to commemorate the twenty-first anniversary of the founding of the association in 1955, Norman Kerr, the executive director, wrote in the foreword that the association was established to heighten men's interest in clothes by promoting "a unified industry campaign." The promotional materials produced by this alliance included articles for consumer magazines and broadcast media, fashion reports in January and June, and press kits and supplements for hundreds of newspapers in the fall and spring. Other campaign efforts featured "back-to-school," "active sportswear," "Father's Day" and other holiday materials; slide kits for retail stores; videotapes for some one hundred television stations every six months; and even promoting awards such as the Cutty Sark Men's Fashion Design Awards and the Lulu Awards for fashion journalism. In addition to recounting the history of the association's work and fashion changes for men, it includes many advertisements for men's wear to commemorate the occasion.

Sears's Everyday Fashions are again featured in 1981, this time with reprints of catalog pages from the 1920s. Stella Blum, costume curator at the Metropolitan Museum of Art, New York, provides the introduction and a comment on each year for 1919 through 1930-1931, which helps the reader see the trends and influences. A visual reminder of what products were for sale to the public, the presentation of clothing on people allows the viewer to see hair styles and accessories, such as shoes and hats, as well. Blum points out that the catalogs offered a reflection of Paris fashion about a year later than introduced in Paris. The advertisement text itself with prices adds to our knowledge of the attitudes and economics of the decade, just as the models themselves portray the white population, to the exclusion of any minority presence. A similar publication, *Everyday Fashions of the Thirties*, also edited by Blum, appeared in 1986.

Ellen Melinkoff *What We Wore: An Offbeat Social History of Women's Clothing, 1950 to 1980* reflects her interest in people, clothing, and journalism. A freelance writer in Los Angeles, she presents signed excerpts from women's letters reflecting on their own clothing experiences during the 1950s, 1960s, and 1970s. Entertaining reading (remembering "'falling' off those darned high platform shoes"), the letters reveal common issues and attitudes. A special feature is the last chapter, "Fashion Magazines in General and *Mademoiselle*'s College Issue in Particular."

The photographer's view is artfully and colorfully presented in Richard Martin and Harold Koda *Jocks and Nerds: Men's Style in the Twentieth Century*. This oversize volume groups men and their attire into twelve categories that represent "persistent style modes of the twentieth century. The introductory and chapter text present analysis as only these two fashion experts could provide. The choice of photographs, most of them from the United States and Europe, does begin to present a reflection of society as it is, with people from minority groups appearing: "The Jock" contains three men of color out of twenty-eight whites; "The Worker," three of thirty-four; "Military Man," one of twenty; "Sportsman," one Asian out of fifty; and "The Dandy," three black out of fortynine. No minorities are seen in the sections on the "Businessman," "Cowboy," "Hunter," "Joe College," "Nerd," "Man about Town," or "Rebel." The authors point out that because tradition is so important in men's clothing, even a subtle change in dress, such as the color of a man's socks, can alter "the role and the man." Many photographs are of famous entertainers and artists; clothing advertisement and "fashion editorials" are included as well. All photographs are documented. The bibliography provides an excellent look at the literature on men's clothing.

Women are featured in Jane Gaines and Charlotte Herzog edited volume, *Fabrications: Costume and the Female Body*. Movies provide the evidence to support their views on how women and their bodies are represented to the public. "Fabrications" was chosen to symbolize "fictions for the eye. One essay, for example, by Herzog, is entitled "'Powder Puff' Promotion: The Fashion-Show-in-the Film." A few of the eleven individual essays are reprinted materials. In 1992 Elane Feldman, writer and adjunct assistant professor at New York University, published an eyecatching volume, *Fashions of a Decade, the 1990s*. Obviously unable to review the whole decade, she features a few themes, such as the influences of sportswear, relaxed office wear, miniskirted suits, clothes for larger women, and "ecowear," or the reflection of various societal causes and other influences on fashion. She also talks about the future. Geared to a young audience, the book includes a glossary and mostly colored photographs with original drawings by Robert Price. The volume is part of a new series, *Fashions of a Decade*, edited by Valerie Cumming, Museum of London. Sears catalogs were again featured by Dover in 1992 with *Eveveryday Fashions of the Forties*. Continuity of the Dover series and text is provided by costume curator JoAnne Olian of the Museum of the City of New York. Popular clothing of that decade examined includes the Chesterfield coat, cardigan sweaters, denim play clothes, and Roy Rogers cowboy-type clothing for children. One value to the Sears catalogs is that they offer a look at clothing and accessories available for men, women, and children. Newer publications include *50s Popular Fashions for Men, Women, Boys and Girls* by Roseann Ettinger.

Exhibition catalogs identified that feature twentieth-century costume include the 1975 Metropolitan Museum of Art's *American Women of Style* whose exhibit included "fashions designed by and/ or worn by 10 wellknown American women." Diana Vreeland and Stella Blum provide the text; nineteen illustrations are included. In 1979 the Indianapolis Museum of Art complemented an exhibition of American costumes representing the period 1900 to 1927 with a catalog entitled *A Rustle of Silk: Costumes from the Caroline Burford Danner Estate*. S. P. Schoelwer describes the costumes and provides biographical information on Danner and her two dress designers, Girolamo D. Giuseffi and Geroge P. Meier, Wearable art, including costumes, hats, and shoes, is featured by *Maximum Coverage: Wearables by Contemporay American Artists* sponsored by the Kohler Arts Center in Wisconsin for a 1980 exhibit. *Mystique and Identity: Women's Fashions of the 1950*s held at the Chrysler Museum in Virginia in 1984 featured the "feminine mystique" as seen in clothing, advertisements, and cartoons. The text by Barbara A. Schreier includes a historical discussion covering the period. Some of the more popular advertisements for products, which might help create such "mystique," are Warnaco's Merry Widow Bras, Helena Rubenstein's "How-to-Be-Blond" promotion, and Revlon's "Fire & Ice" makeup. Most of the costumes were from the collection of Jean Outland Chrysler; thirty black and white photographs and twelve colored plates are included in the catalog.

In 1985 the Kohler Arts Center produced an exhibition catalog on a very different theme, *Hmong Art: Tradition and Change*, with essays by Timothy Dunnigan , Amy Catlin, and Joanne Cubbs. Changes experienced by Laotian Hmong refugees in the United States are reflected by various handmade artifacts. Hmong ceremonial clothing, color significance in their clothing, and jewelry are included in an essay written by Cubbs on their art. Their experiences with adapting to the United States are also explained. Back at the Metropolitan Museum of Art in New York, *Diana Vreeland; Immoderate Style* was produced as a boxed edition containing catalog and portfolio in 1993, with text by Richard Martin and Harold Koda.

Most theses identified dealing with the twentieth century explore influences on clothing. The impact of war as a drastic event is researched by Janet Eiger in her "Effects of World War II Shortages and Regulations on American Women's Fashions, 1942-1945" and by Melissa Fullam in "Just for the Duration: American Women's Fashions during World War Two". Less violent and more general societal influences are researched: effects on the fashion silhouette work outside the home for women's fashion 1939-1948 women's rights movements sociocultural reflections on women's clothing, 1919-1929 costume and Anglo-American social history, 1900-1925 socioeconomic effects of the Texas Spindletop oil boom about 1990 on female fashions in Beaumont, Texas and social aspects of middle-class 1950s clothing.

Design or artistic influences are represented by two studies on the flapper fashion design, by Barbara Allen and Paulette Kontos analysis of "Fashion Curves in Women's Clothing Styles, 1930-1979" by Marilyn Burns and "Art Deco Influences on Women's Dress from 1915 to 1925" by Robyn Gibson-Quick. Paul Poiret's influence for the period 1905-1915 was studied by Catherine Young and his influence on "Society Women's Fashions as Reported by the San Francisco Chronicle, 1910-1915" was studied by Willette Cantua. Chanel's impact on women's fashion was covered by Florence Bailey. Hollywood film costume influence in the 1930s was researched by Susan Prichard.

Other design influences include those from groups within the United States to foreign influences generally. In 1957 Edith C. Donaldson studied effects of Navaho costume on southwestern fashions, and Sandra Sibson examined the French influence on women's clothing, 1917-1927, in 1965. Two theses cover the impact of Egyptian fashion: Insaf Nasr in 1966 and Sara Pape in 1983. "Indian Influence on American Costume from 1960 to 1975" was studied by Hye Kim in her 1990 Ph.D. thesis.

Ethnic group clothing itself is represented by Virginia Anderson 1957 study of Montana Flat Head and Kutenai Indian reservation costume, Margaret Hunter's 1960 study of selected Indian clothing and its relation to culture change, Mary Jacobsen's 1972 work on Norwegian-American ethnic clothing, and Pamela Sandage's 1977 study of Mexican-American clothing. Young people's clothing is researched by Sister Marie Mayer in her 1956 inventory of teenage girls' clothing and by Ann Stroup in her 1967 study of children's dress, 1930-1941. Women's "consciousness" and "identity" are reflected through clothing studies in 1981 by Kathy Sherman for the 1920s and in 1986 by Catherine Cerny for a group of Minnesota quilters. One comparative study concludes the review. It compares selected clothing in Salt Lake City, Utah, with those in New York City, 1900-1909, and was by Karen Janes in 1972.

❑❑❑

3

ESTABLISHING IDENTITY ON FASHION

Introduction

Fashion is an odd jumble of contradictions, of sympathies and antipathies. It exists only by its being participated among a certain number of persons, and its essence is destroyed by being communicated to a greater number. It is a continual struggle between "the great vulgar and the small" to get the start of or keep up with each other in the race of appearances, by an adoption on the part of the one of such external and fantastic symbols as strike the attention and excite the envy or admiration of the beholder, and which are no sooner made known and exposed to public view for this purpose, than they are successfully copied by the multitude, the slavish herd of imitators, who do not wish to be behind-hand with their betters in outward show and pretensions, and which then sink, without any farther notice, into disrepute and contempt. Thus fashion lives only in a perpetual round of giddy innovation and restless vanity. To be old-fashioned is the greatest crime a coat or a hat can by guilty of. To look like nobody else is a sufficiently mortifying reflection: to be in danger of being mistaken for one of the rabble is worse. Fashion constantly begins and ends in the two things it abhors most, singularity and vulgarity. It is the perpetual setting up and disowning a certain standard of taste, elegance, and refinement, which has no other foundation or authority than that it is the prevailing distinction of the moment, which was yesterday ridiculous from its being new, and to-morrow will be odious from its being common. It is one of the most slight and insignificant of all things. It cannot be lasting, for it depends on the constant change and shifting of its own harlequin disguises; it cannot be sterling, for, if it were, it could not depend on the breath of caprice; it must be superficial, to produce its immediate effect on the gaping crowd; and frivolous, to admit of its being assumed at pleasure by the numbers of those who affect, by being in the fashion, to be distinguished from the rest of the world. It is not anything in itself, nor the sign of any thing but the folly and vanity of those who rely upon it as their greatest pride and ornament. It takes the firmest hold of the most flimsy and narrow minds, of those whose emptiness conceives of nothing excellent but what is thought so by others, and whose self-conceit makes them willing to confine the opinion of all excellence to themselves and those like them. That which is true or beautiful in itself, is not the less so for standing alone. That which is good for anything, is the better for being more widely diffused. But fashion is the abortive issue of vain ostentation and exclusive egotism: it is haughty, trifling, affected, servile, despotic, mean, and ambitious, precise and fantastical, all in a breath – tied to no rule, and bound to conform to every whim of the minute. "The fashion of an hour old mocks the wearer." It is a sublimated essence of levity, caprice, vanity, extravagance, idleness, and selfishness. It thinks of nothing but not being contaminated by vulgar use, and winds and doubles like a hare, and betakes itself to the most paltry shifts to avoid being overtaken by the common hunt that are always in full chase after it. It contrives to keep up its fastidious pretensions, not by the difficulty of the attainment, but by the rapidity and evanescent nature of the changes. It is a sort of conventional badge, or understood passport into select circles, which must still be varying (like the water-mark in bank-notes) not to be counterfeited by those without the pale of fashionable society; for to make the test of admission to all the privileges of that refined and volatile atmosphere depend on any real merit or extraordinary accomplishment, would exclude too many of the pert, the dull, the ignorant, too many shallow, upstart, and self-admiring pretenders, to enable the few that passed muster to keep one another in any tolerable countenance. If it were the fashion, for instance, to be distinguished for virtue, it would be difficult to set or follow the example; but then this would confine the pretension to a small number, (not the most fashionable part of the community), and would carry a very singular air with it. Or if excellence in any art or science were made the standard of fashion, this would also effectually prevent vulgar imitation, but then it would equally prevent fashionable impertinence. There would be an obscure circle of *virtu* as well as virtue, drawn within the established circle of fashion, a little province of a mighty empire the example of honesty would spread slowly, and learning would still have to boast of a respectable minority. But of what use would such uncourtly and out-of-the-way accomplishments be to the great and noble, the rich and the fair, without any of the *eclat,* the noise and nonsense which belong to that which is followed and admired by all the world alike? The real and solid will never do for the current coin, the common wear and tear of foppery and fashion. It must be the meretricious, the showy, the outwardly fine, and intrinsically worthless that which lies within the reach of the most indolent affectation, that which can be put on or off at the suggestion of the most wilful caprice, and for which, through all its fluctuations, no mortal reason can be given, but that it is the newest absurdity in vogue! What shews the worthlessness of mere fashion is, to see how easily this vain and boasted distinction is assumed, when the restraints of decency or circumstances are once removed, by the most uninformed and commonest of the people. I know an undertaker that is the greatest prig in the streets of London, and an Aldermanbury haberdasher, that has the most military strut of any lounger in Bond-street or St. James's. We may, at any time, raise a regiment of fops from the same number of fools, who have vanity enough to be intoxicated with the smartness of their appearance, and not sense enough to be ashamed of themselves. Everyone remembers the story in Peregrine Pickle, of the strolling gipsy that he picked up in spite, had well scoured, and introduced her into genteel company, where she met with great applause, till she got into a passion by seeing a fine lady cheat at cards, rapped out a volley of oaths, and let nature get the better of art. Dress is the great secret of address. Clothes and confidence will set anybody up in the trade of modish accomplishment. Look at the two classes of well-dressed females whom we see at the play-house, in the boxes. Both are equally dressed in the height of the fashion, both are *rouged,* and wear their neck and arms bare both have the same conscious, haughty, theatrical air the same toss of the head, the same stoop in the shoulders, with all the grace that arises from a perfect freedom from embarrassment, and all the fascination that rises from a systematic disdain of formal prudery the same pretence and jargon of fashionable conversation the same mimicry of tones and phrases the same "lisping, and ambling, and painting, and nicknaming of Heaven's creatures"; the same every thing but real propriety of behaviour, and real refinement of sentiment. In all the externals, they are as like as the reflection in the lookingglass. The only difference between the woman of fashion and the woman of pleasure is, that the one *is* what the other only *seems to be;* and yet, the victims of dissipation who thus rival and almost outshine women of the first quality in all the blaze, and pride, and glitter of shew and fashion, are, in general, no better that a set of raw, uneducated, inexperienced country girls, or awkward, coarse-fisted servant maids who require no other apprenticeship or qualification to be on a level with persons of the highest distinction in society, in all the brilliancy and elegance of outward appearance, than that they have forfeited its common privileges, and every title to respect in reality. The truth is, that real virtue, beauty, or understanding, are the same, whether "in a high or low degree"; and the airs and graces of pretended superiority over these which the highest classes give themselves, from mere frivolous and external accomplishments, are easily imitated, with provoking success, by the lowest, whenever they *dare Biographical note* William Hazlitt was an English writer. As the son of a Unitarian preacher who supported the American revolution, his childhood was spent in Ireland and North America until the age of nine. In his late twenties, he studied painting, worked as a portrait painter, lectured on philosophy, and produced his first book. He later worked as a parliamentary reporter, an art, literary and theater critic, and biographer. His essays are known for his humanist philosophy.

National Costume

A recent writer closes an article on "Licentiousness in the Fine Arts" with these words: "Let us have a Christian art if need be, an American Christian art and if the great artistic world contemn us, we can pity it till it learns better." To this we heartily respond, and beg leave to add, Let us have a *Christian costume,* and, if need be, an *American Christian costume;* and if the fashionable world at Paris and elsewhere sneer at us, we ought to be able to bear it till they shall have learned to imitate us.

If, as a nation, we are in some danger of marring our innate modesty while taking the corrupt art of the old world, especially European art, for our mode, no more can we go on imitating the costume and manners of one of the most corrupt cities of the old world without a corresponding loss in our morality and native good taste. Costume, it is true, is no more identical with morals than taste is, yet one may and greatly does influence the other, as, for instance, no one would expect to find an immodest costume on a Christian woman of refined taste, any more than he would look for a neat, modest, and elegant attire on a courtesan.

But what *is* costume? Webster defines it to be "an established mode of dress." According to this definition, then, nothing of the kind had existed among us during the last one hundred and fifty years; for in a period of less than one hundred years, from 1760 to 1850, we find more than twenty of the most distinct fashions in existence, to say not one word of the numberless *variations* of these fashions during the same time. Perhaps most of our women have a dim recollection of reading somewhere of such a thing as Japanese, Spanish, or Italian costume for females; well, we assure them no historian or chronicler of veracity will ever venture to tell the world what is the *national* costume of American, English, or French ladies. He might, indeed, go so far as to say, that the women of these countries wore certain articles of dress called bonnets, hats, shawls, cloaks, mantillas, and gowns, of every imaginable size, shape, color, and material; but a more definite description he could not venture on. And he might add, as an incontrovertible truth, that, as a general thing, in matters of dress the French took the lead, and the rest of the enlightened world, regardless of health, climate, comfort, or even modesty, acquiesced in all humility. But all must see that it is at war with our form of government, to be dependent on the nod of a foreign aristocracy for the form and material of our dress; and in the abstract not so abstractly either it is at war with national prosperity. For an extravagant, foreign costume, presupposes a corresponding style of living, both of which are a sure and speedy means for the depletion of either a private or public treasury. And during the process of this depletion we must take into account how often and sorely peace and justice are trampled under foot; for be the extravagance whatever it may, it is the bone and sinew of the land the laboring masses who must apply the means for its gratification. We will not stop to say how much the national prosperity has advanced since the discovery of gold in California; but it is surely of little avail to the country that one vessel after another arrives at New York laden with its million, or half-million of gold dust, if an equivalent sum is as often shipped to Europe to pay for foreign goods, which the country could well dispense with, if our women had a little more of the spirit of the elder Mrs. Adams.

If anyone has doubts as to the increasing extravagance of costume among American women, he has only to glance carefully over the statistical tables of imports, to convince himself that costly foreign goods form something more than moderate items in the list. Indeed, to such a degree of insanity one can call it nothing else have a class of American women arrived, that it is asserted that merchants and milliners find it no easy matter to procure goods sufficiently high-priced to suit their taste and purses; they, to their shame and folly be it said, being more particular about the price than the quality. American women at Paris, and other places, are known to purchase articles of dress at prices which would startle a duchess, whose annual income alone amounts to more than the entire fortune of some of these would-be aristocrats. No wonder crashing, ruinous failures follow in the footsteps of such inexcusable imbecility no wonder if these dear Europeans point their fingers at us, and ask sneeringly among themselves, to what quarter of the globe we have cast our former re-publican spirit. Why, it is not so very many years ago since our fathers fought, and bled, and died, and *conquered* in the struggle to secure an independent government for us; and our mothers, scorning the luxuries of the old world, spun and wove, and cut and made the clothing for their entire household; have their children degenerated so *soon'}* Is it true that Americans, and especially American women, have already become so incompetent, so utterly wanting in the article of ingenuity, that they can not even contrive to model for themselves a costume at once neat, comfortable, and elegant; and which might be regarded by other nations as something of an index to their professed democratic principles?

But even greater than the necessity which exists for reform in dress and which in fact must precede it is the want of a spirit of independence, which will enable Americans to be more emphatically *themselves;* for it is folly to deny that this grand emblem of nationality is painfully wanting in the so-called "society," who claim the privilege of giving tone to manners and morals. It is plain to every observer, that if the mass of our people were as deficient in patriotism as this exclusive class, our form of government would crumble to dust in a twinkling. And, so long as the "exclusive few" continue to spend their energies in making as close an imitation to European life as their means and position will allow, it is useless to expect they will exert themselves much in behalf of the elevation of their own countrymen. Happily enough, however, the country can tolerably well dispense with them; for it is the intelligent, independent, and patriotic masses who are the pillars upholding government, and who alone give a practical voice to religion and politics, to morals and customs.

For we hold that individual culture must, to a great extent, precede all permanent elevation of the masses; there may, indeed, be individual culture without this elevation of the whole, but most assuredly no permanent elevation of the mass without the exclusive culture of the individual. Nor need this again be the least discouragement, but rather otherwise as it leaves each woman free to act, speak, and improve herself for whatever her own judgment dictates to be her proper sphere; provided, always, that at no time she steps beyond the bounds of propriety, religion, and her domestic duties. For every true woman is a law unto herself, and needs not that the public should prescribe rules for the regulation of her life, any more than for the expense or mode of her wardrobe; the most she needs is a word of encouragement to keep her in that path of duty, which she has already marked out for herself. And every true woman can, ought, and will do something for her own individual culture and elevation, independently of what society expects and academic halls prescribe. And if at any time she be lacking in motive to exertion, she has but to bear in mind who plucked the apple, and what the consequences have been; she will then soon learn that, as through her man fell, so also through her must she rise again to his former estate. But before she can ever achieve this restoration, she has first to learn more thoroughly for herself, that as an intellectual being, an immortal soul, the food for her mind is of infinitely more importance that the raiment for her body, and the intelligent mastery and guidance of her own spirit, worth ten thousand triumphs in a fleeting world of fashion.

Biographical note Mary Fry was a regular contributor to *The Ladies' Repository,* a monthly periodical dedicated to literature, arts, and religion, published during the nineteenth century. In the mid1800s, she published eleven articles in *The Ladies' Repository,* with topics that ranged from dress to writing manuscripts for publications.

Psychology of Woman's Dress

The advances which modern life has made over savagery are represented at some points by a very thin line. Old practices are refined, the old forms are presented with slightly different coloring and arrangement, and the emphasis is placed at different points, but we do not get clean away from the old patterns. Savage life, in its turn, borders very close on the animal, and sociology and psychology must continually go back to the simpler conditions of animal life to pick up the cue. Man is naturally one of the most unadorned of animals, without brilliant appearance or natural glitter, with no plumage, no spots or stripes, no naturally sweet voice, no attractive odor, and no graceful antics. But, thanks to his hands, he has the power of collecting brilliant objects and attaching them to his person, and he thus becomes a rival in radiance of the animals and flowers. Rapid rotation style is a device to attract attention not known to animal life and not systematically used in the Orient. The woman of the Far East uses expensive and attractive materials, but she wears them, as she does jewels, for a long period. Among Occidental women the discarding of dress is not only seasonal but, if it can be afforded, diurnal. The constant change is not only striking in itself, but the economic ability to make it distinguish both the woman and the man whom she represents. What Mr. Veblen happily terms "conspicuous waste" is a means of distinction which the masses are not in a position to copy.

Personal display is dangerous ground for woman, since it involves disgust in the spectator when overdone, and she would never be bold enough to carry it to such outspoken lengths if she were not operating in a flock. She is timid about emphasizing herself except as one of a flock, but she is anxious for all the conspicuousness she can get in the flock, and is above all concerned to be a member of the most distinguished flock. At this point she shows some independence of man and almost loses sight of him (after marriage, at least) in her interest in outstripping other women. Men would prefer her more simply dressed; but this is her game indeed, it is almost her business.

As society advances there is a tendency in man to give up ornament and in woman to take on more of it. This is not because man is naturally less inclined to display, but because he has undergone a great reform in his habits, the greatest perhaps in the history of the world. Primitive man was pugnacious, unsocial, ostentatious, and lazy, but capable, crafty, and masterfuly our true adventurer, but endowed with an inventive imagination and capable of splendid bursts of energy. This was the wild-oats period of the race, and its vestiges are still seen in the gamester, the artist, the wild youth, and the dissipated husband.

But when man exhausted the game which had been his principal pursuit and began to take up the settled manufacturing and agricultural interests which had been chiefly developed by woman, and to buy and sell, he brought with him more ingenuity than woman had ever developed, a freer movement, a greater power of organization, and at the same time less domestic responsibility, and he gradually transferred some of his interest in the pursuit of game to the pursuit of business. But business lies, so to speak, outside the region of appearances. It is primarily a matter of judgment, efficiency, and energy, and if a man has efficiency and wealth in abundance he is attractive enough without ornament. No one ever completely loses an interest in bright objects, but business men take advantage of this fact to display their goods, not their persons. The color sense and the sexual interest are recognized in the display, wrapping, and advertising of wares. The glaring billboard and the beautiful lady on the cigar-box saturate the goods with color and sex, and we buy them on that basis. But pretentiously housed business and a handsomely gowned wife are also capital advertisements; they are signs of business success, and "nothing succeeds like success."

The dress of woman has, in fact, become so incorporated in business that, as Sir Henry Maine has pointed out, the greatest calamity which could be conceived as befalling great populations would be, not a sanguinary war, a desolating famine, or a deadly epidemic, but a revolution in fashion under which "women should dress, as men practically do, in one material of one color. There are many flourishing and opulent cities in Europe and America which would be condemned by it to bankruptcy or starvation, and it would be worse than a famine or pestilence in China, India, and Japan." That is to say, any great change in our industrial system must be gradual not to be calamitous.

But, while woman's demands occupy so large a place in the industrial world, it is noticeable that she is herself only a pawn in the industrial game played by man. Her individual possessor uses her as a symbol of his wealth, and the captains of industry make her and her changeable and expensive fashions the occasion of a market for the costly and changeable objects which fashionable habits force her to accept. New fashions are not always beautiful; they are even often ugly, and women know it: but they embrace changes as frequent and as radical as the ingenuity of the mode makers can devise. Women do not wear what they want, but what the manufacturers and trades-people want them to want. The people who supply them also control them.

This does not, however, alter the fact that the general tone and pace of social life are deeply influenced by woman's emphasis of finery and form. There is an old story of a lady who purchased a pair of brass andirons and then by degrees persuaded her husband to refurnish the whole house to match them. Just so, when silks and furs and gems and lace and the unminted gold are attached to the person of woman, it follows also that the household and the world in which she moves are transformed to harmonize with her showy taste and appearance. Beginning with the rugs, tapestry, porcelain, silver plate, fine linen, and the rich and gaudy furnishings of the home, the factitious personality of woman pervades and bedizens everything. The baffling array of silver at the twelve-course dinner and the costly box at the costly opera are equally a part of woman's dress. This situation is the despair of men, but it is "society."

The effect of this situation on the character of woman is altogether bad. One interest expels another or prevents its development. The proverbially hollow mind of the very beautiful woman is not due to the exhaustion of nature's resources on her exterior, but to the fact that her attention is so bound up with the expression of her own charm that it stops with that. And the homely woman who competes with her has a still more absorbing problem. The foolish and disrespectful customs of courtesy which men practise toward women are also a product of woman's dress, and tend to keep her helpless in mind and body. The helplessness involved in lacing, high heels, undivided skirts, and other impedimenta of women has a certain charm in the eyes of man. Their helplessness shows him off better by giving freer play to his protective and masterful instincts. It is his heroic opportunity since the disappearance of large game and in the "piping times of peace." To flatter this disposition of man, woman therefore assumes even greater helplessness than she possesses, and the most romantic periods in history are those characterized by tight lacing and purposive fainting.

The role of "half angel and half bird" is a pretty one, if you can look at it in that way; but it denatures woman, makes her a thing instead of a person, a fact of the environment and an object of man's manipulation instead of an agent for transforming the world. It leaves society short-handed and the struggle for life harder and uglier than it would be if woman operated in it as the substantial and superior creature which nature made her. We have a machine-made civilization which has introduced class inequalities, hatred, and suffering unknown in savagery or barbarism. We are wealthy but not humanized. Man is pursuing business on the same pitiless principle that he formerly pursued game. Women have a base of maternal feeling that makes them more social than man, and if the economic value of the superfluity of their dress and the energy and attention they waste in following the fashions were devoted to humanistic enterprises we should be in a fair way to add the elements lacking to make our machine system a civilization. But there is no use trying to talk fashions down. The change will come gradually, as women become more intelligent and independent and of themselves "experience the expulsive power of a new affection."

□□□

4

Fashioning a Cultural Approach to Dress

Introduction

The emphasis on the creation of linear chronologies and stylistic progressions that art historical directions dictated at the time has to some extent influenced the nature of much fashion history writing since. Various approaches have subsequently been adopted following the self-conscious establishment of a school of new art historical thinking in the late 1970s, in which social and political contexts were prioritized over older concerns of authorship and appreciation or connoisseurial value. The arising debates undoubtedly challenged those assumptions that had underpinned the serious study of fashion in the first place. Indeed many of the defining aspects of new art historical approaches, which drew on ideas from Marxism, feminism, psychoanalysis and structuralism or semiotics, encouraged a fresh prominence for debates incorporating problems of social identity, the body, gender and appearance or representation. These are issues that lie at the centre of any definition of fashion itself, though it might be argued that their effect has been to nudge concentration away from the artefact towards an emphasis on social meaning. Rees and Borzello, in their introductory text on the new art history, use instructive examples of the resulting paradigm shift which had broad implications for the study of fashion history. In their definition of the more cultural scope of new art historical approaches, they state that "when an article analyzes the images of women in paintings rather than the qualities of the brushwork, or when a gallery lecturer ignores the sheen of the Virgin Mary's robe for the Church's use of religious art in the counter-reformation, the new art history is casting its shadow".

However close it came to interrogating the cultural meanings of objects depicted in paintings and other forms of cultural production, the new art history remained largely concerned with issues of representation, the relationship between culture and image. Design history, a relatively young discipline compared to the history of art, has perhaps been able to take on board the complexities of social considerations, economic implications and cultural problems that inform and are informed by objects in a less fixed and self-conscious manner. The relationship between production, consumption and the designed artefact, which has always been central to any definition of the discipline, demands an investigation of cultural context, and is well suited to the study of historical and contemporary clothing. As design historian Josephine Miller has stated:

> *This is a multi-faceted subject and in some ways can be seen to relate to almost every area of design and many aspects of the fine arts. It needs to be placed firmly within a cultural context, against a background of technological and industrial change, literary and aesthetic ideas. In the post-industrial period, the marketing and retail outlets, together with developments in advertising and publishing techniques, have brought a new set of considerations with them. Moreover, the study of dress and its production cannot be separated from women's history.*

Ten years on, the expansion of post-colonial studies and the examination of masculinity and sexuality might broaden her list, but it stands as an indication of the potential held in clothing for a design historical and broadly cultural approach. It is surprising then, that despite its fitness for the field, the study of dress and fashion still remains marginal to wider design historical concerns. This perhaps reflects the discipline's roots in industrial and architectural design practice, with their modernist sympathies. A theoretical and inspirational aid to students of industrial and graphic design, design history as originally taught in art and design colleges tended to prioritize production in the professional "masculine" sphere, re-enforcing notions of a subordinate "feminine" area of interest, into which fashion has generally been relegated. The relatively late establishment of fashion-design courses in British art colleges and polytechnics during the 1960s further encouraged a separate provision for contextual and historical studies in clothing and textiles that has probably influenced the semi-detached nature of fashion in the design historical canon ever since.

Related disciplines, including cultural studies and media studies, have arguably taken the politics of identity and appearance "fashion" closer to their core, but tend to concentrate on contemporary issues and confine themselves, in tandem with art history, mainly to the study of representation and promotion, using social anthropology and semiotics as tools to define meaning. Significantly, cultural studies finds its history in a literary rather than a visual tradition, and objects of study reflect those roots, existing as texts to be decoded in the present, rather than reflections or remains to be recovered from the past. Whilst much of this work has found its way through to the teaching of fashion students with their more pressing contemporary interests, broader historical issues have remained largely beyond their concern. This brings me to my own limited intervention in the field, a textbook designed to present fashion history in the context of contemporary historiographical debate. In the face of a potentially confusing and contradictory conflict of interests, I aimed to incorporate elements of art historical, design historical and cultural studies approaches in an attempt to offer a coherent introduction to the history and interpretation of fashionable dress. Used together carefully, these methods promised to provide a fluid framework for the study of fashion in its own right. They could also be set within a wider argument concerning the nature of cultural history generally, which has fostered concepts of diversity rather than prescriptive or narrowly defined readings of historical phenomena. Roger Chartier in his essay that appeared in Lynn Hunt's anthology of new historicist writings outlines the problems in his discussion of the concepts of "popular" and "high" culture, an area especially pertinent to the history of fashionable clothing and the dynamics of cultural studies:

> *First and foremost, it no longer seems tenable to try and establish strict correspondences between cultural cleavages and social hierarchies, creating simplistic relationships between particular cultural objects or*

> *forms and specific social groups. On the contrary, it is necessary to recognize the fluid circulation and shared practices that cross social boundaries. Second, it does not seem possible to identify the absolute difference and the radical specificity of popular culture on the basis of its own texts, beliefs or codes. The materials that convey the practices and thoughts of ordinary people are always mixed, blending forms and themes, invention and tradition, literate culture and folklore. Finally the macroscopic opposition between "popular" and "high" culture has lost its pertinence. An inventory of the multiple divisions that fragment the social body is preferable to this massive partition.*

It is the central contention of much recent work which places clothing in the cultural sphere that clothing has played a defining, but largely uncredited role in the formulation of such differences, microscopic, highly subjective, and deeply personal though their manifestation in dress may be. Fashion therefore requires a method of analysis that takes account of multiple meanings and interpretations. Reductive connections between social influences and fashionable appearance have dogged much fashion history, unaware as it has sometimes seemed to be of the difficulties and complexity of agency. It is here that the new cultural history, in tandem with more recent work in cultural studies, is of use, presenting a more questioning framework which allows for explanations that are multi-layered and open ended. The historians Melling and Barry have presented a model that acknowledges difference and tensions between new cultural approaches, suggesting a more positive use for the harnessing of divergent directions:

> *It would be misleading to present all these changes as moving in harmony and in a single intellectual direction. For example, there is a clear tension between the emphasis laid by some, notably literary critics, on the autonomous power of the text and language, compared to the interest of others in recovering the intentions of historical actors. Put crudely, the former are seeking to deconstruct the identity and rationality of historical actors, while the latter strive to reconstruct them. To some extent we are seeing, within the concept of "culture" as a basis of historical explanation, a revival of the standard sociological debate between "structure" and "action". Should culture be considered as a given system or structure within which past actors are predestined to operate? Or does the emphasis on culture place higher priority on human creativity, on self conscious action by the individual or society to change their condition. It would be ironic should this false dichotomy become too well entrenched, since the notion of culture has in many*

ways been invoked precisely to avoid the need to choose between structure and action, but the danger remains, if concealed by the inherent ambiguity of "culture" as an explanation.

These are useful suggestions for considering the relationship between fashion and culture, though the passage also introduces the deeper problem of pinning down the notion of culture as a neutral descriptive category in the first place. T.S. Eliot in a famous passage from his Notes towards the Definition of Culture could state categorically that "culture includes all the characteristic activities and interests of a people: Derby day, Henley Regatta, Cowes, the Twelfth of August, a cup final, the pin table, the dart board, Wensleydale cheese, boiled cabbage cut into sections, beetroot in vinegar, nineteenth century gothic churches, and the music of Elgar." Ten years later at the birth of cultural studies in Britain as a specific discipline, Raymond Williams rejected this largely pastoral, romantic and commodified vision to present what he saw as a more inclusive, realist definition of culture that encompassed "steel making, touring in motor cars, mixed farming, the Stock exchange, coal mining and London transport". Forty or fifty years on, both readings of English culture are marked by the effects of nostalgia and the subjective positions of their narrators, but Williams, together with Richard Hoggart, incorporated the idea that culture is a contested and social field in which production and consumption find no easy union and the activities, customs and philosophies of the working class conflict with, or differ from, those of the gentry. Their work established that culture is political as well as aesthetic in its forms and effects.

Between the two positions evolved the formation of a modern school of British cultural studies which aimed to examine precisely the circulation of such constructions and their social power. A purer history of the discipline would trace its roots back to the Frankfurt School and the Institute for Social Research established in Germany in 1923, before moving to the United States, with its largely pessimistic and critical take on the effects of mass culture. There isn't the space here to outline the continuing development of cultural studies as a discrete discipline, and I'm not sure that I could do it the justice it deserves anyway. Graeme Turner's recent British Cultural Studies: An Introduction provides a more than adequate overview of the historiography and its emergent methods. What I do propose to offer instead is a broad discussion of the key areas in which cultural considerations have made a direct impact on the writing of fashion history over the past decades. These fall largely under the categories of textual analysis (semiotics, film and magazines), the consideration of audience and consumption (ethnography, history and sociology), the role of ideology (hegemony, subcultures and pleasure) and the political question of identities (race, gender, sexuality). These are obviously neither comprehensive nor mutually exclusive divisions, but they do indicate the key ways in which clothing and fashion have finally become a vehicle for debates that now lie at the heart of visual and material culture studies.

Fashion and Signification

The deconstruction of image or product as text lies at the heart of any totalizing definition of a cultural studies methodology. In direct opposition to traditional art and design history and literary criticism methods, cultural studies offers a way of studying objects as systems rather than as the simple product of authorship. Borrowed from European structuralism, most specifically the work of linguist Ferdinand de Saussure, the theory of language "looms as the most essential of cultural studies concepts, either in its own right, or through being appropriated as a model for understanding other cultural systems". The structures of language, deployed through speech or text, have been shown to reveal those mechanisms through which individuals make sense of the world: "Culture, as the site where that sense or meaning is generated and experienced, becomes a determining, productive field through which social realities are constructed, experienced and interpreted". In the most basic of terms, the science of semiology pioneered by Saussure and later Roland Barthes offered a more refined mechanism for applying the structural model of language across the wider range of cultural signifying systems, allowing the scholar to examine the social specificity of representations and their meaning across different cultural practices: gesture, literature, drama, conversation, photography, film, television and, of course, dress. Central to this method is the idea of the sign, an anchoring unit of communication within a language system, which might be a word, an image, a sound, an item of clothing, that placed in juxtaposition with other items produces a particular meaning. That meaning is further communicated by the process of signification, the division of the sign into its constituent parts: the signifier (its physical form) and what is signified (the mental concept or associations that arise). Any meaning generated by the sign emerges from the subconscious or automatic relationship of these parts, which is usually arbitrary and culturally relative rather than fixed. It is a meaning that shifts through time and context, so that the ways in which such a shift or relationship might occur are of central importance to cultural studies, because, as Turner notes "it is through such phenomena that it becomes possible to track cultural change", and also cultural value and cultural associations. Barthes famously attributed the term "myth making" to this production of social knowledge and meaning through the manipulation of the sign, and its cultural and political power is difficult to over estimate.

Fashion historians have of course been utilizing this power for a long time. Every time the clothing in a portrait is "read" (for its literary associations, the symbolic power of its various textiles and elements of decoration, the value entailed in its material and production that might together offer evidence of status, nationality, age, sexuality or date) representation is being decoded as text, associative meanings combed out and cultural systems established. But the process has rarely been perceived in a self-reflective or critical light. Culture is often taken as an historical given rather than a constructed system in which the portrait or the dress plays its constitutive part. Elizabeth Wilson must take the credit in her highly influential work on the cultural meaning and history of fashion for questioning and opening up the field. In her aim to ally fashionable dressing with other popular or mass leisure pursuits she has taken the graphic and literary reproduction of dress into a system of mass communication and consumption, hinting at the possibility that more traditional dress history has been toiling unnecessarily in its efforts to use fashion journalism, historical advertising and other popular documentary forms as evidence for actual fashion change or cultural conditions. In her account of the role of clothing in the formation of normative understandings of status and gender, and its capabilities in terms of dissent and deviance from those roles, Wilson has liberated the fashion plate and magazine column from the narrower, linear readings of established dress history:

> *Since the late nineteenth century, word and image have increasingly propagated style. Images of desire are constantly in circulation; increasingly it has been the image as well as the artefact that the*

> *individual has purchased. Fashion is a magical system, and what we see as we leaf through glossy magazines is "the look". Like advertising, women's magazines have moved from the didactic to the hallucinatory. Originally their purpose was informational, but what we see today in both popular journalism and advertising is the mirage of a way of being, and what we engage in is no longer only the relatively simple process of direct imitation, but the less conscious one of identification.*

The conception of fashion as a magical system, which might benefit from textual or linguistic scrutiny, is an area also well tested in the field of film theory and history. The dress historian can draw useful methodological parallels from the way in which authors such as Jane Gaines, Pam Cook and Christine Gledhill take examples of cinema and describe the manner in which filmic images interact with women's perceptions of themselves in terms of fashion, sexuality, maternal and marital duty and work. Gaines makes the connections with cultural studies' linguistic and political concerns explicit:

> *There is a significant link between the notion of woman displayed by her dress and woman displayed by other representational systems. In addition, one might say that contemporary feminists have understood woman's inscription in the codes of contemporary representation because they themselves know too well what it is to be fitted up for representation. We are trained into clothes, and early become practised in presentational postures, learning, in the age of mechanical reproduction, to carry the mirror's eye within the mind, as though one might at any moment be photographed. And this is a sense a woman in western culture has learned, not only from feeling the constant surveillance of her public self, but also from studying the publicity images of other women, on screen, certainly, but also in the pages of fashion magazines.*

Recent dress history, predicated on a cultural studies understanding of the power of the sign, together with film theory, revels in the ambiguity of fashion and its shifting signifiers, which moves the discipline away from earlier reductive or moralistic approaches. From Thorstein Veblen through Quentin Bell to James Laver, historians and commentators from all political persuasions had perhaps taken too many liberties over their ownership of a received understanding of female psychology and supposed predisposition towards luxury, whilst second-wave feminism simply equated fashion with patriarchal oppression. A similarly puritanical strain in early cultural studies echoed a mistrust of fashionable or popular consumption. Such a condemnation of fashion and fashion history implied a dismissal of the women and men who enjoyed its possibilities, and ignored what Gaines has termed "the strength of the allure, the richness of the fantasy, and the quality of the compensation", which their consumption of image and object allowed.

Though to follow recent cultural theory on the instability of the sign to its illogical limits presents a particular set of problems that both cultural studies and fashion history have had to address. As Gaines states: "the more extreme contention of post modernist theory the idea that the image has swallowed reality whole obliterates the problems endemic to comparisons between images and society. If the image now precedes the real, engulfs it and renders it obsolete as a point of comparison, do we any more need to show how representation is ideological?".

The artificiality of fashion texts and representations would certainly seem open to similar interpretation, so how can they in this sense be tied in to any discussion of inequality, power and manipulation, or the simple actions of consumers themselves? Here the poststructuralist approach of Gaines and others and the broader concerns of cultural studies, with the argument that the image of fashion and femininity is a construction, a textual product of its society, relying only on the reality of the moment, allows for a clearing up of any confusion. The constructed image can be held up for further scrutiny, the construction made clear and the seventeenth-century broadside, the nineteenth-century fashion journal or the twentieth-century film revealed as representational systems. In this way fashion and its associated publicity can be shown to rely on current ideologies, and the "obliterated" problems of image and society reinstated for discussion. The arising affinity between fashion and textual analysis has probably constituted cultural studies' major contribution to the discipline of dress history or, more precisely, dress studies.

I choose the term "dress studies" over "history" because that contribution has remained largely within the field of twentieth-century and contemporary concerns. The incursion of cultural studies methods into historical discussions of dress has remained more circumspect, and where examples of a convergence between dress, history and the focus of cultural studies on theory and discourse exist, the texts lie on interdisciplinary boundaries, largely on the peripheries of social, literary and art history, and are by authors who often find it necessary to stress their distance both from traditional forms of their own disciplines and from dress historians themselves. The relationship between cultural studies and history has never been a straightforward or easy one, but some of the crossovers have produced interesting studies of historical clothing practices. The source of the disparity between historical and cultural approaches lies in the necessity of the latter to frame itself within a broad theoretical structure. The problem of conceptualizing the social relationships that make up popular cultures is that it defeats contained empirical analyses and therefore led to a split in terms of methodology and theory between structuralists and culturalists at the moment when cultural studies was gaining ground in Britain during the 1960s.

Structuralists viewed culture as their primary object of study, with the forms and structures that produced meaning drawing their attention at the expense of cultural specifics, empirical quantitative evidence and the process of historical change. Culturalists, amongst whom most British social historians of the left placed themselves, resisted this trend as overly deterministic and comprehensive in a word "ahistorical". For E.P. Thompson in particular, human agency retained a stronger hold than abstract ideology and the work of British culturalists tended to look inwards to English historical experience rather than outwards to European theory. The two positions rather falsely represent polar opposites for the sake of illustration and more recent work predicated on a broad cultural studies perspective productively knits ideology and experience together through the notion of "discourse". This is a term, owing much to the work of French theorist Michel Foucault, that "refers to socially produced groups of ideas or ways of thinking that can be tracked in individual texts or groups of texts, but that also demand to be located within wider historical and social structures or relations". Here the scope for dress history has been wide, as it has for art history and literary criticism, and in my view some of the most exciting examples for a cultural dress history have resulted from this vein. I would offer the work on shopping, department stores and the negotiation of class and gender in the nineteenth century as one manifestation of the approach, incorporating as it does authors as varied as Rosalind Williams, Rachel Bowlby, Valerie Steele, Philippe Perrot, Mica Nava and Elaine Abelson. It is perhaps significant that only two of these would associate themselves with the discipline of dress history, though all have something to contribute to the development of the discipline.

Pleasure and Politics

Another outcome of the argument between structuralists and culturalists was a repositioning of focus in cultural studies and history that has had further ramifications for the study of fashion. Abstract debates about theory and methodology were superseded in the late 1970s by the opening up of new, previously hidden areas of study and fresh perspectives on old political problems. In social history, those receptive to cultural studies concerns oriented around the formation of the History Workshop Journal, which aimed to move discussion away from the academy and into the realm of working people's lives, stressing the importance of feminist and other hidden voices, utilizing the power of oral and non-traditional historical sources that lay outside of the "official record", and claiming that theory might provide answers to social and political problems learnt from the past. In cultural studies, associates of the Birmingham Centre for Contemporary Cultural Studies, founded by Richard Hoggart in 1964, and later directed by Stuart Hall, drew in methods from sociology and anthropology and saw a similar shift in emphasis. Histories of everyday life focused especially on subcultures, examining their construction, their relation to dominant hegemony, and their histories of resistance and incorporation. Much of this work examined the rituals and practices that generated meaning and pleasure within, precisely, that fragment of the cultural field which earlier pioneers from Frankfurt through to Hoggart had dismissed: urban youth subcultures. Dick Hebdige's work on this phenomenon arguably laid the foundation for several studies of fashion and the young which have fed back in to the dress history mainstream. culminating in both the Streetstyle Exhibition at the V&A and the earlier collected essays published under the title Chic Thrills.

The whole notion of a "pleasurable" consumption of clothing, which subcultural studies partly raised, is an idea that has now become familiar in fashion histories spanning a broad chronology. But its substance formed the basis of the last political crisis to rock the cultural studies field. The rise of postmodernism, with its questioning of value and authenticity together with the economic effects of Thatcherism and the Lawson boom in the mid-1980s, placed the issue of pleasure and consumption at the centre of the cultural studies debate. Summarized by the term "New Times", the discussion was taken up by Marxism Today and signalled, according to Angela McRobbie, "the diversity of social and political upheavals in Britain including the success of Thatcherism, the decline of a traditional working class politics, the emergence of a politics of identity and consumption, and most importantly the challenge these represent to the left". It cannot be easily claimed that fashion history has arisen out of a political consensus in the way that cultural studies obviously has, but nevertheless the implications of the New Times debate have important repercussions for the study of objects which cannot be divorced from questions of status, gender, sexuality and national identity. Though the terms of New Times were complex and inward-looking, the emergence of a new politics of identity and consumption offered genuine opportunities for novel approaches and arguments, represented particularly in works on clothing, fashion, shopping and gender. Recent publications, from Caroline Evans' and Minna Thornton's overview of fashion and femininity in the twentieth century, through to Frank Mort's study of Burton's in the 1950s or Sean Nixon's examination of menswear and men's magazines in the 1980s, show some residue of the arguments. Any discussion of consumption and its discontents requires precisely the kind of close political analysis that cultural studies methods can provide, and used in conjunction with other, more empirical methodologies its application can often lead to the most provocative and exciting insights.

It is a shame then that the cultural studies slant often seems to raise aggressive or defensive shackles amongst dress historians, as it does amongst historians generally. It is undoubtedly a field riven with disagreements, and coming to a consensus on what the study of culture actually entails is a minefield. In this sense it would be a mistake to isolate cultural studies at all as a desired or necessarily coherent position, more valid than any other. It is an interdisciplinary field where certain concerns and methods have converged. The usefulness of this convergence is that it can enable us to understand cultural phenomena and social relationships that were not accessible through other disciplines, thus enriching our knowledge of an object category (fashion) that has clearly always played a central role in cultural/social processes. It is not a unified field, but one of argument and division as well as convergence, and therein lies its strength and promise. The dress historian Lou Taylor's recent review of John Harvey's book Men in Black (itself a model of interdisciplinary endeavour) offers encouraging signs for the future:

> *In Harvey's book we see a very effective shattering of the protective barriers we have erected between academic disciplines. Of course no one person can be "expert" on everything but an open mind set on reading the inner meanings of externals, has demonstrated the great advantages of knocking away the walls of academic protectionism. What is this book? Dress History? Literary Criticism? Cultural History? Gender Study? Visual Culture? Who cares? Read it.*

❑❑❑

5

Fashion and Glamour

Introduction

The people who live it the clothes that scream it the make-up that makes it'. Yet quite what glamour is frequently remains unclear. When fashion and women's magazines from time to time conduct enquiries into the meaning of glamour, they invariably seek opinions from a range of experts and celebrities, whose views are strikingly contradictory. Confusion arises over the gender connotations of glamour, whether it is an intrinsic (charismatic) phenomenon or a manufactured one, and whether it is permanent or temporary. In addition there is disagreement over its application to age ranges, places and situations. Such is the lack of common ground that it is tempting to agree with lexicographer Eric Partridge who, as long ago as 1947, included glamour in his list of 'vogue words' which had gained a momentum of their own whatever the original impulse had been. For Partridge, glamour was a word without meaning that had been invested with high status and picturesque connotations by authors and journalists.

One enduring feature of glamour is its identification with fashion. In a recent analysis of fashion photography, Clive Scott contrasted 'glamour' with 'sophistication'. He found that in the fashion press glamour was: youthful, dynamic, pleasure-seeking, extrovert, voluble, short-term, gregarious, uncultured, volatile, public (and thus downmarket). On the other hand sophistication was seen as: mature, poised, restrained, introvert, taciturn, long-term, solitary, cultured, controlled/severe (and thus upmarket). In other accounts fashion and glamour are taken to be synonymous. Jeanine Basinger takes this view in her analysis of classical Hollywood cinema and its female audiences. However, she also states that 'Glamour goes beyond mere fashion. Although the concept of glamour includes fashion, it ultimately involves more than what a woman puts on her body. It deals with the lady herself.' The movie stars she refers to usually occupied a median position between the two poles identified by Scott, thus rendering his differentiation meaningless.

In the context of such confusion, an attempt to identify what glamour is, where it comes from and how it works is surely timely. In this chapter three moments of glamour will be explored. In keeping with glamour's associations with the immediate and the commercial, the first of these will be the present. Older meanings will be considered in relation to contemporary uses in the press and advertising. Second, the root of many of the gestures and stereotypes of modern glamour Hollywood cinema of the middle decades of the twentieth century will be examined. In the final section, consideration will be given to the transformation of the nineteenth-century city which, it will be argued, was the original site of glamour as it is used and understood today.

Contemporary Glamour

The term glamour is employed continuously in connection with fashion, showbusiness and entertainment, beauty and beauty marketing and the social worlds that are determined by, or associated with, these industries. It is scarcely possible to open a copy of *Marie Claire, Vogue* or *Hello!* without finding the word used to underline the allure of an occasion, a dwelling, a product or a person. Even the broadsheets make use of the word's evocative power in presenting leisure, fashion and entertainment features. In all these publications, glamour is used primarily, although by no means exclusively, in association with the public presentation of fashion. The 'fashion weeks' of London, Paris, Milan and New York give rise to ample coverage of runway shows by leading designers which are conceived precisely to capture press and media attention. The concentration of designer brands, fabulous frocks, name models and celebrity guests, all under the glare of publicity and fêted with lavish hospitality, amounts to an irresistible cocktail of all that is desirable in contemporary commercial culture. The pre-eminence often given to the presentation of the new Versace collection on such occasions is testimony to that design company's mastery of the language of allure.

Glamour's appeal is by no means limited to top-of-the-range publications. It is equally used by teenage magazines like 17 and 19 and by the in-house magazines of stores like Debenhams and Fenwicks. In these sorts of publications, it is rare to see top fashion models and designer garments. Rather the emphasis is on explaining to ordinary people on average incomes, and teenage girls of limited means, how they can acquire a touch of glamour for a special occasion or a night out. For example, the Winter 1997 issue of the Debenhams magazine featured on the cover the model Caprice. Inside, she modelled three versions of a 'dressed-up' look, each featuring clothes available in the store. Caprice's function in this context is clear. She is neither an aloof catwalk model nor a homely Page Three Girl, but the sort of woman whose polished California-style beauty functions as a vehicle of general aspiration. Although young and apparently flawless, she has enough personality and sophistication (she first came to public attention in Britain as a friend of socialite Tara Palmer-Tomkinson in the 1996 ITV documentary 'Filthy Rich: The It Girls') to be able credibly to impart fashion and beauty advice in her own right. Her image is that of the high-maintenance, groomed woman whose immaculate look is achieved by judicious choice of clothes, cosmetics and beauty treatment.

As an American, Caprice stands outside the British class system. Her Californian origins give her what Jason Cowley describes as 'a certain exotic appeal, a glamorous *difference*'. But her glamour also derives, in addition to her beauty, from the flash-bulb narrative of her life. Thanks to the able management of public relations expert Ghislain Pascal, Caprice was constantly in the public eye following her launch in the 1996 documentary. She featured on the front pages when she appeared at the 1997 National Television Awards wearing a transparent black lace Versace gown. Her calendar enjoyed enormous sales. She advertised pizzas, California prunes, Wonderbra, hair products and even the cricket world cup. She presented her own travel show and posed for men's magazines *GQ* and *Playboy*. In addition, her relationships, including in 2000 the hint of a liaison with Prince Andrew, have been carefully staged and widely reported.

Caprice appeals because she is an invented personality. In reality she is not a socialite, but a brightly-packaged vehicle for individual dreams and aspirations. As a product she can exist only in the world of the media, where the values she embodies are highly regarded and well-rewarded. Her surface image and shallowness ensure that she conserves certain general qualities that allow people to identify with her. She offers herself as a perfected version of the ordinary woman, while at the same time, through advertising and advice columns, promising to assist women to improve themselves.

Even brief consideration of an example such as Caprice enables us to identify the elements which go to make up what everyone would recognize today as glamour: fashionably attractive, a polished, slightly unreal appearance, physically and sexually appealing, mysterious origins, a touch of the exotic, highly visible. Glamour, in short, seems to be a quality which is rooted to some extent in the real but which is largely manufactured and which exists in the realm of that second-order reality that is sustained by and in the mass media. As a quality that is intended to fascinate a mass audience, it is not very subtle and, indeed, might be said to verge on bad taste. An example of this may be seen in the magazine *Take a Break*. In a story published in June 1995, two women who had paid for a photograph of themselves after a 'Hollywood makeover' lamented the fact that, far from achieving the sophistication they had dreamed of, they seemed like 'a couple of tarts'. Ignoring the sexual and showy elements that are always present in glamour, they had aspired to the polished, confident look so frequently found in upmarket women's magazines.

In order to render these notions more precise, let us examine dictionary definitions of the term. Despite the vagueness of its usage, the etymology of glamour is reasonably clear. According to *The New Fowler's Modern English Usage* the word was originally Scottish. It was an alteration of the word grammar that retained the sense of the old word gramarye ('occult learning, magic, necromancy'). The *Oxford English Dictionary* also highlights its Scottish origins and derivation from grammar, although this is indicated to mean magic, enchantment and spells rather than necromancy and the occult. According to Fowler's, glamour passed into standard English usage around the 1830s with the meaning of 'a delusive or alluring charm'.

For *Websters Third New International Dictionary*, glamour is 'an elusive, mysteriously exciting and often illusory attractiveness that stirs the imagination and appeals to a taste for the unconventional, the unexpected, the colourful, or the exotic'. In its secondary meanings glamour is said to be 'a strangely alluring atmosphere of romantic enchantment; bewitching, intangible, irresistibly magnetic charm; personal charm and poise combined with unusual physical and sexual attractiveness'.

Today, this world of illusion, mystery, seduction and enchantment is to be found almost exclusively in media representations but, as the magazines referred to above show, this world is connected to everyday reality in many ways. Through consumer products women are promised instant transformation and entry to a realm of desire. In December in particular, women's magazines suggest ideas to assist their readers in preparing for the Christmas party season by presenting photographic spreads of red gowns, black evening dresses and sultry cosmetic treatments. On occasion, the message can be remarkably simple. In 19 of September 1994, for example, the 'glamour look' is reduced to bright red lipstick, a party frock and high heels.

Where did these ideas come from? When and how did glamour become a general phenomenon, indeed even a routine feature of contemporary culture? Why is it associated almost exclusively with the feminine? Quentin Bell and Daniel Roche both suggest that glamour's origins are to be found in the *ancien régime*. Sumptuary laws reserved the use of certain colours and precious fabrics for the aristocracy and the court in feudal Europe. In consequence, elegance, luxury and seductive appearances were confined to the top of the social system. Other authors, including John Harvey, have shown that the bourgeois revolution witnessed the renunciation of colour and flamboyance by men of all classes. In the nineteenth century, black became the habitual masculine colour, while decorativeness, luxury and seduction became a feminine prerogative. According to another interpretation, glamour as it is understood today, as a structure of enchantment deployed by cultural industries, was first developed by Hollywood. In the 1930s, the major studios, having consolidated their domination of the industry, developed a star system in which dozens of young men and women were groomed and moulded into glittering ideal-types whose fortune, beauty, spending power and exciting lives dazzled the film-going public. Writing in 1939 about American film stars, Margaret Thorp defined glamour as 'sex appeal plus luxury plus elegance plus romance'. 'The place to study glamour today is the fan magazines,' she noted. 'Fan magazines are distilled as stimulants of the most exhilarating kind. Everything is superlative, surprising, exciting. Nothing ever stands still, nothing ever rests, least of all the sentences. Clothes of course are endlessly pictured and described usually with marble fountains, private swimming pools or limousines in the background. Every aspect of life, trivial and important, should be bathed in the purple glow of publicity.'

Neither of these seems to us to be persuasive as a starting point for the analysis of glamour, although both, with their common emphasis on image and spectacle, are important components of any examination of the phenomenon. Hollywood, in particular, as the most systematic producer of glamorous images in the twentieth century, requires analysis if the functioning of glamour in contemporary commercial culture is to be understood. Before embarking on this, however, let us set out our own definition of the phenomenon. Glamour, it may be argued, is an enticing image, a staged and constructed image of reality that invites consumption. That is to say, it is primarily visual, it consists of a retouched or perfected version of a real person or situation and it is predicated upon the gaze of a desiring audience. The subjects of glamour, which may be things or people (usually reified through a process of manufacture), seduce by association with one or more of the following qualities (the more the better): beauty, sexuality, theatricality, wealth, dynamism, notoriety, leisure. To this list might be added the feminine, because display and consumption have been heavily connoted as feminine since at least the nineteenth century. Femininity moreover is often considered to be a masquerade, the construction of an image that matches cultural expectations. As Basinger observes, 'a woman is her fashion and glamour, rather than her work'.

Golden Age of Hollywood

Hollywood had shed many of the trappings of glamour that had characterized it in the 1930s and 1940s. Only on select occasions, such as Oscar Night, does the modern-day movie industry seek to dazzle its public with a glittering gathering of stars dressed to the height of elegance. If Sharon Stone is sometimes referred to as the only current star of the old type, it is largely because she made it her business from the 1990s always to present herself as elegantly groomed, perfectly coiffed and sexually alluring. Yet the image of the stars of the past and their lifestyles is still strongly evident in contemporary commercial culture. Perhaps more than anything else, the Hollywood golden age constitutes the benchmark for what today is understood as alluring and glamorous. On numerous occasions fashion magazines feature models made up and photographed in black and white as Lauren Bacall, Marlene Dietrich or Ava Gardner. Moreover, in recent times, Pretty Polly tights has deployed in advertisements images of Rita Hayworth, while Mercedes and World of Leather have used Marilyn Monroe, Elena Mirò Ava Gardner, Luciano Soprani fragrances Hedy Lamarr and Gap Steve McQueen. All these images refer back to the period between the 1930s and the 1950s, when Hollywood cinema conquered the world and shaped the collective imagination with its stories, style and stars.

The 'glamour of Hollywood' was precisely an image that was constructed through a variety of media: the films themselves, still photographs and portraits, publicity material and press and radio coverage of the lives and loves of the stars. In reflecting on this image, two elements deserve particular attention. Sex appeal on the one hand and luxury on the other constituted the cornerstone of Hollywood's strategy to capture and hold mass interest.

On screen, all direct references to sexual intimacy inside and outside of marriage were strictly taboo following the adoption of the Hays Code in 1932. By introducing this element of self-regulation, the American movie industry hoped to pacify respectable opinion and win recognition as a mainstream component of American society. Yet sex appeal was always important in Hollywood movies. In 1950, anthropologist Hortense Powdermaker observed in her study of America's 'dream factory' that the physical presence of actors was vital to the films' appeal. Heroes were always virile he-men, she noted, while heroines exuded an obvious sex appeal. The immediate and unambiguous attraction between the two protagonists (even if at first disguised by a comedy of hatred) was part of the theme of most movies. Hollywood, she argued, stressed the 'look at me', 'look at my body' type. Close-ups emphasized the intimate details of the physical being of actors. They were also known by parts of their bodies, that which was deemed most worthy of attention. Thus a husky voice, beautiful breasts, or a dimple in the chin came to sum up the entire persona of a star. The reduction to parts affected women more than men, although Powdermaker did reveal that one (unnamed) male star was known as 'the penis'. Newcomers to Hollywood were obliged to perform a long apprenticeship, part of which involved them in revealing as much flesh as possible for 'cheesecake' and 'beefcake' shots. As Edgar Morin remarked, 'stars reveal their spirits, starlets exhibit their bodies'.

Prior to the Hays Code, many films featured a more obvious sexuality and laid considerable stress on experience. In the 1920s and early 1930s, stars like Greta Garbo and Marlene Dietrich played world-weary women who had seen everything and were shocked by nothing. Frequently, as in Garbo's *Susan Lennox* and Dietrich's *Shanghai Express,* they played women who had been abandoned by lovers and had turned to prostitution. As Lea Jacobs has shown, 'fallen women' movies exercised a great appeal during the Depression years because they legitimated the use of sexuality as a means by which women could escape poverty and hardship. These images also drew on the theatrical tradition of the femme fatale that had been established in the nineteenth century by writers like Théophile Gautier and actresses such as Sarah Bernhardt. Garbo and Dietrich were both enigmatic, even exotic, European women whose allure was enhanced by costumiers like Adrian at MGM and Travis Banton at Paramount, as well as the art of the best cinematographers in Hollywood.

The movie capital sometimes liked to give the impression that the seductiveness and beauty of its stars was a natural phenomenon. All the industry had to do was discover the star quality and present it unalloyed to the public. One example of this can be seen in *The Barefoot Contessa.* In an evening scene, Humphrey Bogart tells Ava Gardner (playing a simple Spanish singer, Maria Vargas) that the moon illuminates her face just like a key light, revealing her potential for movie stardom. Of course, Gardner was already a star and the 'moon' was in fact a key light. The fiction of naturalness served to disguise the fact that the beauty and photogenic qualities of the stars were in reality highly constructed. To turn Margherita Cansino, a simple girl of Spanish-Mexican origin, into the all-American glamour girl Rita Hayworth required considerable art and expertise, and the same talents moulded Norma Jean Baker into Marilyn Monroe. Even Garbo and Dietrich were very ordinary, rather gauche women before being thoroughly reshaped by the studios. The sex appeal of the stars was not an intrinsic feature, although 'personality' was a quality the industry regarded as vital to star creation; on the contrary it was a manufactured, artificial phenomenon that the studios conferred on their protegés.

The inventor of sex appeal in American cinema was the English novelist Elinor Glyn, who arrived in Hollywood at the invitation of Jesse Lansky in 1920 and subsequently worked for MGM. Glyn, author of the scandalous novel *Three Weeks* and the short story *It*, believed that sex should be disguised as romance. She also believed in the creation of an aura of mystery to arouse public interest. Working with Gloria Swanson and Rudolph Valentino, she taught them poise, elegance and seductive techniques (such as Valentino kissing the palm rather than the back of a woman's hand) which fuelled the atmosphere of sensuality. In the course of the 1920s and 1930s, Hollywood set design and costume applied the lesson of deflected or displaced sexuality by incorporating the exotic or the sensual (shimmering fabrics, shiny surfaces) into the structure of film-making. Actors were also moulded through cosmetic surgery, cosmetics and flattering lighting.

Perhaps the most extraordinary and enduring examples of Hollywood glamour are provided by the stills of great studio photographers like George Hurrell and Clarence Sinclair Bull. These portraits, for which the stars often posed reluctantly at the end of a day on the set, are today gathered in numerous volumes. Moreover, when an occasion presents itself, contemporary actors are more than willing to allow themselves to be photographed in the studio manner of the 1940s because they know that the allure of those images is unrivalled. In the sultry black and white photographs of the past, actors were turned into icons. They appeared almost as gods and certainly as archetypes, their individuality giving way to a generalized image of seduction. The perfection of the images did not derive from the beauty of the subject but rather from the invention of the photographer.

Speaking in the 1980s, Hurrell said that he regarded glamour as a synonym for 'giving a sexier attitude' or creating a 'bedroom look'. 'You know, glamour to me was nothing more than just an excuse for saying sexy pictures. In other words my interpretation was entirely one of saying "Come on, we're going to take some sexy pictures".' To achieve this effect, he employed light, floating materials, posed his subjects lying on their backs or wet, or bathed them in light and shade. Each of the images was heavily worked over and blemishes were eliminated through retouching. Although the typical shots involved women, men were given the same treatment. Lead was put on the negative, sometimes on both sides, or images were improved through dyes and brush work. Hurrell claimed that his job was easier if the actor already had a sensual quality or attitude, but where this was absent sex appeal could be conferred as a total invention.

As far as luxury was concerned, this became a hallmark of Hollywood with Cecil B. De Mille, who believed that opulent scenes and fabulous costumes would make people stop and gasp. Several of the moguls had begun their working lives in the garment industry and were alert to the importance of fine clothing in weaving an image that audiences would find seductive. With the aid of Glyn and a few other style advisors, Hollywood conferred on itself an upper-class image of wealth and elegance. The widespread use of eye-catching wardrobes including furs, feathers and jewellery roused some contemporary critics to anger. It was felt that, by covering 'fallen women' with the trappings of luxury in tales of irregular social mobility, a direct exchange between sex and money was being suggested. The accusation that Hollywood was condoning prostitution and offending moral standards was a key factor in the adoption of the Hays Code. However, the emphasis on luxury in the films of larger studios like MGM and Paramount did not diminish. Even by today's standards, the opulence of the upper-class settings of many movies of that era is breathtaking.

What was the reason for this emphasis? First, it should be remembered that Hollywood before the Second World War was not respectable. The moguls who had founded and run the studios were typically Jewish immigrants who were social outsiders. For all his power, Louis B. Mayer of MGM could not join the Los Angeles Country Club because Jews were not allowed. Given this situation, it is not surprising that Hollywood shared the emphasis on exterior appearance that marked immigrant behaviour in early twentiethcentury America. Stuart and Elizabeth Ewen have spoken of an impulse to finery in immigrant communities, in which marginalized individuals struggled to fit in by emulating their 'betters'. Even among the poor, self-hood could be achieved through the construction of an appearance that contained no outsider traits. Given the American ethic of success and social mobility, the upper-class look of those whom Veblen described as the 'leisure class' stood as the maximum aspiration.

A second, connected, reason for the sumptuousness of Hollywood films concerns the rapid development of consumerism in America in the 1920s. In this decade, the Ewens argue, consumption became central to Americanism. The message was communicated particularly strongly to immigrants that by purchasing goods they could transform themselves and become fully-fledged citizens. As Hollywood was developing and becoming a national and international industry at precisely this time, it naturally evolved in tandem with the consumer society. Indeed, even more than advertisements, the movies offered a compelling, enticing image of capitalism. Hollywood's linkages to consumerism were numerous but perhaps the most striking involved the stars. Because the stars were conceived as marketing devices for films, they could also be used to market a range of other products, and these secondary advertisements or endorsements could drum up further business for given films. In an important essay, Charles Eckert examined how tie-ins became a key part of the way stars were presented to the public. Industry found that sex appeal generated excitement which could assist in the sale even of the most demure products.

Stars were the perfect consumers. They were new men and women who were upwardly mobile and rich. They, more than anyone else, were obliged to consume and to display their wealth in order to prove their status; their lifestyles acted as a focus for the aspirations of the masses. However, their explicit association with the material culture of consumerism was not felt by all to be positive. Producer David O. Selznick, for example, thought that tieins undermined the mystique that the studios had built up. He also disapproved the free endorsements that actresses gave to Max Factor and Lux soap. Morin, by contrast, sees no contradiction between the star as goddess (*star-déese*) and the star as product (*star-merchandise*). It may be suggested that the growing links between the film industry and consumerism did in fact herald a change in the nature of stars. As Morin himself notes, stars of the sound era were less exotic and exceptional and more projections of the typical. In this context they became themselves industrial products, manufactured in series like Ford cars. Sometimes, the objectification of the star, especially where the personality was weak and the elements of 'type' strong, resulted in a sense that the objects had taken over. For example, there are some photographs of Lana Turner taken in the 1940s which depict her coiffed, made up and adorned in every conceivable fashion accessory: hat, gloves, fur stole, brooch, earrings. The human element appears to have disappeared almost completely.

There is something standardized about all the icons of glamour produced during the Hollywood golden age. Like shop mannequins and the fashion models of more recent times, their blankness and apparent hollowness leaves a space which enables people to 'buy into' them and project themselves and their aspirations on to them. While upper-class and established middle-class people regarded Hollywood as vulgar, brash and impossibly nouveau, lowerclass people viewed it as the epitome of refinement. Certainly, it was a great educator, with its stories of physical and social mobility, its encouragements to self-transformation and its mail order catalogue aesthetics. Yet, Elizabeth Wilson has pointed out that star images are frequently characterized by an air of the haunting and the unnatural. So still and lifeless are the composed images that their subjects appear almost embalmed and laid to rest.

The capacity of capitalism for reification, for turning everything, even people, into things was first noted by Gyorgy Lukacs in 1923. It can be argued that the de-humanized, dead look that marks glamour proves its intrinsic link to urban, industrial society. Divorced from nature, this society poses the transcendence of nature as an objective. For the first time, abundance was configured as a real possibility by industry. 'Consumerism posed nature as an inhospitable force, a hopeless anachronism,' write the Ewens. 'Industrial production and enterprising imaginations claimed for themselves the rights and powers of creation.' Because these forces were developed most fully in the United States, so too is glamour a phenomenon that in its purest form can be analysed through the prism of Americanism. The level of abstraction required could be developed most easily in the context of a country that was itself invented and unburdened by the weight of the past. Within the context of America, Hollywood was the maximum expression of the artificial, a community created in the middle of nowhere and dedicated to fiction. The lives of the stars, no less than the backlot, was a staged reality, a theatrical construct designed to entice an audience. Consequently, it offered the most powerful and seductive form of glamour and the Hollywood film star became the most glamorous figure to have existed.

Nineteenth-Century City

At the root of glamour, however, is a set of social and cultural changes that took place in the late nineteenth century, in particular in the great modern cities. Broadly speaking, this period may be said to have seen the decline of rigid social hierarchies and the eclipse of aristocratic control of culture, politics and society. Instead, a civilization based on money took shape, in which luxury, visibility and elegance were not reserved for a closed elite, but were open to whoever could pay or be paid for. Increasingly, a cosmopolitan category of *nouveaux* riches bought into the old high society or, where access was obstructed, emulated its forms and rituals. As part of this process, monetary values of ostentation and display enjoyed prominence as industrialists and financiers struggled to establish their status through conspicuous consumption. At the same time, a range of secondary changes served to render more open and visible the public dimension of the life of the elite, which took on the characteristics of a tableau or narrative for lower social classes. For example, the theatre and high society enjoyed closer relations, and both for the first time in the modern period established links with the street, which was redefined as a place of shopping and display. In Paris, Benjamin's 'capital of the nineteenth century', the boulevards, the arcades and the theatres of Montmartre became centres of frivolity and luxury that were not hidden behind the closed doors of the palaces of the aristocracy.

In such a context, dazzling facades produced by families and individuals seeking to win recognition mingled and mixed with commercial displays, the bustle of the boulevards and the gaiety of the world of entertainment. Enticing images became part and parcel of the modern city. What were the sources of this new visual language of display? In part they were conventional ones. Royal courts, like that of the French Second Empire prior to its downfall, or the events of the London Season, provided a focus of attention. But as an established elite lost its monopoly of splendour, the sources were widened to include the *demi-monde* or what eventually was termed 'café society'. Among the low cultural forms that provided inputs into the dynamic image of the city were popular theatre, the *cafés* chantants, the display windows of the arcades and the department stores, and the world of commercial sex. The seductive imagery that defines glamour, it may be argued, was forged through the mixing of these low and high sources. From the latter came the exotic, bright colours (notably red), and a sleazy, vulgar element, while the former supplied an injection of luxury balanced by good taste and refinement. Sex and the theatrical mixed openly in the vibrant red-dominated posters of Toulouse Lautrec.

The figure who symbolized the new language was the courtesan. Like the film star of later years, the courtesan was an emblematic figure who was recounted, evoked, described and analysed in novels like Zola's Nana, newspapers, studies and memoirs. As a professional of illusion and makebelieve, she was a central figure in the new culture of appearances and surfaces. At bottom a prostitute, she was also in parts actress, fashion icon, celebrity and professional beauty. The very grandest courtesans lived in palaces, where they were maintained by a team of wealthy sponsors eager to pay vast sums in return for sexual favours. They lived on the margins of respectable society, but exercised considerable influence through their liaisons and their trend-setting role. At once vulgar and elegant, showy and fashionable, the courtesans captured the attention and occupied a place in the collective imaginary. According to art historian T.J. Clark, the courtesan was prominent because, by embracing luxury, she adopted a facade of respectability that at least partially concealed the uneasy intersection of money and sexuality that was such a widespread phenomenon in Paris.

However, if the courtesan acted as the inspiration for a new language of allure, it took artists to give this language a concrete, reproducible form and develop it into a recognisable trademark style of modern celebrity. Several artists contributed to this enterprise, but none more than the Italian portrait painter Giovanni Boldini, who painted nearly all the prominent figures to pass through Paris between the late nineteenth century and the First World War. Boldini is not today regarded as an important painter, but in many ways he pioneered a type of edgy, fashionable portraiture that summed up the Paris of the Belle Époque. He forged a new pictorial language by combining the sensual atmosphere and bright colours of the worlds of prostitution and popular entertainment with the conventional society portrait. Boldini painted many leading exponents of café society, as well as prominent artists and some aristocrats. His favourite subjects were mainly wealthy women, who revelled in the sexy, scandalous air he conferred on them and which they took to be quintessentially Parisian. He achieved this effect in part by elongating them and twisting their bodies as though they were rotating on an axis. Many of his subjects courted notoriety, like the eccentric Marquess Luisa Casati and Lady Colin Campbell, protagonist of one of the most controversial divorce cases of Victorian England. Being painted by Boldini conferred on them a theatrical kudos and turned them into icons of their era.

Boldini was not only a fashionable painter but also a painter of fashion. He was a master at conveying the effects of a variety of materials and accessories and he was careful to ensure his subjects were clothed in a flattering way. By working quickly and employing indefinite slapdash strokes, often sharply diagonal, he created an air of movement and frivolity. The result was a dazzling surface appearance that was extravagant and dramatic. Worth, Doucet and other designers were happy to lend him their creations because they knew that good publicity could derive from being incorporated into what Boldini's biographer describes as 'a highly potent pictorial *maison de beauté*'. The flamboyance of Boldini's work owed much to fashion and to the creative collaboration he forged with the designers who produced the luxurious gowns women wore to society occasions. He was not interested in psychology or, in general, in character, but in image and effect. The concern with the exterior and artifice led some critics to label his work kitsch. Certainly, they owed more to popular taste than to any idea of refinement.

Many Boldini portraits were displayed publicly in salons, they were illustrated in newspapers and openly discussed. Just as, in later years, society photographers would contribute to the celebrity of their subjects, so too did a striking portrait by Boldini lend allure and status. Thus the painter may be said to have contributed to the birth of modern celebrity culture. Around the turn of the century, the interlocking spheres of high society, fashion, theatre and the *demi-monde* gave rise to figures who were the object of gossip and curiosity. Confirmation of this development is provided by the 1889 Paris Exposition, which featured a circular building holding a canvas entitled 'Le Tout Paris'. Customers paid in large, but not overwhelming, numbers, to see around 800 portraits of the rich and the beautiful. 'Like other panoramas,'

Charles Rearick observes, 'this one catered to a taste for skilfully wrought realism in illusion and a burgeoning touristic desire to see the most touted sites quickly and easily.' Boldini's work is interesting not just because many of his subjects featured in the press but because he developed a standardized and codified visual language of allure at the very beginning of the media age. Although the public that was interested in and familiar with his art was quite restricted, the related dynamics of celebrity and the popular press were contributing to a marked widening of the potential audience. The development of photographic reproduction and the illustrated press fuelled this trend. With the invention of *Vogue* in United States in the 1890s (and European editions in following years), the cafe society became a systematic phenomenon sustained by the media and commercial culture. In contrast to aloof and private members of the old social elite, actors, playboys, courtesans, financiers and young aristocrats were happy to disport themselves before the public gaze. They thus offered a facade of elite life that the public could relate to more easily because it was not based purely on class and inheritance.

This development coincided with the expansion of consumer culture. Department stores, the cosmetics industry and advertising drew on innovations in the arts but they also gave a new impulse to glamour. For marketing purposes, they cultivated royal and aristocratic patronage while also seeking to entice customers with a phantasmagoria of plenty. Bright colours, seductive atmospheres, exotic décor and theatrical razzamataz were employed as techniques to transport shoppers into a realm of fantasy where goods became symbols of values that were as much imaginative as utilitarian. Stores, like theatres, were open to the public, yet they also traded in exclusivity. Many were built like palaces, staff acted like servants and customers treated as honoured guests. From the 1920s, cinemas too presented themselves as people's palaces, where luxury was combined with democracy. The purpose of such techniques was to create appropriate spaces for the selling of luxury goods but also, crucially, to invest ordinary goods with associations of luxury and desirability. In this way they could be sold for premium prices. In fashion and cosmetics, glamour still serves precisely this purpose today.

Originally forged in the great capital cities of Europe, the commercial language of allure fed directly into Hollywood cinema. Between the 1910s and the 1930s, numerous cosmeticians, retail experts and window designers left a politically turbulent Europe for the United States. Several ended up in movie studio art departments. One of these was Ernest Dichter who, having designed stores and advertisements in Vienna, became an influential set and costume designer for Paramount. The most famous such emigre was Max Factor, cosmetic artist to the royal opera in St Petersburg and later to the Tsar's family, who migrated after the Russian revolution to the USA. Following a brief commercial experience in New York he moved to the West Coast where he quickly established himself as the leading purveyor of makeup to the movie industry. On the strength of this success, he developed lines of cosmetics bearing his name that were marketed to the general public through department stores. By buying products such as Max Factor's 'pancake' make-up, women were invited to buy into the world of glamour that they saw on the screen and in magazines. The commodification of aristocratic allure in this way completed its cycle.

Glamour and Modernity

We have shown that glamour is integral to capitalist modernity. It emerged at a specific point in history characterized by: the shift in terms of the general order of meanings and priorities from a society dominated by the aristocracy to one governed by the bourgeoisie; the extension of commodification into ever wider public and private spheres; the development of a new urban system of life permeated by consumerism and the importance of fashion; the closer proximity of the theatre and high society; the creation of patterns of leisure shared by virtually all urban classes; an obsession with the feminine as the cultural codifier of modernity's tensions and promise.

Glamour became more important as modernity spread and the mass media developed. Popular magazines, cinema, radio and, later, television provided opportunities for staging, representing and inventing people, events and commodities. For this reason they were seized on by retail and cultural industries. Over time, a language of commercial seduction evolved and was codified. It may be suggested that, in recent times, the forms taken by this language have tended to be nostalgic or to employ pastiche. The fashion spreads that appeared in the leading magazines at the time of the glamour revival of 1994, for example, had a dull and familiar feel to them. Caprice, as a contemporary embodiment of glamour, seems more like a reminder of American television shows like Dynasty and Baywatch (which themselves were influenced by classical Hollywood cinema) than an original. There are several reasons for this. One is related to the sheer quantity of glamorous images that have been produced over the last century. Today we live in a complex, highly visual culture in which the iconic images of the past have, through repetition, acquired more resonance than everyday reality. Thus contemporary images of glamour tend to work off other images, creating a self-referential cycle that reinforces artificiality. The original social referents have become lost in time.

We offered our definition of glamour. In conclusion, it is appropriate to ask if it is possible to construct a theory. Any theory would have to take account of the imaginative appeal of glamour, its seductiveness and artificiality. It would also need to refer to persistent class divisions, the alienation of modern capitalism and the frustrations as well as the temptations of consumer culture. Although a great deal of work has been undertaken in recent years on consumerism, fashion, photography and the media, there is not as yet any theory of glamour. It may be suggested that early sociologists like Werner Sombart, Georg Simmel, Thorstein Veblen and Siegfried Kracauer still have much to offer. Their contribution is important because they were writing about luxury, fashion, conspicuous consumption and cinema towards the end of the moment that has been identified here as having witnessed the birth of glamour. Perhaps the most important starting point, however, is Walter Benjamin's concept of the decline of the aura of art in the age of mechanical reproduction. Through reproduction, art may gain commercial potential, he argued, but it loses authenticity. Something similar can be sustained in relation to high society or fashion. Rita Felski argues that even woman loses her aura in an era of technical reproduction since femininity as nature is demystified and downgraded. These ideas stem at root from Marx's theory of labour and value in capitalist society. The problem is that, without aura, imagination is impoverished and commercial potential is undermined. Glamour therefore is the manufactured aura of capitalist society, the dazzling illusion that compensates for inauthenticity and which reinforces consumerism as a way of life.

❑❑❑

6

Dress, Style and the National Brand

Introduction

We must say that the idea of emancipation is intimately linked to the fascist goal of projecting an image of a nation with a strong identity that would no longer permit it to be dismissed as it had so often been dismissed: that is, as the greatest of the small powers, but the smallest of the great ones. In the context of fashion, however, "emancipation" meant two main things; first, to build a textile industry able to compete in the foreign market and second, to create a distinctive style recognizable as Italian and admired abroad as such. Indeed, as Gundle has recently noted: "For Mussolini, style, beauty and appearance were central to the fascist project." In the ideological plan of fascism, fashion was identified as a privileged terrain that would make a significant contribution to the achievement of the nation's sense of self. This process, however, was extremely complex and intertwined with various and opposing forces. If on the one hand, we can pinpoint the conservative project to discipline the language of fashion, as in the case of the intentions of Meano's text; on the other, we cannot but fail to note that the steps taken by the ENM, especially in the field of textiles and synthetic fibers, represented a modernizing project whose outcome, together with the individual creativity of designers, was to form the basis for what much later would be identified as the "Italian style" and the "made in Italy."

Major achievements in terms of production and experimentation with textile and design occurred, in fact, in the autarchic phase, at a time when the Italian nation, because of foreign-imposed sanctions, was forced to be self-sufficient. First and foremost, economic reasons pushed Italian industry in general, and the fashion industry in particular, to rely on and to exploit domestic resources and inventiveness. In fact, a number of articles in the fashion magazines of the late 1930s emphasized that the consumption of fashion items desperately needed to gravitate around Italian products. In addition, then, to a concern to Italianize the language of fashion, the regime gave great attention to the need to foster the consumption of domestically produced goods. This was argued by Maddalena Santoro who, writing in 1934 in the *Almanacco fascista del popolo d'Italia,* brings the nationalistic agenda inherent in the fashion discourse to the fore. She writes that:

> *This season's fashion is rich in elements that can satisfy everyone's taste Even those with little spending power can wear, with a few light and wise changes, the clothes, cloaks and hats that were worn last year. This season's fashion also extends an invitation to those who are more fortunate to become even more beautiful and elegant, not only to satisfy egotistical whims, but also and above all to drum up business, not in the interests of individuals, but of the nation.*

In the background of such appeals is the issue of Italy's emancipation. Fascism, according to the Duce, represented a "new" course in Italian history, a break with the liberal past that had enabled Italians and their country to regain the dignity it once enjoyed in more glorious and past epochs, such as imperial Rome and the Renaissance. By achieving emancipation, the implicit message sent by the fascist regime was that previous liberal governments had been unable to serve the best interests of the Italian peninsula. Hence, the emphasis on both recovering and inventing an identity, that of *italianità* which would penetrate through massive propaganda everyday life in customs, manners and lifestyles. Perhaps the most marked trademark of *italianità,* which survives even to our day, is the myth of the *bella figura.* As we have noted in reference to the Renaissance, *bella figura,* a concept and a practice common both to the upper and lower classes, is indicative of a deep sense of the importance of taking care of one's appearance. This has become a central part of Italian culture and identity that joins, as so rarely happens in Italy, North and South, lower and upper classes. It is also central to the romanticization of the idea of Italy abroad and its stereotypes. Paradoxically, the author who theorized the *bella figura,* Castiglione, is absent in Meano's entries and quotations. It is indeed, an absence that it is difficult to explain, either because of an oversight on the part of the author or out of choice, since the discourse on clothing in Castiglione describes an explicit narrative of power that is perhaps too explicit.

Another glaring absence in Meano's work is any reference to uniforms, which played a vital role in fascist dress sense. In fact, the wearing of fascist uniforms inscribed itself in the re-use of the concept of *bella figura,* especially when parades were organized. These became moments when smartly dressed Italians could feel proud of themselves and their appearance as they marched through the streets of their town or city before congregating in the hallowed space for showing off one's *bella figura,* the town or city square. Here, fascist fashion policy squared completely with time-honored practices. Spaces in Italian cities and towns were architecturally conceived with a center and a square where generations of people used to gather on Sundays, after mass, and on holidays. The organization of the urban space also represented a major factor in the performative display of dress and its social meanings. In some provincial places a stroll through the center of town is still an occasion for showing off, for everybody, males and females alike, and is a constant opportunity for gossiping and socializing. During the fascist dictatorship, the *piazze* became the sites for sport-related spectacles and events in which the appropriately dressed local population was invited to participate.

Under fascism, there existed a great variety of civil uniforms, their number increasing in the colonial period because of the differences in weather and lifestyles in the Italian colonies. Interestingly, the whole text by Meano, whose focus is on the aestheticization of appearance where its socio-political meanings are well hidden in the texture of the performance in dress, is completely devoid of entries on *camicia nera* (black shirt) the emblem of fascism *divisa* (uniform, civil or not), and definitions like *piccola* or *giovane italiana* (little and young Italians, members of the fascist-sponsored youth organizations). Only the term *fez* appears, and explanations are offered as to how this headgear of oriental origin had currently become a fashionable accessory in ladies' wardrobes after previously being worn by the Italian *Bersaglieri*. Subsequently the fez was used by the first fascist *arditi* and later passed on to the *balilla*, another fascist youth organization.

Indeed, the absence of an entry such as *vestire alla fascista* is quite surprising, given the emphasis the regime gave to the public display of order, combining uniformity and distinction according to age group, gender, etc. The intent behind all the uniforms, however, was that of putting on display a disciplined social body that belonged to the fatherland and bore allegiance to the Duce. In 1934, prior to the publication of Meano's text, Francesco Salvori, among others, had strongly encouraged the adoption of civil uniforms. In his opinion, they expressed a disciplining of civil society as well as illustrating a sense of modernity. He wrote:

> *We live in a corporative epoch, an epoch of permanent civil militarization. All citizens are split into organizations and categories according to their profession. With military style clothing one can attach badges or the colors of the profession to which each one belongs. In this way, even in private and communal life, and even in external affairs the new social and political organization of fascism would find its harmonious and complete application and the people would feel included in a stronger and more formal manner, always under the yoke (and this is what is most important) of a strict law of discipline, self-control and honor. With civilian clothes this would be almost completely lacking. In a more fluid and acute way, a greater love for one's own profession would flow into the veins of each man, a more marked sense of solidarity and a more intimate understanding that life is discipline and rough weather. The new Italians must live like heroes; if not all of them with magnanimous gestures, which is impossible, at least with their thoughts and desires. Being heroes in style at least is very often the first step toward the substance of real heroes.*

For Salvori, to dress as a fascist and to dress *italianamente* was the precondition for the birth of a new type of Italian, of a new national identity. However, this new type is little more than a discursive construction born of fascist ideology and its cult of beauty. Having deep ramifications in the nation's cultural and social traditions and practices, the cult of beauty meshes with the discourse on style and its impact on the construction and perception of what here is called "substance," the real thing. Moreover, through the author's stress on the relationship between style and the political messages the wearer wishes to convey, we clearly see how fashion works as a system of communication and how fascist propaganda exploited to the fullest this key component of fashion, making style one of the major concerns of fascist ideology and aesthetics. In particular, Salvori seems acutely aware of how the performance of a heroic role achieved by dressing the part makes of the wearer something of a hero. Likewise, dressing as a fascist, for whatever reason, the desire to make a *bella figura* included, makes one something of a fascist, or at least not an anti-fascist. This finds confirmation in Gundle's point that: "In nationalist and right wing opinion, democracy was incompatible with beauty and style. Thus, 'to give style', the aesthetic expression that reflected Mussolini's political aim to transform the populace had as a pragmatic counterpart the expression 'to fascistize'."

This is the reason why Meano privileges a more general cultural politics of style and the new codes of beauty and identity operating within civil society, rather than lingering over the more external and less subtle projection of fascist style through a focus on official military uniforms, of which he has very little to say. In this regard, some of the entries contained in Meano's text are illuminating, especially the very first one: *Abbigliamento,* a term that in the Italian language contains ramifications with verbs such as *abbigliarsi* (to adorn oneself, to dress), hence the common Italian expression *farsi belli* (to make oneself beautiful). Here, Meano aims at emphasizing the acts of dressing and adorning oneself, which he exemplifies by quoting from D'Annunzio, who championed the exaltation of the aesthetic features of the *bellezza italica* and of a intimate link between aesthetic and politics in its most elite manifestations. Indeed, in this entry, the aesthetic is strongly emphasized over the practical. And at the end of its treatment, as complementary links, the author suggests reading the entry *toletta* a process of dressing, preparing - the Italianized version of the corresponding French term *toilette* - meaning *abbigliamento* - commonly used. However, what is at a stake in the *abbigliamento* entry is a fascist cultural politics that defines the right appearance of the body according to accepted codes of elegance and style that have their ground in national mythologies such as the cult of the *bella figura*(looking good) and the nationalistic ideology of D'Annunzio's aesthetics. And nowhere could young Italian men and women show off the care they dedicated to their appearance and to their bodies in the projection of their *bella figura* better than in sports, to which we now turn.

Sport, Gender and Models of Femininity

Sport and its related activities occupy a large number of entries in Meano's dictionary. As mentioned in the previous chapter, the entry *Abbronzare* (suntanning) testifies to the change in the codes that established the idea of the kind of beauty that was promoted in a given society. Indeed a strong connection is overtly made between beauty and outdoor activities for women:

> *There was a time when milk, roses and lilies had no rivals for illustrating the skin color of women. In Italian poetry, the famous rose took its proper place. Then, even a light shadow of sun-tan or the slightest trace of peeling would have offended beauty and poetry, women and their admirers.*

After this, Meano goes on to quote a poem by Giosué Carducci in support of this new model of beauty and femininity. Then, the text continues:

> *And today? From the passion for sport and the outdoor life, on which we have commented many times, was born the myth of strong beauty, just as from the passion for pathetic meditation came the myth of an evanescent, languid, sighing beauty. The bronze color of athletes, of soldiers in the field, of reapers and explorers brought an ideal of beauty that was not only masculine, but also feminine, if not more so. So, good-bye to roses and lilies, to the sweetness of dawn, to ivory shoulders and snow-like cheeks. The sun of the mountains, of the beaches, and of city balconies was called into action (see: entries on Sun, Sport) and, as the rays of the sun did not suffice we had recourse to artificial means, and oils and creams to color the skin were invented (see: entry on Make-up).*

The spread of sport in the Italy of the 1930s represented a major change. Starting in the second half of the nineteenth century, sport had played in Western countries, and later in Italy, a major role in the progressive modification of dress and appearance, especially for women. Benjamin is keen to point out that the appearance of posters portraying women riding bicycles was an important sign of the changes taking place in female identities and in a new idea of attractiveness. Moreover, this is acknowledged by Benjamin as the first manifestation in society that sport was destined to affect the future of fashion and dress: "The costume of the cyclist, as an early and unconscious prefiguration of sportswear, corresponds to the dream prototypes that, a little before or a little later, are at work in the factory or the automobile."

Meano, in the entry dedicated to sport, recalls Isabella Inghirani, one of the first female aviators, who in 1909 attempted to adapt her voluminous gown so she could manipulate the controls of her plane with greater ease: "She tied a cord around her skirt so that the pleats stuck more closely to her legs." Meano uses this example in order to show the stark changes undergone by women's roles in the present. Magazines such as *Lidel* often contained articles that illustrated and heaped praise on the importance of sport for women, as well as offering chronicles of pioneer female aviators. Although Meano focuses on women as the subject of his analysis, he stresses at the beginning of the above quotation and later in the text that males are not excluded. He explicitly refers to the "many discourses of fashion" and how, in the 1930s, street-fashion was more oriented towards sport: "Many speak of sport, and on the street we see many clothes made for walking."

In the articles contained in *Lidel,* a few common ideological threads can be traced. The pictures portraying women in public events wearing sports uniforms and performing activities are always accompanied by pictures of domesticity and maternal care or, if not visually, in the text these traditional female roles are highlighted and strongly starred as a fundamental achievement. Moreover, praise for sport and women is often justified by the fact that outdoor sports contributed enormously to the "improvement of the race," as we find in the title of an article published in *Lidel* in January 1933. In the same issue, a world record in female aviation achieved by Carina Negrone is celebrated. In the photographs accompanying the article she is portrayed in several poses and outfits; first, wearing her flying uniform and then on the following page smiling while embracing her baby son, followed by a glamorous picture of Carina, soon after her adventure in the sky. In this photograph, she is wearing a stylish white suit with a short blazer wrapped over her shoulders, her hat in her left hand, wearing a tight striped knitted blouse surrounded, on her left and right, by handsome men, impeccable in their uniforms. These images convey a message that Carina is a strong woman, happy with herself and completely at ease in a male world. Indeed, she has become famous for having engaged in traditionally male activities. Hence, the glamour emphasized in the pictures where her "traditional" or "expected" femininity in dress, appearance, as well as motherhood are both reaffirmed and undiminished by her sport activity.

Although women appeared as very diversified subjectivities, at times depicted as contradictory female types in the fashion magazines, as well as in women's writing, Meano portrays above all a paternalistic and conservative model of femininity. In fact, the *maschietta,* on which we commented earlier, is moralistically condemned and considered out of fashion. Nevertheless, the changes in culture that had nurtured these new models of femininity did not completely disappear and the iconic message of females engaged in sports and outdoor activities exhibiting strong bodies inevitably suggested a dynamic vision of women. In this regard, it is interesting to see the pictures and read the testimonies of the women who attended the female Orvieto Academy, which had been founded in 1932 as a counterpart to the male Farnesina Academy in Rome. The *Accademia Nazionale di Educazione Fisica Femminile di Orvieto* (The national academy for female physical education of Orvieto) was founded in order to fulfill the regime's aim to promote sport as well as using it as a means of educating the masses, in this case women. Sport and social rituals became a key component of the celebration of the nation, the Duce and patriotism, and an opportunity, as in any ritual, to keep the community together in a display of unity and control. Indeed the "fascist nation" was in many ways also the "sporting nation."

Under fascism, there was, then, a very real double take on women. The fashion of the 1930s proclaimed a return to the old days: *Torniamo all'antico* (Let's go back to the way things were) was, in fact, the title of an editorial by Lina Putelli in the periodical *Per voi signora,* which became, together with *Bellezza,* the official mouthpiece of the ENM. Here Putelli reports on the latest French fashions that abandon the simplicity and linearity of the *garçonne* style in favor of a more elaborate one, echoing the second half of the nineteenth century with its long and elaborate gowns and more romantic taste. In the *Commentario,* we find descriptions of women from different social classes, from the high society *femme fatale,* who wore dresses that covered their necks but revealed their completely exposed backs to the modest women who work in a Piedmontese workshop and learn how to continue the tradition of local embroidery called *bandera*. This latter description emphasizes the work of such women in a populistic language that is ideologically in line with the fascist project of promoting regional artisan and craft traditions. One of these was lace, which occupied a prominent role for different kinds of dress decoration. Magazines and newsreels, as well as the publications of the ENM, went out of their way to emphasize Italian tradition in this decorative art. Meano, in fact, has an entry dedicated to *Merletto* (Lace) in which he gives an historical account on the spread of the art of lace and in which he emphasizes the role Italy once again had played in the Middle Ages and the Renaissance. He explains how this important skill was passed on by Venetian merchants to Germany and other countries and gives a detailed account of various styles and lace production techniques perfected in Italian cities, all of which had their own distinct traditions.

The emphasis on traditional roles also spills over into an overtly misogynistic view. This is what informs Meano's description of the *intellettualità della donna* (Intellectual ability of women, 205) in which his main aim, perfectly in line with regime policy, is to emphasize women's qualities as bearers of children instead of their intellectual work. Interestingly enough, Meano, while stressing the feminine side of fashion and the relationship between women and fashion, minimizes the relationship between men and fashion. He puts men in what he calls the "zona neutrale immobile" (Neutral immobile zone), which is to say that men lack audacity in the cut of their clothes and in the use of vibrant colors. Meano, in fact, praises this neutral zone, the "calm little stream," stating that this sober style is indeed in line with the notion of virility, heroism and strength that the regime wishes to reinforce and maintain. In support of his argument, he makes references to past historical epochs such as the eighteenth century when males, in his view, were no less fashion victims than their female counterparts. He argues, in fact, that men, then, did not project and convey in dress their best "virile" qualities.

At stake, however, in the text is not a representation of women or of gender relations per se. Rather, the text offers a view on men's functional role in the building of a national image for Italian fashion through a series of rules and forms of language that ensure the creation of a domestic tradition. It is in this vein, in fact, that Meano returns as a recurrent source of inspiration to the Italian Renaissance, identified as a crucial point for defining an "authentic" Italian identity. The references to Renaissance authors and art are countless in the text and especially in the entries where the process of inspiration and creativity is involved. This historical interest in the art and costume of the Renaissance is also confirmed in a series of articles published in several periodicals that highlight Renaissance Italy's innovative arts and crafts and showed the connections existing between painting and the decorative arts. In some of the articles, for instance, Leonardo Da Vinci's interest in textiles is highlighted; in another, attention is paid to Pisanello's wellknown drawings which, as we have seen in the previous chapter, also inspired Genoni's search for Italian models. In "Arte dell'abbigliamento" (Art of dressing), Meano states that:

> *We will discover in our Renaissance artists lines of beauty that we should never have forgotten, and we will be surprised to learn that fashion has not always been of our age. Leonardo and Botticellli have much to say about this. It is vital that we know the forms of the human body, a body that, as Leonardo said, is the model of the world. Let us hope, then that in our schools young intelligent minds are turned to an understanding of the supreme harmony of the lines of our body; and better still if this happens in our State-run schools. We will have, in this way, worthy architects of Italian fashion, creators and when we go ahead in our study for other ends we will have men who are more self-aware.*

The notion of the self-awareness of one's own identity, in this context, must not be considered from the merely individual perspective. Rather, this awareness, according to Meano, acts as a necessary step to the achievement of an original creativity. If, once again, we strip the text of its pompous fascist rhetoric and selfcentered nationalism, we see how such concepts were at the core of the initial claims for an Italian fashion made by Genoni, who belonged to a completely different political environment. Following Genoni, the other fervent advocate of an autonomous Italian style and fashion, De Liguoro used nationalist and patriotic language to convey similar messages. What I would like to underline here, however, are two points: first, as we have already stated, a line of continuity links prefascist and fascist Italy in the search for a national fashion; and second, the strong political dimension with which fashion is charged both in its making and in its varied uses. And this is so still today in our contemporary society.

We cannot dismiss from this discourse the personal side of fashion, since it is central to the articulation of a complex and dual structure that aims at commodifying, standardizing and proliferating a plurality of sometimes imagined selves and identities. Indeed, one of the most elaborate entries in Meano's text is *Personalità* (Personality). Here the author discusses at length the impact and function of creating a personal style and of adorning oneself in terms of the construction of an individual appearance, which inevitably creates a micro-narrative of our being in the world. He writes: Women often speak of personality, women and men. Today it is very common and not always reproachable to note the pride with which one of us keeps alive and clear his or her specific qualities, all of which make up the personality. In the field of fashion, then, this is the strength that presides over one of the most delicate and most representative functions, that of the choice of clothes, it being always the desire of women to find clothes that reveal their personality to the world. But how do clothes go about this? They carry out this function through what they themselves say, because each article of clothing and fabric, like each hat and scarf, always says something, and in most cases they say it very clearly seeing that they draw on a language of images.

But what was the efficacy of a text such as Meano's? Did it effectively discipline the language of fashion and the way Italians dressed? Strangely enough, given its premises and its length, the *Dizionario* is something of a disappointing text. Similarly to the absence of entries describing the *Vestire alla fascista*(Dressing like a fascist), one is also surprised to note relatively few references to foreign terms. Indeed, far fewer than one would have expected, given the scope of the text. The aim of purging the Italian language and the fashion jargon of foreign words especially French is somehow half-hearted. For the most part, in fact, the French words in use are simply Italianized, as in the case of *paltò,* or given a translation like *palline* (polka dots), instead of *pois;* or the pathetic example of *Cignon* translated with *cignone*. In addition, the important entry *Taielleur*(Suit), such a classic item of ladies' wardrobes appears under the male counterpart *Completo,* which is a translation once again of the French *complet,* from which expressions such as *Completo a giacca* for men and *abito a giacca* are derived, the latter replacing *taielleur.*

Even today in the Italian language, the French term is commonly used. For the rest, the result is a mixture of fascist propaganda as in entries such as *Moda in Italia* (Fashion in Italy) or those reserved for the synthetic fibers. *Moda in Italia* is, in fact, one of the most propagandistic entries and reiterates the fact that Italy held an hegemonic position in Europe for fashion and style during the Renaissance and traces how in the following centuries the sway had passed to France. However, Meano affirms that Italy, thanks to the fascist steps taken following to the creation of the ENM, is gradually regaining its leading position in terms of style.

More than on the actual act of disciplining styles and body exposure, the importance of this text lies in its emphasis on the complexities of language and discourse and their bearing on fashion. The book calls attention to the production of a discourse on fashion and the attempts made by the fascist regime to nationalize it as well as to control the customs of the Italian people. An immediate effect of the publication of the book was, especially in the periodicals, the observation of the order to Italianize the names of the models shown in the magazines, as well as their captions. In addition, as we have seen, articles were also published in support of the Italianization of the language of fashion. However, on the whole, this nationalizing process was not literally observed and automatically applied. A review of Meano's *Commentario* by the linguist Alfredo Panzini that appeared in the daily newspaper *Corriere della sera* focuses on the difficulties inherent in Meano's project, likening it to the sumptuary laws of the Renaissance, and even pokes fun at, without ever actually criticizing, the regime's attempt to discipline fashion, language and women:

> *To discipline women's fashion will be less easy than you think. At least up until today, the strictest sumptuary law was shown to be impotent Similarly, it will be a difficult thing to discipline the language of fashion. And here we are already in the middle of the great wood of French locutions.*

In this context the relationship with the verbal structure of fashion as exemplified in the names of fashion items assumes a political valence that also bears on the "aura" associated with the name given to a particular dress. Indeed, it was against this aura, which had been codified in strictly French terms, that projects like Meano's struggled and lost. In "Verso l'autarchia della moda"

(Towards an autarchic fashion) Mario Peter, writing in *L'informatore confidenziale della moda,* takes up once again the issue of French terminology, as well as the fascination experienced by the wearer of clothes that "speak" French:

> *By now there are very few Italian women who are stubbornly faithful to the Parisian model. These are women who consider superior products everything that comes from abroad or carries a foreign label. But there are still those who continue to delude themselves that if they call it a* taielleur *the work will be carried out better than if it was called an* abito a giacca.

Returning to Panzini's review, we see that as well as poking fun at Meano's project of disciplining fashion, it also contains other interesting strands. For one thing, despite his opinion that there is little point in trying to rid the language of fashion of French terminology, his review is overtly nationalistic, recalling a declaration by Arnaldo Mussolini made in 1931 on the importance of the campaign to promote national products. The praise Panzini reserves for Meano's project is occasioned by the fact that it exalts the Italian present and connects it with the glory of the Renaissance past, to the time of Isabella D'Este when Italy had an hegemonic role in terms of art, style, and the manufacture of sumptuous and beautiful clothes. In conclusion, what Panzini emphasizes is the effect that the formation of an institution such as the ENM would have in breathing new life into the national fashion industry, as well as promoting the Italian tradition of clothing and textile. But Panzini also seems aware that the real future enemy of Italian fashion would not be France, hence perhaps his relative lack of concern about French influence, but the USA. The gradual changes in the economy, new models of consumption, the transformation of cultural models to which sport and cinema had contributed led to a different perception of the social body and gender relations. It is not by chance, then, that Panzini's review, in underplaying French hegemony, points the finger at the USA, the new emerging world power that would gradually impose its political, cultural and economic weight on Europe. This, in the field of fashion, is translated into the fact that the US ready-to-wear industry was developing at a great speed and introducing its products onto the European market.

Yet, if Panzini saw the threat on the horizon coming from the USA, Italian fashion still had to deal with the present threat, still represented by France, still the nation that held a hegemonic position, still the enemy, but an enemy that was paradoxically also the source for inspiration, the model to imitate. In this regard, Elvio Fenoglio in his article "La creazione della moda" (The creation of fashion), published in the 1933 Christmas issue of *Per voi signora,* uses as an epigraph an excerpt from a Parisian daily newspaper that reports how several parties and balls given by the French aristocracy had the effect of boosting the sales of the French luxury goods industry. These socialite gatherings ensured a domestic market for the production and consumption of luxury goods and haute couture, their public display underlining the flair of Parisian chic. Drawing on this excerpt, Fenoglio illustrates the importance of fashion on the national economy, not without paying homage to the Duce in his final words:

> *A flip through a Parisian daily newspaper of two years ago is enough to confirm the importance and the repercussions that fashion can have on the economic life of a nation. This is why it is important to have in our hands the leadership of this movement so we can direct it according to our own needs.* In a word, to achieve what the Duce wants and, that is, create fashion.

Whether as enemy to be defeated or as model to be imitated, or both at the same time, France, and above all Paris, remained firmly in the sights of the Italian fashion industry in the 1930s. To get a closer idea of this troubled relationship let us now turn to the film *Contessa di Parma*(Countess of Parma) directed by Alessandro Blasetti in 1937, a film that dramatizes how Italian fashion at least dreamt of exorcising that threat.

Fashion, Film and the Politics of the Regime

Although specialized periodicals and fashion magazines had a considerable weight in the campaign for supporting Italian fashion, it is undeniable that cinema established itself as a much more popular medium able to reach out and guarantee a larger audience, which in Italy was composed of a population where the majority of people were hardly able to read and write. The popularity of cinema was not, however, a solely Italian phenomenon. Other European countries and the USA had, in fact, undergone a similar development and trend. In Italy, however, cinema was even more crucial as a form of entertainment and "education" in fascist terms, since there were still, in addition to a very high degree of illiteracy, stark contrasts between North and South and between urban centers and rural areas.

The fertile terrain out of which Italian cinema in the 1930s grew was the product of a group of creative film directors and intellectuals. This was a potential that the fascist regime was quick to recognize and harness to its own purposes. Indeed, especially in the 1930s, cinema was given particular prominence, first with the formation of *Cines* in 1930-1, and later of *Cinecittà in* 1937 as well as the *Centro sperimentale di cinematografia*. In addition to the massive production of Italian films, foreign films, especially American ones, were also widely distributed and available. Despite, or perhaps on account of, the popularity of US cinema, the regime began to regulate it only in the late 1930s, and increasingly in the early 1940s as Italy entered the war against the USA.

Irene Brin, a sharp observer of her contemporary culture and styles, published an article in 1943 entitled "La moda e il cinema" (Fashion and the cinema) in the journal *Cinema*. Here, she stressed the popularity, especially among the female audience, of myths such as those created by the screen personae of Greta Garbo, Marlene Dietrich and Joan Crawford. In her opinion, and not surprisingly, their imported ideals of beauty and elegance exercised a stronger appeal and power of imitation on the Italian female audience than their homegrown domestic actresses who were then forced to imitate the glamour of their foreign colleagues. Similarly to the advertising pages in fashion magazines, Hollywood divas represented a magic carpet on which bored housewives or women conducting ordinary lives could fly and, for a moment at least, live out their dreams: "These women need romance," writes Roland Marchand, "they crave glamour and color." Hollywood films "cast such magical spells that housewives and women workers could daily see themselves as *femme fatales*, as Cleopatra or Helen of Troy," and so glamorize the monotony of everyday life.

Hollywood actresses were also one of the sources for fashion and trends. Brin sarcastically states that, thanks to Garbo and her medium length page-boy hair style, women could at last abandon their short Eton haircut inspired by the model of the 1920s, that of the *maschietta*. Writing a few years after the initial impact of the Garbo phenomenon, she notes:

> *Our childhood, surrounded by mothers with shaved necks, bigger sisters sporting Eton haircuts, was full of heartfelt questions and fearful sentences: "Hair looks good very long or very short. What will we do when it grows out. Garçonne style or braids, nothing is worse than medium length hair." Yet, the triumph was entirely that of medium-length hair and the pageboy style of Greta is still with us, after 12 years. And the basque beret, the dark overcoat, the sporty well-worn trousers, which she alternated with fabulously scintillating evening gowns. Greta was always splendid and delicate.*

The face of Garbo was so ever present in fashion magazines' advertising either for make-up, perfume or fashion. So strong was the power exercised by her image that other models sought to look like. As Barthes has written in his *Mythologies:* "Garbo belongs to that moment in cinema when capturing the human face still plunged audiences into the deepest ecstasy, when one literally lost oneself in a human image as one would in a philter, when the face represented a kind of absolute state of the flesh, which could be neither reached nor renounced." Hollywood Star look-alike competitions thrived during fascism, even more so in the post-war years. Gundle reports that in 1932, the MGM company held a Greta Garbo look-alike competition that was won by Romilda Villani, Sophia Loren's future mother.

As the case of Garbo shows, fashion and cinema have an intimate link in the creation of mythologies and identities either to be imitated for those who could afford it or simply fantasized about. For Italian women, the cinema has always represented an important source of inspiration for the reproduction of dresses, especially when and where magazines were not available. Hollywood films played a key role, both in the USA and in Europe, as merchandisers of goods, especially fashion and beauty products. As we shall see, films of the white telephone genre, such as Blasetti's *Contessa di Parma* which is mentioned in Brin's article and *Grandi magazzini*(Department stores), directed in 1939 by Mario Camerini, show a number of similarities both in film and commercial techniques. Both films contain, in fact, explicit tie-ins for clothes and accessory items, a marketing ploy, akin to the more recent "And now a word from our sponsor." Such a ploy had already been tried out in 1930s Hollywood films such as *Stolen Holidays,* made in 1937, *Roberta,* made in 1935 or *Mannequin,* made in 1938. The dresses worn by the actresses in the movies were, in fact, reproduced on a mass scale and sold in American department stores. In Italy, cinema began to rival the specialized periodicals as a source of inspiration for the skills of those *sarte* and *sartine*(dressmakers), of whom there were many, who catered to mainly lower-class customers. Indeed, for women who were not living in big cities and who for economic reasons could not pursue a higher education, it was very common to work as a seamstress or as a *ricamatrice*(embroiderer). For less privileged women, this was an opportunity to gain a relative independence. In fact these women could work outside the paternal home before marriage while acquiring a skill to be used to earn money after their apprenticeship was served. Moreover, the majority of women could put their sewing skills to the service of the needs of their families. This was also an opportunity for them to sew their own *trousseau* before getting married.

If Garbo "The Divine," represented the elitist and aristocratic myth, a more democratic myth, closer to the actual lifestyles of the average woman film viewer, but a myth nonetheless, of the young self-made woman was incarnated by Joan Crawford. Here is how Brin speaks of this latter:

> *Joan Crawford's story seemed to complete the elegy of the disdainful face of inexpensive clothes, of the self-made girl. Summing up a thousand other stories that seemed dramatic and close to us, female clerks swarmed out of their offices after work firmly convinced that they looked like she did and deserved, as she did, a villa with a swimming pool in California.*

Brin's article illustrates the important changes and social transformations that were taking place both in Europe and the USA and their repercussions on the formation and spread of new models of consumption and styles. Indeed, she points out that Hollywood cinema became a powerful vehicle for the spread of images of goods to be acquired and models to be imitated, reproducing them on a mass scale. Brin, in fact, goes out of her way to state that American films such as the already mentioned *Roberta* or *Mannequins* did little to hide at all their propagandistic and advertising aims. As a result, affordable reproductions of the dresses launched in the films were sold nationwide at the big US department stores. In a similar vein, she notes that, although in a less organized manner, in Europe as well, imitation of the fashion present in the movies was gradually picking up. Icons of glamour, sport and a mysterious life, such as the black sunglasses worn by Garbo, became very fashionable accessories to be sold even at "UPIM [an Italian department store] for two lire." As the Italian couturier based in Paris, Elsa Schiaparelli noted: "what Hollywood designs today, you will be wearing tomorrow."

For reasons such as these, some of the Italian commercial films produced in the second half of 1930s are interesting texts when considered in the light of the politics of fashion and its commercial and narratological potential. In this way, white telephone films, borrowing ideas from Hollywood, readapted and Italianized the glamour of the characters, their representation and stories. As with Hollywood films, however, commercial films amused and entertained, their political intent, although present, well embedded in the drama of the plot.

The ENM had a role to play in the Italian film industry. In fact, it extended its regulations regarding the Italianization of fashion and required that Italian films made in the 1930s featured only domestically made clothes for their costumes. This was no bad deal for the fashion houses as, naturally, commercial films could become a powerful, and cheap, means of advertising. Costume designers Gino Sensani and Nino Novarese were among those who ensured that the costumes worn in historical films were of a high standard. It goes without saying that *Cinecittà* lacked the structure and the organization of Hollywood studios in terms of fashion consultants, make-up artists, photographers and designers such as Adrian (MGM) or Edith Head (Paramount), but there was, indeed, a concern and an awareness to create a more attuned relationship between the fashion houses and film production. Indeed Blasetti's *Contessa di Parma* will help to see this issue in a clearer light. Morever, the history of Hollywood costume designs is complex and a distinction must be made between costume and couture design, as Stella Bruzzi points out in her study on the relationship between clothing, identity and the movies. When Coco Chanel received an offer to design for MGM in Hollywood in 1931, her stardom and personality created her well known conflict with Gloria Swanson and led Chanel to leave the USA. Couture resisted the demand to adjust to the character and the narrative needs of the film. Rather, it sought to create a show of its own. But it was through Hollywood and cinema that the USA supplanted and ultimately undermined the Parisian influence on domestically produced fashion, as we have noted earlier in the spread of its icons of style via stars such as Garbo, and Crawford in the puff-sleeved dress she wore in *Letty Lyton*. Lucio Ridenti, a regular contributor of *Bellezza* does not miss the opportunity to underline in his articles on "Moda e Cinema" (Fashion and Cinema) the importance of this almost magical binomial, a project on which the ENM embarked. Ridenti, however, stresses the need to develop and reinforce this link in the relationship between the fashion houses and the ENM in such a way that clothing in the film must be ahead of fashion instead of *following* it, as was still the case in Italy. This was a lesson, Ridenti believes, that Hollywood had learnt very well when, in order to free the American market of French fashion, it started to produce films dealing explicitly with fashion and thus spread an imposed "American" fashion to Europe. Going back to Italy, the fascist regime understood via Hollywood that an important link existed between fashion and cinema and that these were both powerful weapons to spread national models, to mold identity and consciousness and also to advertise images of modernity and glamour. And this could also serve the purpose of reaching out culturally and commercially to domestic and foreign markets. In both fashion and cinema, however, there was still space for fantasy and desire. Along these lines we may note that even in the midst of WWII, the ENM commissioned a lavishly illustrated volume entitled *Moda e Cinema* (Fashion and Cinema). Here, in the opening pages of the book, we read that:

> *the volume aims at illustrating the intimate relationship between the arts and fashion, which is here to be understood not only in its aesthetic function but also in its ramifications with the national industry through the relationship between fashion and cinema it is possible to gauge to what extent the big screen, via an enormous diffusion of easy to assimilate images, is able to influence the majority of its audience. Italian cinema, deliberately Italian, is also an international cinema and thus a vehicle for the spread of art, attitudes and tastes, which are the key element of Italianness.*

It is clear from this paragraph that not only did the project of building a national cinema and a national fashion go hand in hand, but also that the project was launched with the intent to export abroad domestic products. Indeed, a nationalistic intent always entails the projection of such models abroad that can be recognized as such. This assumption finds confirmation in a series of articles that appeared in *Bellezza* on "Moda italiana per gli stranieri" (Italian fashion for the foreigners):

The aims set by the ENM, which began its activity in Turin and was founded by the Duce's will, are well known. The first aim was to conquer the domestic market of the garment industry: this necessitated two tasks, one harder than the other - the organization and greatest valorization of all the artistic, crafts, industrial and commercial forces operating in the national field of fashion, while at the same time engaging in the struggle against the Francophile preference of the customers and their groundless diffidence towards Italian production. The second aim is a natural consequence and development of the first went in the direction of expansion abroad and conquest of foreign clothes markets to the benefit of our own production the foreign market.

In the volume *Moda Documento,* we find a series of photographs illustrating the spaces and the activities of the *Centro Sperimentale di Cinematografia* (CSC), the school for acting and directing, the gymnasium where various sports were practiced, followed by another illustration of *Cinecittà.* In an article following the illustration of the CSC and *Cinecittà* the important function that Hollywood cinema had for the diffusion of fashion and models incarnated by the female and male stars to be imitated emerges forcefully. The article, however, stresses the importance for both Italian cinema and fashion of keeping their distance from Hollywood models of femininity and masculinity. The question posed here is whether Italian cinema could spread "ideas of a previously unknown elegance, so true and real that they create a process of imitation in the audience and educate it to taste." As we can imagine, the answer to this question is yes, Italian cinema can convey and achieve these ends with the support and collaboration of "great constructor tailors and fabrics." Meano, the author of the *Commentario Dizionario della moda,* also writes here on the relationship between fashion and cinema. While emphasizing the function of propaganda in film, he refers to the production of several costume dramas set in the nineteenth century like *Malombra.* He links this return to the nineteenth century to the time of the Italian Risorgimento, which can be compared, in his view, to the wars in which Italy was then involved.

Several steps taken by the fascist regime confirmed its attempt to institutionalize the relationship between the construction of both a national cinema and a national fashion that went hand in hand with the projection of an attractive and modern image of Italy and Italians. It is with these premises in mind that we now turn to a close analysis of Blasetti's *Contessa di Parma.*

From Hollywood to France and From France to Italy

The Italian capital of fashion chosen by the fascist regime and where the official initiatives of the ENM took place - *Contessa di Parma* represents a rich reference point from which to observe the ideology of the regime in its quest to create a national fashion. Blasetti's film, in fact, is a useful means to illustrate not only this, but also to document the fascist politics on fashion and how it was interrelated with other activities such as sport and its impact on cultural models. *Contessa di Parma* is, then, something more than just a remake of an American commercial film. Rather, it is a film whose subtle and hidden complexities can be seen only through the lens of fashion and its interrelations with gender and politics. This is a film that reveals the manipulative power of the media in a totalitarian regime, but just as importantly, in giving hints of the entrepreneurial quality and role of women who worked in the fashion apparel industry, it also presents interesting twists in gender relations and representation.

Of interest, then, is the representation of gender relations offered by the film in which rather than a unified model of female identity, we see several models. Present in the film are several identities - differing in age and economic power that portray a mixture of traditional female roles that are not pulled apart by the quest for independence and self-determination. Indeed, Blasetti's cinematic eye surveys a sophisticated terrain on which one can explore both the politics and aesthetics of the representation of gender and its interrelations with fashion.

The film's establishing shots are images of art deco buildings onto which credits are projected as if they were advertising signs. These are illuminated against the dark background so that the images have a pictorial quality and transmit an aura of both tradition and modernity. The establishing shots also introduce a commercial message, as we are informed, first, that the clothes in the film, "all with a certificate of guarantee," have been supplied by Matté, a well-known fashion house in Turin; and, second, that the fur coats worn in the film are from Viscardi, which had successful branches in Rome and Turin. Further confirmation that this is designed to be a film with domestic concerns is found in the rational architecture of the buildings in the opening shots, which resembles that of the buildings in the Luce newsreels that chronicled and publicized the national exhibitions of fashion and textile held in Turin at the *Palazzo della moda.*

The film, a love story between Gino Vanni, a stylish and handsome football player in the Italian national team who looks more like a male model, and a mannequin in the guise of an aristocrat. This guise is supplied by the very elegant dress she wears that bears the name the *Contessa di Parma.* She wears this dress at the very beginning of the film when she first exchanges glances with Gino. Despite the predictability of this love story and its happy ending, the plot reveals interesting aspects of gender relations. From the start the viewer enters a fashion house and sees its patronizing director who is depicted as a faithful supporter of French fashion, seduced by its allure and chic. The viewer, who for these kinds of films was mainly female, also becomes immediately aware that the director treats the mannequins as commodities, there to serve his advertising purposes. Throughout the film, the director of the Maison is portrayed as effeminate and pretentious, dropping French words here and there in his conversation. His entire persona and affected mannerisms are depicted as a caricature and as the exact opposite of *sprezzatura.* Even the name of the firm he directs has a French name *Printemps,* like the well-known Parisian department store. When at the beginning of the film, one of the employees of the fashion house informs him that a new person from Milan, the widow Marta Rossi, has acquired the business and that she is arriving soon, he promptly answers that he has no time for her (or anybody from Milan) since he is about to leave for Paris and needs to buy his ticket at once: "Macche Milano," he says, which is best translated as "Forget Milan, I'm leaving for Paris." He delivers his line with an air of arrogance and mystery that is soon to be ridiculed by his affected and pretentious demeanor. Unlike him, the true aristocrats appearing in the film are depicted as chic solely on account of their family names. These are aristocrats on the downward slide, forced to do what for them is demeaning work. In fact, circumstances dictate that they cannot hide their desperate need for money and are forced to sell their titles and agree to become paid escorts for the fashion models at the high society balls and horse races where the fashion house shows off its goods. We soon learn that the fashion house, whose interior is elegant and refined, has been acquired by a female Milanese entrepreneur, Marta Rossi, who happens to be the wealthy aunt of the male protagonist, the soccer player Vanni. Rossi, as opposed to the previous effeminate director, anxious only to breathe Parisian air, is depicted as a very masculine, independent woman who has at heart the project of the Italianization of fashion and its spread. Most importantly, she feels no sense of inferiority towards French couture, convinced as she is of the high quality of Italian clothing. Here, already, we see a twist in gender representation. From Milan, the city that, no less than Turin, had a well-established tradition in fashion and textile (which is why the regime's choice of Turin rather than Milan as the official capital of fashion generated some resentment in the Lombard city), Rossi is shown to have the managerial and advertising skills completely lacking in the male manager, who exhibits an extreme case of love of all things French, and whose obsession consisted in passively imitating Paris fashion. We wonder why a woman was chosen to represent this new entrepreneurial figure in Italian fashion. In the film, the female characters are, indeed, portrayed as innovators who have a better understanding of the facts of commercial life, which they know does not consist solely of the glamorous gatherings of high socialites. Female characters, then, come out of this film much better than their male counterparts. Although the new owner Rossi shows a greater sense of solidarity with the women working as models at the firm she has renamed *Magazzini Primavera,* Italianizing the name, she also has a hasty manner. But her virile manners are not to be confused with those of the 1920s *maschietta,* whose slender, young and sexy image was condemned by the regime. Rossi's virility proves to be a positive plus for the success of her business while at the same time never being a source of any attraction or sex appeal. She is an older woman, content not to be forced to appear younger than she is in her choice of clothes, hairstyle and make-up. She has the effect of reassuring both the audience and her employers with her motherly and yet authoritarian figure. By contrast, the former Francophile manager with his effeminate manners had a paternalistic attitude and treated the models overtly as goods.

At the beginning of the film, when we first see Marcella the female protagonist, the director of the fashion house introduces her and another model to the two aristocrats who have fallen on hard times and who have been hired to accompany them to the Opera and, the next day, to the horse races held at Mirafiori. Here Marcella is wearing the evening gown whose name, as we previously mentioned, is a French aristocratic title, *La countesse de Parme*. This mode of advertising which had been practiced since the turn of the twentieth century by French *couturiers* - is here, once again, re-proposed. As they dance, the models at the ball slip their firm's business card into the pockets of the tuxedos worn by their wealthy dance partners. This, and other French inspired modes, were all encouraged by the "bad guy" of the film, the former manager of *Printemps*. However, they are seen to be commercial failures as the models themselves complained of being treated as commodities to be used by males looking for sexual amusement and with little interest in buying clothes for their wives. Indeed, from the opening shots of the film, Marcella is depicted as a young woman who rejects the logic of commodification simply by virtue of the fact that she is a model and a beautiful woman. In fact, while they are driving towards the horse races at Mirafiori, she states that she is not interested in engaging herself in any intimate conversation or relationship with her male partner. As a result the Duke says to Marcella: "That dress you're wearing has given you airs above your station, remember you're just a poor model." To this she promptly responds that it is he who rather than she is at the low end of things since he has agreed to accompany her to social gatherings so he can pay off his debts. Marcella adds that hers is a job that she performs with dignity and for which she earns money, whereas the aristocrats like the fallen Duke have lost all dignity. It is at this point that the Duke, angered by her non-servile and feisty behavior, leaves Marcella alone in the car once they arrive at their destination. While left alone in the car, Marcella sees Gino with whom she had already exchanged a few admiring glances the previous night at the opera.

Confirmation of Marcella's determination not to be considered solely as a sexual object comes with her claim that the fact that she needs to work in order to make a living does not mean that she is put in the weaker position of being the target of sexual harassment. This was, in fact, her reaction, in the middle of the film, to the advertising campaign of *Printemps* that took place at a ball where models promoted the evening wear of the Maison's collection. The male guests showed more interest in the models' bodies than in buying the clothes that were destined for their respective wives.

It is at this point that Rossi accuses the former manager of incompetence in his job and suggests that rather than using balls to publicize the company's clothes they organize a fashion show in the trendy ski resort of Sestrières. Fashion shows at this time were becoming popular as a means of advertising and promoting the sale of Italian clothing and accessories. Especially during the autarchic phase, shows like this were organized during the national exhibitions organized by the ENM in Turin, in local branches of the *Rinascente* department store, at Mirafiori, and at the Villa D'Este in Como, in conjunction with the textile industry.

Since her first meeting with the new Milanese owner, Marcella is considered her protégée. One of the reasons for the immediate sympathy established between the two women is the fact that Marcella is wearing a suit borrowed from the collection sent from Milan by the new owner that she wore for a show. Later, she wears it on her first date with the football player, who still believes, on account of her clothes, that she is an aristocrat. But as she enters Gino's car she accidentally rips the upper sleeve out of the dress, and is now terrified by what has happened. Marcella's outfit costs, in fact, 2500 Lire, a substantial amount, if we consider that earning 1000 Lire a month, as a popular song of the day says, was considered one of the highest salaries. The outfit itself is of black velvet and features a jacket with a revers in white ermine. This is something that Marcella could never afford. In fact, on the following date she has with Gino, she timidly tries to reveal her true identity when she tells him that on this occasion she is wearing a 200 Lire dress, something that a milliner or a modest seamstress could afford. To this, Gino, fast becoming the male hero of the film, promptly replies by saying that it is not the price of the dress that reveals the style of the wearer, but the person wearing it who ensures the attractiveness of any outfit, expensive or not. Gino also adds that in any case he would never be interested in going out with somebody like a seamstress or, even worse, someone with a dubious reputation like a mannequin. It is at this point that Marcella feels ashamed of her real identity and decides not to reveal it in order to continue her relationship with Gino. Her fear is that it is the mysterious countess who attracts Gino's imagination more than the *brava ragazza* (good girl) who makes *polpette* (meatballs), as is suggested by the football player's aunt Marta Rossi.

Titles and appearances, then, play a huge role in this film, aristocratic titles and exotic names given to dresses being shown in the film as devices for attracting possible buyers. While never putting the workings of this commercial mechanism in doubt, the film does fulfill the nationalist intent of fascist fashion policy by translating these names into Italian. The film, then, seeks to persuade us that the quality and style of clothes made in Italy are not inferior to or less attractive than French ones. This becomes clear when during a fashion show in the now renamed *Primavera* fashion house, the Francophile former manager says the clothes from the new collection on display look so chic as to convince him he is breathing Paris's sophisticated air. At this, one of the assistants remarks that the models being presented did not come from Paris but from Milan. Faced with this revelation, the manager is so disconcerted that he disdainfully says he has changed his mind and that he does not like the new collection any more. By exaggerating the manager's Francophile attitudes to such a degree that he becomes a caricature, the viewer is led to condemn all of his actions and consider his opinions completely irrational, especially when we see the actual beauty of the chic outfits that appear on the screen. In displaying luxurious and elegant female and male dress - Gino, too, is impeccable in his well-tailored suits, complemented with fine accessories like the snugly fitting leather gloves or hats he wears - the film becomes a powerful advertisement for Italian fashion and style. Through its narrative techniques and the popular love story format it adopts, the film attracted big audiences, especially among women, and sent a message whose efficacy was more powerful than that of other media. Blasetti himself, in an interview, affirmed that, indeed, his film was tangible proof that fascism took very seriously the idea of promoting and building a national fashion. He added that, at that particular point in his career, he needed work and making a film with the attractive ingredients of *Contessa di Parma* was a recipe for guaranteed success and pecuniary reward.

It is interesting to note that Blasetti's film can be considered the Italian counterpart of the aforementioned Hollywood films that adopted similar techniques designed to give the best possible visibility and publicity to the clothes on display, such as several close-ups of details emphasizing the cut, decoration and accessories of the outfits. In fact, this is a film in which the way the outfits worn by Marcella are filmed, dwelling on their seductive power, leaves a very strong impression on the viewer. When asked in an interview about the provincialism of Italian fashion in the 1930s, Blasetti replied: "I never believed that Italian fashion had been literally negative. Even then it had its positive side and I remember beautiful toilettes, of good taste too, that were prepared for my characters." Marcella's black velvet suit, ermine trimmed, fitted jacket, and her black beret with a light and transparent black half-veil delicately touching the white revers of her jacket represent the height of her elegance, her status and her seductive power. Here the sophisticated use of the camera plays its part as angles, and close, medium and long shots all ensure the audience gets a complete picture of the details of her outfit, almost to the point of fixation. Even the tear on the jacket's sleeve provides an opportunity to emphasize and revisit the seductive power of the dress. The (predominantly female) audience, then, is put in the position of being able to gauge every possible nuance of the dress and "assess the exactness of its fit" so that it could be either acquired by wealthy women, so promoting domestic production, remembering the name of the fashion house given at the beginning of the film, or copied by skilled dressmakers for less wealthy customers.

This ploy is emphasized in the grand finale of the film - the fashion show of the entire collection presented at Sestrierès, where the various narrative threads come to a head. Again here, we find a very similar context and similar advertising techniques to those analyzed by Charlotte Herzog in "'Powder Puff' Promotion: The Fashion Show-in-the-film" for American films such as *Stolen Holidays* or others in which fashion shows are part of the film narrative. At the fashion show, organized at the ski resort chosen by the new management, the camera cuts backstage where Marcella and other mannequins are changing their clothes and interacting with other characters. Here, the narrative of the fashion house and that of Marcella and Gino intermingle and find their respective moments of denouement. The audience's enthusiastic reaction to the show is the forerunner of commercial success, and the two lovers Marcella and Gino finally cement their relationship on solid ground.

Interestingly, the narrative of the fashion show we see in the film's closing scenes is tailored along the lines of a traditional story, the protagonist being a woman whose wardrobe features clothing worn from the day of her debut in society. The show then follows all the stages of her personal life, her first kiss, and on to marriage, the show concluding triumphantly with the protagonist - Marcella, of course - dressed as a bride. This is also the moment of revelation for Marcella and Gino who, although they do not realize it, are going to play bride and groom on the catwalk. Here the camera cuts backstage again to Gino who in order to make her jealous announces to Marcella, who is wearing a Russian-style suit with pants and a long Cossack jacket, that he is engaged to be married. As a rejoinder,

Marcella invents the lie that she too is getting married and wishes to show Gino her wedding dress in order to ask his opinion. It is here, still backstage, that the camera lingers once again on very elaborate shots of Marcella's wedding dress, thanks to which the female audience can grasp the details of length, fit, and the precious lace decorations that form part of the head gear and frame Marcella's face in a widescreen close-up. Suddenly, as they talk in close proximity, Marcella and Gino are transported onto the center of the stage in front of the fashion show audience, thrust there by a stagehand acting on Marta Rossi's orders who has activated the circular stage on which the two soon to be lovers were standing. In the meantime, the film cuts backstage again and we see Marta Rossi, who is the director both of the fashion show and of her nephew and her protégée's wedding. The final scene is a close-up of both bride and groom who are enthusiastically applauded by the audience, marking their appreciation of the show. The camera lingers on the bride's dress from different angles showing and emphasizing the details of the precious lace out of which it is made, the fabric of national pride and tradition, the most Italian of fabrics, often on display in exhibitions and magazines of the period. Lace also symbolically represented a strong link to tradition, to the fine regional craftsmanship that fascist policy aimed to valorize alongside its interest in experimentation and modernity. Indeed, feature films such as *Contessa Di Parma* or as we will see later *Grandi Magazzini* are quintessential manifestations of the fact that fascism used the different and often contradictory features of an Italian culture and identity that is suspended between the poles of experimentalism and tradition. It is with lace in mind, and all the connotations that come with it, that we now turn our attention to what was the backbone of Italian fashion, the domestic textile industry.

❑❑❑

7

Motives of Wearing Clothes for Fashion

Introduction

All other creatures being fittingly provided with needle and thread, to maintain their being, it is really not to be believed that we alone should have been brought into the world in this defective and indigent state, in a state that cannot be maintained without foreign aid. So I hold that, as plants, trees, animals, all that lives, are by Nature equipped with sufficient covering to protect them against the injury of the weather, And therefore almost all Are covered either with hides, or else with shells, Or with the horny callus, or with bark so were we; but, like those who with artificial light extinguish the light of day, we have extinguished our proper means with borrowed means. And it is easy to see that it is custom that makes impossible to us, what is not so: for among those nations that have no knowledge of clothes, there are some that dwell in much the same climate as we do; and moreover, the most delicate parts of us are those which are always uncovered, the eyes, the mouth, the nose, the ears; in the case of our peasants, as with our ancestors, the pectoral and ventral parts. If we had been born on condition of wearing farthingales and galligaskins, I make no doubt but that Nature would have armed with a thicker skin what she has exposed to the battery of the seasons, as she has done the finger-ends and the soles of the feet.

Why does this seem hard to believe? Between my habit of clothing and that of a peasant of my country-side there is a much greater distance than between his and that of a man who is clothed only in his skin.

How many men, especially in Turkey, go naked as a matter of religion! Somebody or other asked one of our beggars whom he saw in his shirt in the depth of winter, as merry as a grig and feeling the cold as little as many a man who is muffled up to the ears in sable, how he could patiently bear it. "And you, sir, he replied, you have your face uncovered; now, I am all face." The Italians tell a tale of, I think, the Duke of Florence's fool, that his master asking him how, being so poorly clad, he could bear the cold, which he himself was hardly able to do: "Follow my recipe, he replied, and pile on all the garments you have, like me, and you will feel the cold no more than I do." King Massinissa could not be induced, even in his extreme old age, to go with his head covered, were it ever so cold, stormy or rainy. The same is told of the Emperor Severus.

In the battles fought between the Egyptians and the Persians, Herodotus says that both he and others remarked that, of those who were left dead on the field, the skulls of the Egyptians were without comparison harder than those of the Persians, by reason that the latter always have their heads covered, first with biggins and afterwards with turbans, and the former are shaven from infancy and uncovered.

And King Agesilaus observed the habit, until his decrepitude, of wearing the same clothing in winter as in summer. Caesar, says Suetonius, always marched at the head of his army, and most often on foot, bareheaded, whether in sunshine or rain.

A Venetian, who had long resided in the kingdom of Pegu, and has but lately returned from thence, writes that both the men and women of that country always go barefoot, even on horseback, the rest of their body being clothed.

And Plato gives this wonderful advice, that, to keep the whole body in health, we should give the feet and head no covering but that which Nature has provided. The man who, following our King, was chosen King of Poland, and who is indeed one of the greatest princes of our age, never wears gloves, nor does he change, however severe the weather in winter, the bonnet he wears indoors. Just as I cannot go loose and unbuttoned, the labourers round about here would feel fettered if they had to button up. Varro contends that, when it was ordained that we should uncover in presence of the gods or the magistracy, it was rather for our health's sake, and to harden us against the inclemency of the weather, than upon the account of reverence.

Biographical note Michel de Montaigne was a French essayist, a widely read writer of the French Renaissance, who lived in Bordeaux. He is generally acknowledged as the inventor of the personal or familiar essay as a modern literary genre. This reading was drawn from what is considered to be his best-known work, a collection of essays published in three volumes between 1580 and 1588, and first translated into English in 1603.

Significance of Clothes

Discriminating and applicable though these theories may be it is obvious that no one of them adequately accounts for the fact of clothing nor sufficiently explains its complexity and variety. It may be, as one writer suggests, that the ancient Britons painted the body with earthy pigments to check the cooling effect of free evaporation from the skin; that the Andaman Islanders plaster themselves thickly with mud in order to resist the attacks of insects; the skin mantle of the Fuegian, shifted to meet the varying winds, and the elaborately fitted fur garments of the Eskimo, are obviously worn in deference to rigorous climate; the gourd or sling of certain South American tribes probably serves as a protection from injury, and the exceedingly small pearl-decorated apron of the Kafir belle is doubtless worn as a means of attraction; vanity, aesthetic feeling, the desire for distinction and the motive of comfort play their part. But as the primitive clothing impulse manifests itself in such varied forms we are justified in retreating beyond these partial hypotheses to one more profound and fundamental which underlies and includes them all.

Too great stress must not be laid on the factor of use, on an assumed end determining the particular form taken by the primitive impulse to decorate or clothe the body. The doctrine of use as a factor in evolution finds less favor than formerly. In the language of

Professor William Patten of Dartmouth College, "The use made of an organ can not be the cause of its origin, for the organ must be present in the first place, in some form or other, before any use can be made of it:" and while to-day we find man by reason of his acquired equipment of reason and foresight working toward definitely conceived ends, it is hardly reasonable to attribute to the primitive creature at the outset of the human career clearly defined motives which determined his acts. As has been pointed out by the naturalists Geddes and Thompson, human nature can not be rightly understood apart from the biological approach, and even in a matter apparently so far removed from the natural as that of clothing there will be found many analogies to zoological and biological facts. Primitive psychological attitudes from what has been termed physiological thought and the instinctive inner urge prompting the acts of primitive man may be not inaptly compared to those special internal conditions which biologists recognize as determining local growths, organs and structure, lower down in the scale of life.

In order adequately to frame a philosophy of clothes it is necessary to view as clearly as possible man's place in nature. Though there are now on earth only isolated examples of hairy men it is probable that the primitive human being and certainly his precursor were covered with hair. We may or may not accept the Darwinian conclusion that the loss of our coat of hair was due to aesthetic reasons, "the members of one sex having chosen as mates those of the other who were least hairy" but the fact remains that man, as Carlyle said, is by nature a naked animal. Moreover he is, broadly speaking, the only naked animal. In the world of living things are displayed fur, feathers, thickened and colored hide, scales, various armors, and integuments, for the tree bark and for all plant forms fitness and beauty of investiture. Man alone is left with an incomplete exterior. His position in nature is anomalous. All other creatures are finished and complete, clothed and with instinct sufficient to form themselves an abode which remains unaltered with the passing of the ages. Man alone must supplement nature. He has progressed by reason of his incompleteness and to what extent his initial advance was due to the lack of a satisfactory and fitting exterior is matter for conjecture. The gods left man naked in order that he might clothe himself: unfinished that he might indefinitely continue the process of development.

Underlying all the various motives which apparently lead man to paint, tattoo, decorate and protect the body is the fundamental feeling of incompleteness, of dissatisfaction with self as it is, and clothing in its origin and subsequent development is the result of his attempt to remedy the deficiency, to replace what he has lost. The covering and ornament which human beings supply for the body stand in lieu of fur, feathers, and all the varied exteriors found in lower nature and further, serve like ends of protection and adornment. The fact of the reputed complete nakedness of certain peoples does not militate against this theory of the primary reason for clothing. While individuals may be entirely nude it is said that in no tribe do all the members remain constantly as nature left them. Study of "our contemporary ancestors" discloses, it is probable, most of the forms of adornment and body covering used by prehistoric man complicated in many instances by contact of the savages with civilized races and as might be expected there are peoples in whom the clothing impulse has not developed, or but feebly, going no farther than paint, the mutilation of some organ or the wearing of a necklace or belt. Man's place in nature must be still further defined if we are to appreciate to the full the significance of clothing. Humanity appears to be a continuation of the main stem of life of which all lower forms are the branches. They diverged from the central stem, advanced a pace and became what Nietzsche would term the goals of nature, plant, insect, animal and bird man, according to the German philosopher's thought, being not a goal but a bridge. The life which was to become human continued to advance though divested of many possibilities. It is not necessary to accept all the implications of Bergson's philosophy in order to make use of his pregnant idea that life, evolving in the direction of man has abandoned many things by the way.

Tendencies which were incompatible with the main trend of life were dropped and set up a subordinate line of development. Applying this conception to the matter in hand we may say that man has left far behind the possibility of a furred or feathered exterior, of blossoms, thorns, horns, tails, and countless other structures and appendages displayed by lower forms of life, plant and animal. It may be said further and here is the crucial point in our philosophy of clothes that these structures, appendages and ornaments which are characteristic of life other than human, survive in man as subconscious dispositions which at various times in the world's history, some in one race and some in another, are embodied in his dress. Actual physical survivals of lower forms of life appear during the development of the human fetus. Certain of these disappear, others are modified to form working parts of the organism, while occasionally one persists as an atrophied structure in the fully developed human being. In the light of these facts we are warranted in assuming the presence of corresponding mental survivals. The variety and vagary of garb are thus not due to mere whim and vagary of the human mind. Man is the epitome of all tendencies and the reason for the complexity of his clothing impulse may be found in the complexity of his mental inheritance which includes all that he has lost physically on the way to man. There is scarcely a covering in nature that has not been utilized or imitated in human apparel; there can hardly be found a protuberance or appendage that may not have served as the prototype for some form of human mutilation or adornment. Fur serves both savage and civilized man. Certain tribes of the Amazon basin fix a covering of feathers on their bodies, daubed with a sticky substance; other tribes insert feathers in perforations in the cheek or nasal septum, while feathers as adornment, especially of the head are found the world over and not least in modern civilized nations. There are striking simulations of horns, notably the head-dress of some African tribes, and in England what has been called "the preposterous horned head-dress" of the reign of Henry V the student of costume will come upon many an arresting likeness of coronet, cockade, neck ruff, stock, and frill, plume, sash, and train, to natural organic characteristics of other creatures and it is interesting to note in passing that a caricature of the date of 1786, entitled "Modern Elegance," shows two women wearing the Bouffon, an exaggerated neckerchief of cambric, and above them the figure of a Pouter pigeon with characteristically inflated oesophagus.

Perhaps the most striking example of physiological habit surviving in man as a mental tendency is that of the tail. This appendage has been so often simulated that it has given rise to the fable of men with tails and even our modern sash and train may, without stretch of the imagination, be referred to a like lowly origin. The student of savage costume comes again and again upon instances of this addition to man's natural equipment and while the claim may be made that this widespread habit is due to imitation of animals it may with greater reasonableness be attributed to the subconscious reminiscence of an actual tail. This view is strengthened by the fact that the taillike ornament is often worn on the front of the body and quite naturally the conclusion is reached that the various forms of the fig leaf, apron and clout may be included in the same category. The tail being one of the most recent of our losses, physical vestiges of this appendage occasionally, it is said, persisting in man, the impulse to thus supplement the body is strong. Deeper than the ends which they serve is the reason for all forms of apparel.

Biographical note Sylvia Hortense Bliss is described as a writer, accomplished musician, and amateur botanist. She studied music in Iowa and at Syracuse University. She taught piano lessons and was a church organist. She sought medical treatment for a speech handicap with Boston neurologists Dr. Morton Prince and Dr. James Putnam and it was during this period that she researched and published articles in the *American Journal of Psychology* and *the Journal of Abnormal Psychology* on subjects that interested her as a layperson.

Dress

DRESS – An analysis of the relations of man's clothing with his development in social evolution will naturally be chiefly concerned with psychological categories. When once instituted, for whatever reasons or by whatever process, dress became a source of psychical reactions, often complex, to a greater extent (owing to its more intimate connexion with personality) than any other material product of intelligence. Some outline of the historical development of dress will be suggested, rather than drawn, as a guide to the main inquiry. The practical or, if one may use the term, the biological uses and meaning of dress, are simple enough and agreed upon. These form the first state of the material to be employed by the social consciousness. Its secondary states are a subject in themselves

Origins The primary significance of dress becomes a difficult question as soon as we pass from the institution in being to its earliest stages and its origin. For speculation alone is possible when dealing with the genesis of dress. Its conclusions will be probable, in proportion as they satisfactorily bridge the gulf between the natural and the artificial stages of human evolution. The information supplied by those of the latter that are presumably nearest to the natural state, to *Protanthropus,* is not in itself a key to the origin of clothing, but, on the other hand, the mere analogy of animal-life is still less helpful.

It may serve, however, to point by contrast the actual continuity of the natural and the artificial stages, the physical and the psychical stages, of our evolution. If we say that man is the only animal that uses an artificial covering for the body, we are apt to forget that even when clothed he is subject to the same environmental influences as in the ages before dress. Again, there is no hint that the approach of a glacial epoch inaugurated the invention of dress. But it is an established fact that the survivors of immigrants to changed conditions of climate and geological environment become physically adapted by some means of interaction and in certain directions of structure, which are just coming to be recognized. The most obvious of these natural adaptations, physiologically produced, to the environment is pigmentation. The skin of man is graded in colour from the Equator to the Pole. The deeper pigmentation of the tropical skin is a protection against the actinic rays of the sun; the blondness of northern races, like the white colour of Arctic animals, retains the heat of the body.

If we followed the analogy of the animal, we should have to take into account the fact that a mechanical intelligence enables it to obviate certain disadvantages of its natural covering. The animal never exposes itself unnecessarily; its work, in the case of the larger animals, is done at night, not in the glare of the sun. Automatically it acquires an artificial covering in the form of shelter. If man in a natural state followed a similar principle, he would be at no more disadvantage than is the animal. A similar argument applies to the other use mentioned above, namely, sexual decoration. What these considerations suggest is that man was not forced by necessity to invent. The reason is at once deeper and simpler. Again, we get the conclusion that one primary use and meaning of dress is not so much to provide an adaptation to a climate as to enable man to be superior to weather; in other words, to enable him to move and be active in circumstances where animals seek shelter. The principle is implicit in the frequent proverbial comparison of clothing to a house.

Dress, in fact, as a secondary human character, must be treated, as regards its origins, in the same way as human weapons, tools, and machines. Dress increases the static resisting power of the surface of the body, just as tools increase the dynamic capacity of the limbs. It is an extension (and thereby an intension) of the passive area of the person, just as a tool is of the active mechanism of the arm. It is a second skin, as the other is a second hand. Further, if we take an inclusive view of evolution, admitting no break between the natural and the artificial, but regarding the latter as a sequence to the former, we shall be in a position to accept indications that both stages, and not the former only, are subject to the operation of the same mechanical laws, and show (with the necessary limitations) similar results. These laws belong to the interaction of the organism and the environment, and the results are found in what is called adaptation, an optimum of equilibrium, a balanced interaction, between the two. The selective process has not been conscious, but neither has it been accidental. It is the result of law. Equally unconscious in its first stages was the adaptation of dress to temperature. This brings us no nearer to the origins of dress, though it clears the ground. Still further to simplify speculation, we may notice some prevalent hypotheses on the subject. Dress being a covering, it assumes, when instituted, all the applicable meanings which the idea of covering involves. But it by no means follows that all of these, or even any, were responsible for its original institution.

There is, first, the hypothesis that clothing originated in *the decorative impulse*. This has the merit of providing a cause which could operate through unconscious intelligence, automatic feeling. It is in accordance with the rule among animals that among primitive peoples the male sex chiefly assumes decoration. Ornaments among the Indians of Guiana are more worn by men than by women. The stock ornamentation is paint; scented oils are used as vehicles.

But this analogy is not to be pressed, though it is sound as far as it goes. It applies, that is, up to a certain point in social evolution. Beyond that point the balance inclines the other way, and for the last five hundred years of European civilization decorative dress has been confined to women.

In practical investigation it is difficult, as Ratzel observes, to say "where clothing ends and ornament begins," or, on the previous hypothesis, where clothing springs out of ornament. Since either may obviously develop into the other when both are instituted, it is idle to examine such cases. Cases where one or the other is absolutely unknown might serve, but there are no examples of this. If an instance, moreover, of the presence of clothing and entire absence of ornament were observed, it would be impossible to argue that clothing cannot be subject to the decorative impulse. In any case, there is the self-feeling, satisfaction in individuality, to be reckoned with, for the impulse to finery is only one phase of it.

The supporters of the ornamentation hypothesis of the origin of dress have an apparently strong argument in the Brazilians and the Central Australians. These recently studied peoples possess no clothing in the ordinary sense of the term. But they wear ornament, and on special occasions a great deal of it. Brazilian men wear a string round the lower abdomen, the women a strip of bark-cloth along the perineum, tied to a similar abdominal thread. This is sometimes varied by a small decorative enlargement. The Central Australian man wears a waist-string, to which is tied a pubic tassel. Corresponding to the last in the case of the women is a very small apron. Leaving the waiststring out of account, we have remaining the question of the erogenous centre. In both the decoration hypothesis and the concealment hypothesis this centre is the focus of speculation. If the Australian tassel of the male sex and the leaf-like enlargement of the Brazilian woman's perineal thread are considered superficially, they may appear to be, if not ornaments, at least attractions. But if this be granted, it does not follow that we have here the first application of the idea of dress. It would be impossible to make out a case to prove that these appurtenances can ever have satisfied the idea of *concealment,* as on the next hypothesis is assumed. This hypothesis is to the effect that male jealousy instituted clothing for married women. The general connexion between modesty and dress is a subject of little importance, except in so far as it has involved the creation of false modesty, both individually and socially. Modesty where there is dress, tends to be concentrated upon it mechanically. When clothing is once established, the growth of the conception of women as property emphasizes its importance, and increases the anatomical modesty of women. Waitz held that male jealousy is the primary origin of clothing, and therefore of modesty. Diderot had held this view. Often married women alone are clothed. It is as if before marriage a woman was free and naked; after marriage, clothed and a slave.

But the fact of dress serving as concealment involved the possibility of *attraction by mystery*. Even when other emotions than modesty, emphasized by male jealousy, intervene, they may work together for sexual attraction.Finally, there is the *protection-hypothesis*. Sudden falls in the temperature, rains and winds and burning sunshine, the danger of injuring the feet and the skin of the body generally when in the forest, and the need of bodyarmour against the attacks of insects and of dangerous animals seem obvious reasons for the invention of dress. But they do not explain the process of invention, which is the main problem. The cloak, the skirt, the apron, cannot have been invented in answer to a need, directly, without any stages. The invention of cloth was first necessary, and this was suggested by some natural covering. The only line of development which seems possible is from protective ligatures. There are numerous facts which apparently point to such an origin of clothing. One of the most characteristic 'ornaments' of savages all over the world is the armlet. It is quite probable that this has an independent origin in the decorative impulse, like the necklace. But here and there we find bands worn round the ankles, knees, wrists, and elbows, the object of which is clearly to protect the sinews and muscles from strains. The pain of a strained muscle being eased by the grip of the hand, the suggestion of an artificial grip might naturally follow, and a system of ligatures would be the result.

Wild peoples, in fact, understand quite well the limitations and the capacity of the human organism in respect to the environment. We may credit them with an adequate system of supplying natural deficiencies, and of assisting natural advantages also. Now, the great majority of the lowest peoples known wear no clothes. Shelter is used instead. But there is very commonly a waist-string, and it is more used by men than by women. We assume that the girdle is the point of departure for the evolution of dress, and the mechanism of that departure will be presently discussed. But for the origin of body-clothing it is necessary to find the origin of the girdle. The civilized idea of a girdle is to bind up a skirt or trousers. This is certainly not its object among the earliest peoples, who have nothing to tie up. It might be supposed that the original purpose of the girdle was that of the abdominal belt, useful both as a muscle-ligature and to alleviate the pangs of hunger. But the earliest girdles are merely strings, and string is useless for such purposes. String, moreover, made of grass or vegetable fibre, or animal sinew or human hair, is an earlier invention than the bandage. Its first form was actually natural, the pliant bough or stem. The waist-string, therefore, being earlier than clothing proper, and being, as we have suggested, the point of departure for the wearing of coverings, we have next to examine the mechanism of the connexion between them. The use of the string as a holder being given, it would serve not only as a pocket, but as a suspender for leaves or bunches of grass, if for any reason these were required. The point to be emphasized here is that the presence of a suspender would suggest the suspension and therefore the regular use of articles for which there had been no original demand. It is unnecessary to enter upon a description of the various zones of the body which require protection, such as the spine at the neck and in the small of the back, against sun and cold, or the mucous membranes of the perineal region, against insects. The use of clothing of certain textures and colours to maintain a layer of air about the skin at a temperature adapted to that of the body, and to neutralize those rays of light which are deleterious to the nervous system and destructive of protoplasm, is also out of place here. We may note, however, that by unconscious selection the evolution of dress has probably followed a thoroughly hygienic course. But no principles of such hygiene, except the very simplest, can have occurred to primitive man. One of the simplest, however, we way admit for tropical races the use of a protection against insects. The perineal region is most subject to their attacks when man is naked, owing to the sebaceous character of the surface and its relatively higher temperature. These facts, no doubt, more than anything else, are the explanation of primitive habits of depilation. But depilation is not a complete protesction. Something positive is required. The use of bunches of grass or leaves is natural and inevitable, as soon as there is something to hold them, namely, the waist-string. A parallel method is the use of a second string depending from the waist-string in front and behind, and passing between the legs. The Brazilian strip of bast used by women, and the red thread which takes its place in the Trumai tribe, though "they attract attention like ornaments instead of drawing attention away," yet, as Von den Steinen also satisfied himself, provide a protection against insects, a serious pest in the forests of Brazil. These inter-crural strings protect the mucous membrane, without, however, concealing the parts, as do leaves and grass. In the present connexion their chief interest is the use made of the waist-string. When cloth was invented, the first form of the loin-cloth was an extension of the intercrural thread.

The protection-hypothesis of the origin of dress may thus be adopted, if we qualify it by a scheme of development as suggested above. When once instituted as a custom, the wearing of leaves or bark-cloth upon the abdominal region served to focus various psychical reactions. One of the earliest of these was the impulse to emphasize the primary sexual characters. It is an impulse shown among the great majority of early races in their observances at the attainment of puberty, and it is, as a rule, at that period that sexual dress or ornament is assumed. Among civilized peoples, in the Middle Ages and in modern times, the impulse is well marked by various fashions the phallocrypt and the tail of the savage having their European analogues. A less direct but even more constant instance of the same recognition is the assigning of the skirt to women as the more sedentary, and trousers to men as the more active sex. The suggestion sometimes met with, that the skirt is an adaptation for sexual protection, need only be mentioned to be dismissed. The Central Australian pubic tassel and similar appendages will here find significance, but it is improbable that such accentuation was their original purpose. Once instituted for protection, the other ideas followed. Another of these, which at once received an artificial focus, was the emotion of modesty. It has been observed among the higher animals that the female by various postures guards the sexual centres from the undesired advances of the male. The assumption of a waist-cloth does not actually serve the same purpose, but it constitutes a permanent psychical suggestion of inviolability. Similarly, the use of any appendage or covering involves the possibility of attraction, either by mere notification, by the addition of decoration, or, later, by the suggestion of mystery. Further than this, speculation as to origins need not be carried. The various forms and fashions of dress, and the customs connected with it, will supply examples of the material as well as of the psychological evolution of the subject.

In spite of the underlying similarity of principles, universally found, dress more than any external feature distinguishes race from race and tribe from tribe. While distinguishing a social unit it emphasizes its internal solidarity. In this latter sphere there is, again, room for individual distinction *Biographical note* Alfred Ernest

Crawley was a British social anthropologist. He was a Fellow of the Sociological Society and an Examiner to the University of London. He also wrote *The Mystic Rose* which contained research on "primitive" and "traditional" societies, such as magical and religious practices.

Customs and Beliefs: Ceremonial

We may now return to the question of the meaning of personal ornament in general. It is a commonplace of psychology that the development of the sense of self is closely connected with the perception of one's own body. It is also generally recognized that the development of the moral and social sentiments in man is dependent upon the development of self-consciousness, of the sense of self. These two important principles will help us to appreciate the hypothesis to which the discussion has now led, that in the Andamans the customary regulation of personal ornament is a means by which the society acts upon, modifies, and regulates the sense of self in the individual.

There are three methods of ornamenting the body in the Andamans, (1) by scarification, (2) by painting, and (3) by the putting on of ornaments. The natives give two reasons for the custom of scarification, that it improves the personal appearance and that it makes the boy or girl grow up strong.

Both these mean that scarification gives or marks an added value. The explanation of the rite would therefore seem to be that it marks the passage from childhood to manhood and is a means by which the society bestows upon the individual that power, or social value, which is possessed by the adult but not by the child. The individual is made to feel that his value his strength and the qualities of which he may be proud is not his by nature but is received by him from the society to which he is admitted. The scars on his body are the visible marks of his admission. The individual is proud or vain of the scars which are the mark of his manhood, and thus the society makes use of the very powerful sentiment of personal vanity to strengthen the social sentiments.

Turning now to the painting of the body, we have seen that the pattern of white clay serves to make both the painted individual and those who see him feel his social value, and we have seen that this interpretation explains the occasions on which such painting is used. To complete the argument it is necessary to consider the occasions on which the use of white clay is forbidden.

Those to whom this prohibition applies are (1) a youth or girl who is akaop, i.e., who is abstaining from certain foods during the initation period, (2) a mourner, (3) a homicide during the period the isolation, and (4) a person who is ill. All these persons are excluded from full participation in the active social life, and therefore the social value of each of them is diminished. It would obviously be wrong for a person in such a condition to express by decorating himself a social value that he did not at the time possess. All ornament in some way marks the relation of the individual to the society and to that force or power in society to which he owes his well-being and happiness. When painting or ornament is used to give protection, it is, as we have seen, the protective power of the society itself that is appealed to, and what is expressed is the dependence of the individual on the society. When ornament or paint is used for display it is again the dependence on the society that is expressed, though in a different way and on occasions of a different kind. We have seen that scarification is also a means of marking the dependence of the individual on the society, and it is very important to note that the Andamanese sometimes explain it as due to the desire for display and sometimes to the need of protection (enabling the child to grow strong and so avoid the dangers of sickness), showing very clearly that there is some intimate connection between these two motives, or at any rate that one and the same method of ornamentation can satisfy both. There is one further example of red paint, which is combined with the pattern of white clay for purposes of display, and is also constantly used in many ways as affording protection.

We are thus brought to the final conclusion that the scarification and painting of the body and the wearing of most if not all the customary ornaments are rites which have the function of marking the fact that the individual is in a particular permanent or temporary relation to that power in the society and in all things that affect social life, the notion of which we have seen to underlie so much of the Andaman ceremonial.

In the various methods of ornamenting the body the two chief motives that we have considered are so combined that they can hardly be estimated separately, and it is this mingling of motives that has led us to the final understanding of the meaning and social function of bodily ornament. Each of the different kinds of ornament serves to make manifest the existence of some special relation between the individual and the society, and therefore of some special relation between him and that system of powers on which the welfare of the society and of the individual depends. One of the most important aspects of the relation of the individual to the society is his dependence upon it for his safety and well-being and this is revealed in all painting and ornament worn for protection. But the society not only protects the individual from danger; it is the direct source of his well-being; and this makes itself felt in the customary regulation by which the use of the more important ornaments used for display is confined to occasions on which it is quite clear that his happiness is directly due to the society, such as a dance or feast. Thus the customs relating to the ornamentation of the body are of the kind that I have here called ceremonial. They are the means by which the society exercises on appropriate occasions some of the important social sentiments, thereby maintaining them at the necessary degree of energy required to maintain the social cohesion.

Biographical note Sir Alfred Reginald Radcliffe-Brown was a leading British social anthropologist. He conducted numerous ethnological studies in Africa, Australia, and North America. The featured reading is drawn from his fieldwork among the people of Andaman Islands of Australia. He is a functional anthropologist. A major contribution was his examination of behavioral patterns and institutions of a social system in terms of how they functioned. His goal was a science of society that would formulate laws, explaining how social systems operated.

Dress

The history of dress there are roughly four fields of study: prehuman behavior, archaeology, primitive peoples and modem civilized conditions. The study of animal behavior emphasizes two facts regarding the origin of clothing. In the first place, human dress, in so far as it is for protection against the elements, has no continuity with any prehuman behavior. Animals in frigid climates grow warm coats, which are transmitted to their offspring by heredity. The opposite technique of invention and traditionally transmitted processes does not occur except in man. In the second place, observation of the higher apes has emphasized the prehuman roots of clothing as self decoration. Kohler describes the naï've delight of chimpanzees in hanging objects about their bodies and trotting about to display them.

Archaeology reveals nothing about the history of dress until the upper palaeolithic era which is far removed from earliest man. Clothing is necessarily of perishable materials, but even ornaments of animal teeth, ivory and shells begin to appear only in the Aurignacian period at the same level at which is found the characteristic palaeolithic development of mural drawing and engraving. From this period date also the characteristically distorted nude figurines of the female form, some of which are wearing bracelets although they are not represented with any other clothing. It is obvious, however, that the distortion of these female figurines is in the direction of fertility symbols, and their nudity furnishes no information as to women's daily wear in the Aurignacian period except that bracelets were worn at this period.

The reasons that have led man to clothe himself can therefore be studied chiefly from a comparison of the divergent behavior of now existing peoples. There is a strong association in western civilization between dress and the covering of the sex organs, but most of the literature concerning the origin of clothing has directed its array of facts to demolish the assumption of the primacy of this connection and to point out that dress did not have its origin in a specific instinct of modesty focused on the organs of reproduction.

It is obvious from any study of primitive clothing that this particular function of dress has very often been unknown in other cultures. The habit of complete nudity has a wide distribution in the tropical regions of South America, Melanesia and Africa. In some cases both men and women are habitually naked, in others only the men, in still others only the women. Even outside of tropical regions habitual nudity is widespread, although a skin may be thrown over the shoulders for protection. Such regions are the Great Basin in North America, California and Australia. Even in arctic regions, where well tailored clothing is universal, the conventions are often such that both men and women are habituated to indoor nudity like all people so habituated exhibit no shame in uncovering. Nansen describes the intercrural cord of the east coast of Greenland, the sole covering of the natives when indoors, as being "so extremely small as to make it practically invisible to the stranger's inexperienced eye".

In more extreme instances that may be brought to bear against this theory of the origin of clothing in an instinct of modesty the very nature of the coverings themselves is the point of the argument. The codpiece which was worn in Europe about 1450 and the custom of the men of certain Papuan tribes who squeeze their members into the opening of a gourd are indicative of the exhibitionist nature of certain forms of dress. Many observers in many parts of the world have commented on the fact that the most obvious function of the genital coverings was to attract attention rather than to divert it.

It is possible therefore to discard the notion that there is a human instinct of modesty that expresses itself in clothing. Modesty is a conditioned reflex and has its roots in the fashion of dress to which any group is accustomed. It is therefore to be expected that, given certain turns of fashion, other regions than the genital will be singled out and this emotion directed elsewhere to the feet, as among Chinese women of past generations, or to the face, as with Mohammedan women. Native Brazilian women are extremely unwilling to remove their nose plugs and Alaskan women to remove their enormous labrets. Feelings of shame may also be associated with types of behavior not connected with clothing. Perfectly naked savages, for example, show acute feelings of shame at seeing anyone eat in public.

All the other theories of the origin of clothing contain varied amounts of truth. The advocates have erred only in too generalized a support of their particular positions. It is not necessary to deny any of them, once one has granted that human custom has no unique root but in different parts of the world has been the result of quite different circumstances and habits of mind variously interacting.

Thus Frazer and Karsten argue for the origin of clothing in ideas of magic, as, for example, the covering of the organs of reproduction in order to prevent the evil eye being cast upon them. Amulets hung about the neck or inserted in the lip or the nose are the full scope of clothing among some peoples, and in those and similar cases costume can be most pertinently studied in connection with local magical beliefs. In some regions these have had a profound influence upon the development of dress, but it is not necessary to generalize them as the origin of clothing.

The theory that clothing originated in protection against the rigors of climate is defended by Knight Dunlap. To doubt that weather has ever been a factor would be to cast a gratuitous slur on human intelligence and to ignore one of the great differentiations between human and animal behavior. If it were the primary factor, however, the primitive tribes living in the cold climates of the southern hemisphere would have provided for themselves as well as those living in similar climates of the northern hemisphere. But they have not done so. For the freezing weather to which they are seasonally exposed the Australians and the Fuegians do not make themselves clothing but barely protect their shoulders with a skin. Certainly many other motivations have been as potent in the history of clothing as protection against the weather.

Westermarck considers dress under the heading of "Primitive Means of Attraction." He believes that it is fundamentally rooted in the erotic impulses. Instances of this sort have been given above and he presents many others, both of habitual ornamentation of the pubic coverings and of ornamentation worn for particular occasions, such as dances, especially those of a licentious character. The history of clothing in our own civilization is ample evidence of the degree to which one sex dresses for the other, and certainly the often recurring differentiation of the dresses of the two sexes should be studied from this angle.

It does not seem necessary, however, to single out the one trait of display before the opposite sex when dress is so obviously and so often a self-display on all counts. Sex display in dress may hardly appear in a given area, but display of trophies or display of status may be fundamental. Thus on the plains of North America men's dress is a heraldic display of war counts, and on the northwest coast a man's hat will be built up in cumulative units to designate his rank. As an old explorer said of the Fuegians, "although they are content to be naked, they are very ambitious to be fine." This impulse toward decoration is the most constantly recurring motivation in the history of clothing and, as we saw above, the one which is found also among the higher apes.

Modern conditions have introduced only one important factor into human behavior in regard to clothing. In all that has been said above, modern dress like that of any other period is merely one of many possible varieties all illustrative of the general principles. But there is one fundamental difference. Whereas in simpler conditions, even in untouched rural districts of Europe today, dress is geographically differentiated, in modern civilization it is temporally differentiated. This rise of fashion in the field of dress had begun somewhat tentatively between the tenth and the fourteenth century, but it is with the Renaissance that its full and startling effect is first to be gauged. In rural districts dress remained and has remained to the present time a matter of local individuality perpetuated for centuries with great conservatism. The revolutionary rise of fashion had to do only with the urban population and even more specifically with the court. Its onset in the fifteenth century was marked by those peculiarities that have continued to characterize fashion in the modern world: first, the grotesque exaggeration of certain features, in this case notably the hennin (the fantastically elongated head dress that was held on by a chin band); and second, the personal arbitership of the great lady.

The latter part of the fifteenth century and the earlier part of the sixteenth show some of the most pleasing of all western European fashions, styles that are best known through the portraits of the Italian Renaissance. In the first half of the sixteenth century the woman's hoop skirt was elaborated, and this returned in extreme forms in the mid-eighteenth and mid-nineteenth centuries, in less extreme form in the mid-seventeenth. In the eighteenth century version in the reign of Louis XVI this was coupled with spectacular display of costly material in garments; clothes became a primary means for the ostentatious exhibition of wealth. The greatest excesses were cultivated in the matter of hairdressing; coiffures were a half yard high and prints show the hairdressers seated on ladders in order to reach the upper tiers of their creations. Nor was there any marked improvement during the nineteenth century. Probably the fashions of the period from 1830 to 1900 the desperately constricted waist, the bustle and the heavy dragging skirt were the ugliest and most unhealthful in the history of women's dress in western civilization.

The usual view of fashion is, first, that it is an affair of violent contrasts, each few years' swing of the pendulum reversing that of the preceding; and second, that it is essentially dictated by individual Parisian costumers. Kroeber, however, taking as a test case woman's full dress toilette from 1844 to 1919, has shown that, at least in the measurements he has considered, fashion's vagaries follow definite long time trends. This is clearest in the measurement of the width of the skirt, which for fifty years before 1919 had in spite of incidental variations become progressively more constricted. For almost as long a period previously it had in the same way grown progressively fuller, and its cycle therefore would be about one hundred years. The length of the skirt showed a similar trend. Its cycle for this period was about a third the duration of the width cycle, but even this is too long to be due to the influence of a single gifted designer. Kroeber does not claim universal validity for his examples but draws from them two conclusions: first, in a broader view styles not merely oscillate between two points but work themselves out in cycles of considerable length; second, these cycles are obviously longer than the reign of influence of any one designer and are therefore independent even of the most powerful costumer.

The study of fashion along with a variety of other cultural traits of modern civilization, such as mass production, can derive no assistance from the history of the world before comparatively modern times. Fashion is new in human history and its future course is not known. At present it marks, as Santayana says, that margin of irresponsible variation in manners and thoughts which among a people artificially civilized may so easily be larger than the solid core. It may well be that this swift succession of styles will maintain itself as a fixed characteristic of dress as a culture trait in our civilization.

8

Fashioning Masculinity
Dress for Style

Introduction

Women are fashionable but men are not. This lament is common in western cultures. Indicatively, most studies of contemporary fashion emphasise female fashion and marginalise attention to male dress. Yet the equation of fashion with women and the exclusion of men is historically and culturally specific, stemming from nineteenth-century Victorian and European notions of etiquette, gender relations, and sexuality. In particular, these ideas proposed a radical split between genders and assigned each of them specific roles and locations. An index of this order of sexual division was the continuous recreation of dress codes. Within this process women were gradually assigned the role of the fashionable gender of the species.

Accordingly, the rhetoric of men's fashion takes the form of a set of denials that include the following propositions: that there is no men's fashion; that men dress for fit and comfort, rather than for style; that women dress men and buy clothes for men; that men who dress up are peculiar (one way or another); that men do not notice clothes; and that most men have not been duped into the endless pursuit of seasonal fads. In other words, there is a tendency to underplay if not deny the phenomenon of men's fashion. Yet, pushed a little, people hold very strong and diverse views about men and clothing: commonsense clichés about men's fashions disguise passionate opinions. Men's fashion relates to, but is distinct from, the codes of women's fashion. Whereas contemporary codes of women's fashion have revolved around achieving 'a look' as an image to be admired (spectacle), men's appearance has been calculated to enhance their active roles (especially occupation and social status).

Historically and cross-culturally, the clothing of men and women has been subject to trends in styles and fashions. From the eighteenth century, in western Europe male fashion has received less attention than women's. This chapter examines both the un-fashioning of western men fashion and male bodies. This revival is explained in terms of changing power relations associated with gender relations, specifically in terms of challenges to male-dominated practices of post-industrial societies. As men's power is questioned by women's involvement in the workplace and in assuming responsibilities in the public sphere, men have adopted new codes of clothing conduct, modifying attributes of respectability and authority by incorporating frivolous and narcissistic elements.

There has been considerable debate about the invention of men's fashion: the main claim has been that men have abandoned their studied lack of interest in clothes and devoured the images and looks offered by a spate of designers and fashion stores. A common refrain has been that men have awakened from a fashionless stupor and 'rediscovered' clothes. Yet an examination of earlier generations and centuries-not to mention cross-cultural comparisons-makes this account questionable. Not only is there a history of men's fashion, but codes of wearing and sanctions for ignoring or subverting those codes have, if anything, been stronger for men than for women.

Within European culture, cycles of changes in men's dress have been longer and less dramatic, especially since the eighteenth century. Men's fashions typically have used a smaller range of fashion garments, with a basic wardrobe consisting of shirt, trousers and jacket. Within this range, there has been a narrower degree of adaptation-for example, in the choice of tie, socks or sweater. One analyst has even argued that the barometer of men's fashions can be found in the shaving and trimming of beards! Between 1840 and 1970, beards (a composite measure of sideburns, moustaches and beards) appeared in regular cycles of fashionableness that corresponded to fluctuations in width of skirts. The heyday of the beard was between 1875 and 1895 when the fashion for wide skirts was also at its fullest. Robinson argues that these cycles in 'style preferences' resisted manipulation:

> *The remarkable regularity of our wavelike fluctuations suggests a large measure of independence from outside historical events. The innovation of the safety razor and the wars which occurred during the period studied appear to have had negligible effects on the time series. King C. Gillette's patented safety razor began its meteoric sales rise in 1905. But by that year beardlessness had already been on the rise for more than 30 years, and its rate of expansion seems not to have augmented appreciably afterward. Far from initiating a great style wave, Mr. Gillette rode on one to fame and fortune.*

Not only is it possible to identify cycles in men's fashions but they run parallel to those in women's fashions. Arguably, from the nineteenth century, however, men's fashions have offered fewer choices at any one moment and therefore acted to impose conformity on those adhering to fashion. Normative men have either resisted fashion or conformed to mainstream elements. Conversely, expressive (individualistic or idiosyncratic) male fashion has been confined to particular groups and 'subcultures', such as 'gentlemen', gays, popular entertainers, ethnic groups, and popular subcultural groups. The implication is that these groups are not normative, but articulate non-mainstream forms of masculinity reflected by, and coded in, their choice of clothes. These other 'masculinities' have pivoted around heterosexuality but frequently have invoked parodies of mainstream male mores. As Pumphrey has argued, definitions of masculinity are coded through clothes and the associated politics of style. He suggests that the Western (as history, novel and film) has offered one enduring style from which men's fashions and group identities have derived. Even so, the way in which the Western has figured is ambivalent:

> *The heterosexual norm exemplified in the Western has always been satirised and parodied within gay cultures and, drawing directly on that tradition of resistance, style politics does offer heterosexual men new ways of conceptualising and acting out masculinity-not least because at the immediate level of everyday social life it ridicules the*

> *coercive homophobia that has so fundamentally shaped the processes by which masculinity has traditionally been maintained, and offers new ways in which these men can relate to each other.*

Underpinning Pumphrey's argument is a sense of ambivalence towards the relation between male style and male sexual identity. Contemporary men struggle to articulate the image of male sexuality appropriate to their circumstances. For some, this has an overwhelming importance; for others, little at all-or so it seems. The very act of decorating and displaying the male body in twentiethcentury Europe has been fraught with partially spoken-and often competing desires and fears. The myth of the 'undecorated' male effectively suppresses ambivalence about this process of forming the male social body. In industrialising Europe, men became consumed by employment which could secure status and power. In a conscious move, men disassociated themselves with the idleness and extravagance of aristocratic codes of dress and behaviour. Men dressed to confirm their involvement in the new industrial order. While men competed in the tough world of politics and economics, women were allocated the role of decorating and complementing the public status of men through their clothes and demeanour.

As indicated in earlier chapters, decoration and dress has frequently been a major feature of masculinity in other cultures. New Guinea headdresses are primarily the province of men; body decoration is as much a male as a female pursuit in most non-European societies (such as Africa, South America, Australian Aborigines, North American indigenous peoples, Polynesia); splendid Polynesian capes are worn primarily by men; and so on. But, in European culture, the emergence of our form of civility has involved a fundamental disquiet about male decoration. The presentation of the body and practices of etiquette were central to the formative character of civil society. The sumptuary laws which lasted from the thirteenth to the seventeenth centuries are the most commonly cited example of the attempt to regulate fashion and codify display. These laws specified appropriate clothing according to occupation and social status. In particular, they imposed restrictions on eligibility to wear certain kinds of garments, fabrics and accessories-especially fur, gold, silk and jewels. Since the rules were set by the court, they sought to enhance the status of the aristocracy through sartorial distinctiveness.

Sumptuary laws also had implications for commerce. By prescribing consumer habits precisely, the laws regulated 'the acquisition and exchange of valuable goods'. Overall, they eschewed excessive display for its own sake. But, as with any regulatory code, the act of suppression and articulation of permissible limits, both codified status and created an alternative set of rules and codes. Despite the laws, which were frequently flaunted, especially by the upwardly mobile merchant class, neither fashion nor consumerism was eradicated. Rather, the laws enshrined the significance of clothing and appearance as signs of economic and social position. Clothes were an inherent component of persona. As Elias has shown, a reaction to this legislative imposition from the court was the formation of dress codes among ordinary people, especially wealthy business classes. This gave rise to the phenomenon of 'town fashions'. Thus, it is somewhat misleading to interpret surviving court fashions as indicative of mainstream dress norms of the time.

Civilising Imperative

The history of European court society of the Renaissance reveals that fashion flourished at that time. Indeed, it functioned as a major determinant of position within the court. Although the consumption of clothing had been a preoccupation for centuries, court society turned consumerism into an art form. The most extravagant monarch was Louis XIV who has been called 'the consumer king'. Not only did he himself display an obscene indulgence in lavish and opulent clothing, ornamentation, housing, furnishings, parties and fetes, he set impossible standards for his nobles and those who wished to curry favour. Once admitted to court society, the nobles 'had to spend ruinously to stay there', running up huge bills and indebtedness to the king:

> *State spending increased astronomically. In return for this expenditure, the monarchy gained a dependent nobility which gathered at court because royal power was concentrated there, only to find themselves committed to a level of consumption which further enhanced that power.*

It was a vicious circle. By preying on their vanity, Louis XIV created a circle of 'insatiable consumers' who spent huge sums of money in order to remain in favour with the king, and supported the regime in order to keep their creditors at bay. In the end, the court became a self-perpetuating world out of touch with society at large and wider political forces. Foreigners were 'astounded' by the splendour and excessive extravagances of the French court.

Over time the rigid grand habit of the court was regarded as unfashionable and conservative by the fashionable classes in the towns and by the younger members of the court. Often they ignored the requirements of the *habit de cour* or incorporated elements from town fashion, thereby incurring the wrath of Louis XIV. But the end of the king's reign did not mean the end of consumerism. Citizens had been exposed to glimpses of unimagined possibilities and the power of money. The social structure of European societies had already changed significantly and was continuing to do so. Subsequent developments of a bourgeois class and an urbanised population embodied the desire for material goods and conspicuous consumption. The bourgeoisie wanted to live 'nobly' by acquiring goods 'that imitated aristocratic styles from the past'. This desire to emulate aristocratic elements was a mere affectation confined to a small group and occurred alongside the emergence of explicit codes of fashion and etiquette in civil society.

Trends in clothing and cycles of fashion demonstrated this. Costume collections show that men's clothing-at least for the wealthy-was elaborate and extravagant. For example, seventeenth-century men's dress was based on doublet, breeches and cloak. When resources permitted, these garments were heavily embroidered, sometimes trimmed with silver or gold thread, edged with satin, and featured lace collars. According to Hart, printing and embroidering motifs (what she calls 'decorative abuse of expensive textiles') became fashionable from the late sixteenth century. When the expensive fabric could not be afforded: 'Calicos and cottons were treated to look like silk, while wallpaper with gold floral patterns and chairs upholstered in "Pompadour" style were made for the salons of the middle bourgeoisie'.

Although the influence of court society declined, the desire to decorate the male body did not. However, the aristocratic influence waned. In contrast to the elaborate tops and leggings (breeches, pantaloons, stockings) preferred by the court, in the eighteenth century, the basis of men's wardrobes became the suit, although the jackets were still very full with coat skirts, and the trousers were knee-length breeches. This trend was a trickle-up phenomenon, since it was based on the clothing of working-class men but gradually became the standard dress for men of all classes. The cut and preferred fabric of the coat (embroidered or woven patterned silk or wool) changed each season. In the 1740s, the suit became somewhat plainer and the waistcoat-visible underneath-became the extravagant fashion statement. By the late eighteenth century, these garments were becoming more standardised though still elaborate. A preference for dark colours was also evident. The nineteenth century was a turning point. Changes in tailoring techniques 'concentrated on fit rather than style' by creating waist seams, underarm seams, and introducing Cossack trousers. There were enormous variations in the style of coats and experimentation with different kinds of trousers. But, over time, men's dress became less elaborate, less decorative, and less variable.

Yet despite the trend towards more standardised dress, there were still seasonal fashions and precise rules of dress etiquette. The trend towards plainness occurred against periodic campaigns in favour of extreme decorative male dress. These included the phenomena of the beau (early eighteenth century), Macaroni fashion and the dandy (early nineteenth century) and the aesthete of the late nineteenth century. These are usually contrasted with subsequent plain fashions for men, which are explained in terms of political and economic upheavals, in particular, the French Revolution. Steele, however, argues that the trend towards plainer clothes was under way much earlier alongside the moments of excess in men's fashions. In fact, she suggests, these fads triggered the trend.

Steele argues that there was a battle between men's fashions that accompanied the growth of civil society and the gradual erosion of aristocratic power and prestige in Europe. The Macaronis appeared during 'the peak of aristocratic power'. They epitomised the desire of aristocrats to distinguish themselves from the growing bourgeoisie and minor gentry through their clothes. They drew on images from the French and Italian courts to emphasise that difference and create an impression of solidarity with their European counterparts. This occurred against a background of emerging political awareness among newly empowered groups in England. Inevitably, the tensions between the groups spilt over into vicious attacks on the character and appearances of each. Macaroni fashion became the rich butt of caricatures and satire in anti-aristocratic literature produced by those who despised the values held by the Macaronis:

> *the image of the Macaroni was used to attack the perceived vanity, irresponsibility, effeminacy, and lack of patriotism of the aristocracy, especially (but not exclusively) the Court elite. Elaborate and modish male dress was perceived as symptomatic of corruption, tyranny and foreign attitudes, while plainer male dress was heralded as an emblem of liberty, parliamentary democracy, enterprise, virtue, manliness, and patriotism.*

Typical items of clothing attracting scorn included the Macaronis' shoes with buckles or bows, light silk stockings, accessories, nosegays, neckchiefs tied in a bow, decorative buttons, tasselled canes, watches, trinkets and baubles. Above all, in contempt for the declining fashion for wigs, the Macaronis wore elaborate headdresses:

> *But the Macaroni wig was both new and Frenchified, and it paralleled the current fashion in women's wigs, which, since the late 1760s, had been worn ever higher. Apparently, it was bad enough that 'female macaronis' be subject to the arts of the French* friseur, *but it was utterly contemptible that men should copy them. Many critics suggested that the Macaroni had 'a good quantity of hair for his head produces nothing else', but one writer used a more devastating image that associated external appearance with internal corruption: 'Their toupees imitate their high elevated thoughts, which, teeming with maggots of various kinds, display to the world their humour'.*

Through caricature and denunciations like these, the Macaronis were implicated in a style war between traditional elite arbiters of taste and new groups of cultural nationalists. The mercantile and bourgeois classes in Britain were in the process of consolidating their social identity and distinguishing it from what had gone before at the same time as the elite tried to insist on their superiority and assert their vestimentary distinction. Although there was not yet a clear sense of British civil fashion, the new groups preferred simplicity and drew on images of military, sport and country life. Clearly, the antithesis between the 'country' associations of this code and the court associations of Macaroni fashion was underpinned by deep-seated hostility. Yet despite the strident denunciations of the Macaronis' aristocratic dress, there was also a desire to imitate certain aspects of it. The tensions between the desire to imitate and the impulse to reject aristocratic ways embodied the dominant themes of contemporary political, economic and moral life:

The fashion in men's attire changed as more and more people came to perceive sober male dress as being a reflection of patriotism (versus aristocratic cosmopolitanism), liberty (versus tyranny), country and city (versus Court), Parliament and Constitution (versus Royal prerogative and corruption), virtue (versus libertinism), enterprise (versus gambling, frivolity, and dissipation), and manliness (versus a fribbling, degenerate exotic effeminacy).

The values associated with Macaroni dress had been discredited and rejected. As a consequence, men's dress became plainer. Moreover, it was interpreted as a sign of British patriotism, cultural dominance and economic success. But while clothing became simpler, it did not mean that men's fashion or codes of dress disappeared. Rather, they became more subtle and internalised. Subsequent moments of excess in men's dress were thus posed against this plain backdrop, and were widely resisted precisely because they articulated the values and association that the fashion system tried to keep invisible.

The emergence of consumerism and the growth of bureaucratic and civil society heralded other more accessible sources and conduits of fashion. Success in public life depended as much on the successful management of appearances as it did on economic clout. The extension of industrialism and urbanism created new possibilities for fashion. Individuals could buy the qualities they desired and wished to project:

With a plentiful supply of material goods, the individual's right to possessions, be they gold adornments, furs, silk clothes or heeled shoes, took on a different meaning. Now, the ownership and display of goods became evidence of an individual's accomplishments and attributes. Ownership made an individual appear wealthy, socially mobile, in possession of refined sensibilities and tastes.

Central to the new possibilities opened up by consumerism was the manipulation of appearances. People had greater access to clothes, a new awareness of fashion and fads, and the possibility of buying the look they desired. Accordingly, appearance, complemented by 'artifice and performance', combined in new registers of social etiquette and measures of achievement:

a shift in sensibility took place when the age of consumerism was expanding, in the early nineteenth century, and a new balance was being struck in which the external appearance, particularly of men, was becoming a significant index of political and social interests. At the time, a man could demonstrate his thorough disinterest in the struggles for power and his distance or removal from ancestral wealth in the style of clothes and the mien he adopted.

A new attention to appearance and calculated display heralded the emergence of conspicuous consumption organised around the body. For men, this involved restraint rather more than excess. Social success was predicated on respectability which was gauged by conveying an impression of a serious (business-like) demeanour created by wearing sombre clothes.

In contrast, 'society' fashion adapted these norms in an extreme way, epitomised by the figure of the dandy. The socialite Beau Brummell became synonymous with dandyism. During the early years of the nineteenth century, Brummell was socially ambitious and used his appearance to gain favour with high society. He abhorred the ostentatious display conveyed by the extravagant frippery of the nobility and chose instead simple, understated clothes, and wanted to create 'a new kind of aristocrat' based on 'a purely subjective influence over society'. To this end, he 'concentrated on the body and used his clothing to bring attention to and enhance the human frame' such that 'his social identity was fashioned from his appearance'.

Brummell created a style of dress that was 'more austere, manly and dignified than any before or since'. He chose to wear a well-tailored coat with a tight waist and knee-length skirt, over waistcoat, shirt and cravat, and pantaloons. Although apparently plain, Brummell's clothes were the product of highly skilled tailoring and painstaking care with his toilet. According to Moers: 'Brummell's major contribution to history was his highly original advocacy of cleanliness. It was a matter of pride with him that he did not need perfume: he did not smell'.

Through the judicious choice of well-cut suits and fresh, starched linen neckcloths and shirts, Brummell imposed a new restrained code of men's dress: 'the fashion ideal of understated elegance'. This became the language of dress for the modern man and 'the forerunner of the modern business suit and the necktie'. These clothes 'were suitable for all classes and occupations' that, in the long-term, 'would clothe democracy':

By making simplicity the fashion, Brummell established a style suitable for any man, king or commoner, who aspired after the distinction of gentleman. Without sacrificing elegance or grace, he invented a costume that was indubitably masculine.

The secret of men's dress was a standardised sober suit enlivened by choice of tie and accoutrements. Items like the necktie allowed individual interpretations; indeed, it was Brummell's favourite item. But mostly clothing codes entailed more subtle conventions concerning the cut, fabric and mode of wearing. Even the business suit, the apparent leveller of men's dress, invokes complex and almost imperceptible 'esoteria of fabric, fibre, tailoring and aesthetics' for the cognoscenti. Above all, taste was costly. Modish consumers were locked into patronising the most expensive purveyors. Thus, an elite consumer group developed alongside a democratic one. While the elite group thought they could transcend banal taste and everyday life, the democratic group 'wanted to rescue everyday consumption from banality by raising it to the level of a political and social statement'. The tensions between these two groups marked the character of nineteenth-century male consumer culture.

The irony of the era of the dandy was that this elitism and desire to distinguish themselves from ordinary people by 'spiritual superiority all depended on the vulgar act of shopping'. It was very expensive (ruinous in Brummell's case) to acquire the appropriate dress, furnishings, possessions and lifestyle of the dandy:

> *In consequence, the dandy ideal was not only dragged down to the level of materiality-an unavoidable fall for any human ideal but it was dragged down more specifically, and less necessarily, to the level of the marketplace. The dandy expressed himself as a consumer; dandyism was inherently tainted by commercialism.*

But dandyism was an important moment in European men's dress because it established new sets of relations between trend-setters and fashionable groups, and secured new sartorial codes for men in industrialised societies. The dandy combined vestiges of the peacock with rules for the plain man.

Suited for Respectability

The activities of the dandies, most people were constrained by financial and practical circumstances as well as by more conservative aesthetic considerations. Generally, the nineteenth century was characterised by conservatism in men's dress and resistance to change. This was maintained by successive campaigns against excess in men's dress. According to Paoletti, these campaigns were conducted by endorsing positive role models and ridiculing undesirable tendencies. Specialist shops in the form of gentlemen's outfitters catered for the new male mode and became authoritative sources about men's dress. Male fashion advice came from tailors, columns in men's magazines and etiquette books which described 'the perfect gentleman'.

The 1880s man dressed in a way that was 'inconspicuous to the casual observer, but perfect in its attention to quality, fit and correctness'. There was more concern with men's involvement in the workplace, which required a suitably serious and practical outlook and appearance. 'Conformity and conservatism in dress indicated reliability'. But, in the space of a decade, the well-dressed man became a pale reflection of his earlier self. Now he bought ready-to-wear clothes from department stores and men's clothiers, and primarily wore suits-for work, sport, and leisure. He was 'neat but casual, clean but not fussily immaculate, and versatile, not occasion-specific'.

So, what led to this rapid change in the wardrobe and the image of the fashionable man? According to Paoletti, men became subject to a number of pressures both in the workplace and at home. Attitudes were changing. More men worked in sedentary occupations, especially in office jobs. These required different kinds of clothing, hence the growing popularity of the business suit as a practical, multi-purpose garment and the basis of the wardrobe for the whitecollar workplace. In some occupations, such as the police force, the military and medical workers (doctors and surgeons), uniforms were introduced in order to indicate professional authority. In blue-collar jobs, overalls, dungarees and boilersuits gradually replaced suits as functional and conformist clothing more suitable for the job. These practical garments were colour-coded by occupation: white for laboratory and manual work, blue for engineering, and khaki for operational tasks.

As a fashion garment, the suit was invested with sexual attributes of the new masculinity of the 1890s. This stylistic rhetoric of conversion was accompanied by denunciations of clothes and adornment which threatened 'traditional masculinity or masculine values' and sustained 'ridicule of occasion-specific styles such as the frock coat'. By the late nineteenth century, there was a relentless trend towards plain dress characterised by the uniform choice of colour, style and fabric. Men's suits retained considerable padding throughout the garment to enhance the shoulders and the hips. By tailoring the jacket to feature a nipped-in waist, a rounded effect was achieved which complemented the hourglass figure of the fashionable woman. Some men wore corsets (made of rows of stretched springs) while others wore pantaloons made with rows of drawstrings at the waist which created a full-hipped look. The impression created was one of substantial bulk. Kidwell has noted how the similarity between the nineteenth-century male and female ideal silhouette is often misunderstood and misinterpreted:

> *Even what was similar in men's and women's dress was perceived differently. When contemporary writers made reference to the shape of a fashionable man's body, they most often described wide shoulders, while reporters of feminine fashions focused on narrow waists. Any reference to the apparent width of the shoulders in women's dresses was in terms of how this feature showed off in contrast a small waist. Thus the optical illusion created by the V angle of the lapels on a man's coat and the V angle of the gathers on a woman's bodice were interpreted differently.*

From the 1890s, the rounded male physique gave way to a new look. Suits were tailored in an angular, square mode using stiff, sturdy and durable material allowing freedom of movement. By using a limited range of dark colours and discreet, subtle patterns, the suit became the perfect multi-occasion garment. Complemented by white or pastel shirts, the dour suit was relieved only by the choice of tie or cravat. Ornamentation was viewed with suspicion. The overall impression conveyed the serious disposition of men locked into the industrialising economy. As Finkelstein has noted, the severity of men's dress was reinforced by its contrast with women's fashions. These were made in softer fabrics in light colours, and cut to exaggerate curves and flowing lines which drew attention to the contours of the female body. Not only did these fashions restrict movement and allow only minimal physical exertion, the excessive use of jewellery and accessories underlined the ephemeral interests and frivolous image of nineteenth-century women.

In earlier chapters, we have discussed the rhetoric of the New Woman that accompanied significant changes to the circumstances of women in the late nineteenth and early twentieth centuries. There was also a complementary rhetoric about the New Man. But whereas the New Woman was heralded as a symbol of the new age, her male counterpart came in for heavy criticism:

> *Numerous cartoons depicted a topsy-turvy world of the future populated by strong, domineering women and passive, domesticated men. The challenge to young men of the turn of the century was not only to adapt successfully to the pressures of modern urban life, but to adjust to these changing standards of femininity.*

The ideal of masculinity was no longer the mannered, passive, leisure-seeking 'Gentleman', but a young man filled with ambition and courage: 'energetic, athletic, ambitious and less concerned with style than action'. In accordance with this ideal, the 'Coming Man' spent little time on his clothes and appearance. His wardrobe was based on the business suit with a sack-style jacket: 'Neatness was desirable, but not really expected, as it seems to have been believed to have run contrary to masculine nature'. The new look was advocated in etiquette books as well as through popular magazines and cartoons. Paoletti argues that ridicule of what was deemed to be inappropriate men's dress, especially the Perfect Gentleman as well as unmanly and effeminate looks, was a strong and effective feature of this period. The term 'dandy' was revived and applied to the positive role models associated with the new dress codes-the American equivalent was 'the dude'. These fashions were often uncomfortable and comical. In the 1890s, the Dude was replaced by a companion to the Gibson Girl, the Gibson Man, who was well-dressed but casual, athletic and possessed a cool, square-jaw. This ambitious young man was popularised in advertising campaigns which extolled his modern outlook and business-like mode of dress.

The suit has remained the basis of the male wardrobe throughout the twentieth century. There have been some attempts to challenge the narrow range of men's fashions, notably from the British Men's Dress Reform Party which lasted from 1929 to 1937 and similar groups in other countries, including New Zealand, India, China, Australia, South Africa, Egypt, Costa Rica, Austria, the USA, and Canada. The reform movement aimed to rid men's dress of unhealthy and restrictive clothes by replacing the uniform of suit and shirt. In particular, they targeted the collar and tie, recommending a Byron collar instead. The shirt should be replaced by a decorative blouse making the jacket an optional extra. Breeches or shorts were recommended in the place of tight trousers, and sandals instead of shoes. The movement actively promoted its views in pamphlets and newsletters, fashion parades and competitions. Generally, the reaction was one of ridicule in magazines like *Punch,* and scorn from the general public. One letter to the *Daily Sketch* warned: 'In my experience of life-nearly eighty years-unconventional dress leads to unconventional manners and a lower standard of society'. The Reform Movement also reflected the shifting locus of fashion influence from Europe to the New World. No longer did London and Paris dominate ideas of male dress. Different climatic and working conditions in other countries required different ways of dressing. In addition, mail-order, catalogues, and ready-to-wear became the main forms of selling clothes. The challenge to Europe was especially strong in America which slowly became the main influence on everyday men's clothing as opposed to high fashion.

Although the Men's Dress Reform movement was short-lived, it had a lasting impact on men's swimwear and on outdoor leisure and sports wear-though it is difficult to conclude whether these changes were in the air already or precipitated by the movement. In relation to swimwear, the movement opposed the heavy full costumes in favour of swimming naked or simply wearing slips. It also recommended the use of artificial silk instead of wool in manufacturing swimwear on the grounds that it was lighter and did not become water-logged because it had much greater water resistance. These changes were eventually taken up. The movement also advocated lighter and looser clothing for leisure wear, such as shorts and short-sleeved shirts for tennis. This was a radical innovation. American tennis player Bunny Austin overcame considerable self-consciousness when he first wore shorts at the 1932 United States Men's National Championship:

> *I myself took over two years to summon up enough courage to wear shorts, although for years I had known how much more healthy, comfortable and reasonable they were for tennis. I hovered in my bedroom putting them on, taking them off, putting them on again, wrestling with the problem of Hamlet-'To be or not to be'. At last I summoned up all my courage, put and kept them on, and wearing an overcoat to conceal them as much as possible, went out of the hotel to play. My bare legs protruded beneath the coat and I slunk through the lounge self-consciously. As I passed through the door an agitated porter followed me. 'Excuse me, Mr. Austin', he whispered diffidently, 'but I think you've forgotten your trousers'.*

After some controversy and resistance to the exposure of men's knees and hairy legs, these daring garments gradually gained acceptance. One enduring variant of the suit, shorts and military uniform was the 'safari suit' which was made in light-weight fabrics suitable for sub-tropical and tropical climates. Distinctive as it is, with its military-styled jacket and shorts, the safari suit has retained a loyal following in many post-colonial societies. More generally, innovations like these acted as a catalyst for the manufacture of specialised sports and leisure wear.

But the movement had less effect on business clothing. Despite the practicality of its recommendations, Burman and Leventon argue that 'loose, soft cloths, shortened arms and legs, and unstructured necklines of reform clothes' failed to denote the 'visible authority' associated with tailored suits, stiff collars and formal ties. In other words, by now, a rounded male silhouette was deemed inappropriate for the serious disposition of working men denoted by the rectangular look of the suit.

The dominance of the suit as the appropriate dress for white-collar occupations remained unchallenged. The basis of the modern man's wardrobe was set. Apart from minor deviations and variations, twentieth-century American and European men have been clad in shirt, trousers, and jacket. Fashion commentators have consistently stressed the functional basis of men's clothes. For example, Elizabeth Ewing argues that the development of the motor car led to more protective outer coats for men and women to cope with the breezy ride. Equally, the car (and motorised forms of public transport) induced a preference for streamlined clothes which did not drag or get caught up when entering and alighting from these vehicles. Also in line with increased mobility, sweaters were popularised in the 1920s, enabling the expression of individual taste and giving an impetus to the home-knitting industry.

The necktie generally replaced the cravat and the bow-tie, allowing men to exploit its decorative value as 'an assertion of identity and social status'. There have also been suggestions that the necktie 'links together the physical symbols of virility' (from the larynx to the male sex organ), 'through the desire to enhance the sexual attractiveness of the wearer and to draw attention to the genital organs of the body'. Seen in this light, the infinite variety of the necktie has been interpreted as a potent sign of male sexual identity.

The suit itself has also undergone various modifications in design during the twentieth century. In the early years of the century, men's suits created an oval shape with relatively narrow shoulders, flared coat, wide hips and tapered trouser legs: 'It took a series of revisions in specifications starting in 1926 with a change in the collar, to transform this oval outline to a roughly inverted-triangle silhouette by 1939'. Gradually the shoulders became the focus of the cut while simultaneously minimising the width of the hips. But although the trade magazines advocated the new line from 1926, the majority of men resisted the look until the late 1930s. Hollywood was an important catalyst for popularising the big-shouldered look which lasted through to the 1960s and was revived in the 1980s.

There were attempts to define men's fashions in consumer categories. The American department store Sears, for example, distinguished the snappy dresser, the university or fashion-conscious man, the business man, and the conservative dresser. Minor variations in styles and details were targeted towards these groups.

Restrictions imposed in World War II on clothing had lasting effects through the 1950s and early 1960s on men's fashion. Nonetheless, there were some rearguard responses to these edicts. When, in 1942, the President of the British Board of Trade, Hugh Dalton, introduced measures insisting on single-breasted jackets, minimising the use of pockets and buttons, and limiting trousers to nineteen-inch wide legs, there was a mass objection to a further restriction on turn-ups (cuffs). Despite a plea to parliament by the nation's tailors, Dalton did not budge, responding: There can be no equality of sacrifice in this war. Some must lose lives and limbs; others only the turn-ups on their trousers'. The pared-down suit remained popular after the war though elaborated in other respects. But apart from various male style subcultures, such as the 1940s American 'zoot suit' subcultures, the 1950s British Edwardian look and the Teddy boys, 1950s Australian bodgies, men were incontrovertibly conservative in their choice of clothing.

Pumphrey recalls how older men in the 1950s and 1960s took pride in resolutely 'refusing to take notice of fashion'. Not only were there pressures for men to conform to conservative norms of dress, but there was 'an aggressive indifference to dress and a silent avoidance of bodily display'. By choosing to wear 'doggedly characterless dark suits', men demonstrably rejected 'the frivolous, superficial, ephemeral and trivial'.

Accompanying this display of uncompromising masculinity was a 'pronounced homophobia'. Any indication of attention to dress or decoration by a man was looked on with suspicion. Yet, while aggressive masculinity and homophobic paranoia characterised codes of male dress and social etiquette, different attitudes graced 'the sports field, gym, running-track and beach...where momentarily those sanctions broke down-where the body could be rubbed, oiled, shown off'. Sporting activities not only gave a licence to the display of the body but deliberately transformed the body into disciplined musculature. The male sporting body internalised a 'regimen of discipline, punctuality, obedience and attentiveness' in order that the trained body could be displayed and admired. In contrast to male dress codes, the codes of sporting behaviour valorised exhibitionism, physical contact between men, and the display of physical attributes. Sport celebrated male muscularity which in turn was 'the *sign* of power-natural, achieved, phallic'.

Perversely, normatively homophobic sportsmen have engaged in blatantly homoerotic activities (touching, embracing, kissing, cuddling) which elsewhere they would denounce. In other words, sport has been 'the privileged space of the legitimate gaze of male upon male'. Out of the sporting arena, however, the men have continued to eschew signs of masculinity and sexuality. Insofar as clothes articulate masculinity, they display attributes of strength and power rather than male sexual desire and homoeroticism.

The history of sports clothes demonstrates the slow acceptance of pragmatic requirements of physical exertion over a concern with decorum. It was not until the late nineteenth century that sportsmen exchanged their jackets and flannel trousers (modified forms of the business suit) for customised wear for sports such as football, gymnastics, basketball, baseball, tennis, swimming, riding and cycling. Outfits like the jerseys, knickers and bright-red stockings adopted by the Cincinnati Red Stockings in 1867 were highly controversial at the time, since the freedom of movement they permitted was achieved by figure-hugging garments condemned as 'positively indecent'.

Not only have men been reluctant to wear clothes that exude sexuality but they have also been loathe to indulge in other behaviour associated with sexual display, including shopping. By rejecting consumerism and other activities involving the projection of ideal transformations (through window shopping, romance reading, window displays, fashion parades, and fashion magazines), men have reiterated their serious, materialistic concerns and rejected effeminate wiles.

This situation began to change in the 1960s once some designers decided to take an interest in men's clothes as fashion. It was the start of a process that wrested male clothing design away from tailors, chain stores and wholesale manufacturers. The suit itself changed with the Nehru look, the Mao look and the use of outrageous fabrics. More generally, there was a 'movement towards light-weight, unstructured styles and the popularity of separates and casual clothes'. No longer was the suit the basis of the whole wardrobe. A separate set of leisure garments evolved. A distinction between the fashion of the workplace and the fashion of everyday wear became an important element of men's clothing. From the excesses of the 1960s-at least among some young men-men in general became a little more adventurous in the 1970s and 1980s. They experimented with a wider range of colours than before and were more adventurous in choice of garment and cut.

Recognition of this has come in the growth of men's fashion magazines such as *Vogue Men, Uomo, Cosmo Man, GQ, The Face, i-D* and *Arena*. Other magazines have incorporated special inserts or produced special issues for men. Not only do such magazines promote fashions but a range of other products for the contemporary man. Such strategies have not always been successful and numerous male-oriented fashion and lifestyle magazines have failed. One magazine, *The Hit,* published in the UK, was aimed at 15- to 19-year-old men, but failed after just six issues. Research suggested that the concept was fine, but that:

> *unlike girls of the same age (and women in general) who identify strongly with a community of women, young men baulked at being spoken to as a community of men: 'they might like BMX bikes, waterskiing and the Jesus and Mary Chain, but they don't like magazines to suggest that other men within their age group feel the same way as them'. In other words, speaking to young men as men is a risky business, because it targets men in gendered terms rather than the norm which defines everything else. Masculinity's best-kept secret is broken open.*

The 1980s witnessed a sustained effort by advertisers to capture the male market. Of course, men are not a homogeneous market and advertisers have been at great pains to distinguish different demographic, lifestyle and consumer groups among men. At stake was 'the hyper-cultivation of the male body' around new codes of masculinity, physicality, and dressability.

In order to appeal to male consumers, advertisers and marketers have to play on traditional associations of masculinity, such as individuality, competitiveness, mateship and aggression, while attempting to wean men into consumer identifications and relations. Garments like jeans proved to be useful vehicles for this transformation of men into consumers with dress sense and stylistic aspirations.

Scheuring has examined the way in which the humble pair of jeans was transformed from practical, rural and blue-collar work-clothes into a fashion garment synonymous with youth. The break came in the 1950s when middleclass, white rock singers and film stars (such as Elvis Presley, Eddie Cochran, Gene Vincent, Marlon Brando and James Dean) adopted the Levi Strauss 501 style (with buttoned flies) and black leather jackets to convey a 'tough, rugged, youth-rebel appearance'. Their working-class and black counterparts, on the other hand, wore anything but jeans which were a reminder of their poor roots. Jeans were a symbol of middle-class revolt from the strictures of respectability and conformity. Parents frowned on their jean-clad offspring, some American colleges banned them from being worn on campus, and places like restaurants displayed signs prohibiting customers in jeans.

Perhaps more than any other object, jeans epitomised the values of 1960s youth culture. The success of Levi's meant that young men escaped the pressures of the male fashion industry and clung to this basic garment with minimal variations. Although Levi Strauss has remained a market leader, many other brands of fashion jeans (notably Lee and Wrangler) benefited from this growing sector. The fashion industry was desperate to turn jeans into a fashion commodity, subject to regular variation and stylistic change.

The popularisation of flares (trousers which flared out from the knee) provided new opportunities for jeans manufacturers who produced a range of designs and massively increased sales: 'now changes could be calculated and influenced'. By the mid-1970s, the wearing of jeans was no longer confined to workers and young men. New designs were produced for middle-aged 'swingers' who were young at heart but wide in girth (often with open-fronted shirts and gold neck chains). As the economic well-being of wearers of jeans increased, the fashion industry saw yet more possibilities.

Designer jeans were born. As well as carrying the designer logo and name, these exclusive jeans were cut to suit the particular proportions of the clients of designers. American designer Calvin Klein was the first to market signature jeans. When he introduced his 'refitted, well-cut' Calvin's in 1978, 200,000 pairs sold in the first week, even though they cost 50 per cent more than leading brands like Levi's. Klein capitalised on the exclusive associations of designer jeans, and promoted his clothes through explicitly sexual imagery. His best-known advertisement featured actor Brooke Shields, murmuring, 'You know what comes between me and my Calvin's? Nothing'. It was denounced as 'pornographic' but was highly successful. His success has been attributed to a combination of recognising women's desire to wear casual, comfortable clothes; drawing on androgynous images and designing 'unisex' clothes for women and men; sexualising the image of designer labels; and adding the exclusiveness of a designer signature to the ubiquitous pair of jeans.

Sales of Calvin's jeans reached about $400 million world-wide in 1984. After a slump of several years, Calvin Klein attempted to revive sales in the early 1990s, partly through his use of provocative promotions. An advertising supplement for his denim collection was shot by radical photographer Bruce Weber for an issue of *Vanity Fair* around the theme of 'denim and skin' against images of a rock concert:

> *The collection of sexually ambiguous images features male band members in jeans and leather jackets fondling nude, semi-nude and fully clad women, then undressing themselves and their dates. Included in the narrative are sculpted poses of male and female limbs entwined in bed, and a hunk in a shower engaging in what some interpret as masturbation.*

Although the advertisement created a storm, sales of his jeans rose by 30 per cent the following month, though this momentum was not maintained and Klein's empire remained shaky. Other designers have also jumped onto the designerjeans bandwagon, though not always successfully. The best known include Gloria Vanderbilt, Liz Clairbourne, Versace, Guess, Donna Karan, and The Gap. In the United Kingdom, the label Joe Bloggs has taken 'an intrinsically American product', adapted it with 'embroidery and graphic detail', experimented with a range of colours, and attached very prominent signature labels, thus creating a parody of the signature but a highly distinctive (and therefore marketable) range of jeans.

As a result, jeans have become respectable dress, not only for leisure but for a casual, dressed-up look. While they have remained the mainstay of workers and youth, the latter constantly seek ways to mark out their choice of jeans as different from those of the fashion industry. While young people may tear, rip, appliqué, or tie-dye their jeans, designers produce 'sporty formal' denim suitable for more bourgeois lifestyles. Upwardly mobile men and women can look 'acceptably shabby'. The success of jeans as a ubiquitous fashion and a symbol of youth testifies to the adaptability and opportunism of the fashion industry and to the mercurial tastes of the fashionable classes.

In sum, what is often regarded as the norm of men's clothing-namely, the lack of fashion and the lack of interest by men-is questionable. At most, this has been a recent historical and cultural aberration. While it is true that men's clothing in Europe has become plainer since the eighteenth century, it has still been subject to cycles of fashion in terms of preferred garments, style and cut, choice of fabric, colours, and modes of wearing.

What has marked out changes in men's fashion has been the association with the workplace. Clothes were the index of professional character. In particular, the business suit was associated with authority and status. In the corporate world, the suit was also associated with seriousness in so far as 'a similitude exists between the appearance of the individual and the demeanour, even personal characteristics, which s/he can be expected to possess'. This aura of similitude also extended to moral qualities associated with the position adopted by the wearer. By treating clothes as an index of social and moral qualities, recent male fashions have celebrated the body itself and played down the decorative attributes of clothing and body decoration. The emphasis on the display of masculine attributes constitutes a profound challenge to western conventions of morality.

New Male Modes

Over the past decade, a new term has entered discussions of men and clothing-the New Man. The idea of the New Man has an implied counterpoint-the old-fashioned man. This man seems to be derived from several masculine types: 'the gentleman' who is 'styled and stereotyped as the strong and silent type'; the action man who is 'virile, strong, independent and anomic' and denoted by the cowboy, war hero and Marlboro Man; the slob who is functional but uninterested in speed and style; and the chauvinist who is authoritative and ambitious (but equally ruthless and a misogynist). While all may be recognisable, these types conflict and refer to different cultural attributes of masculinity. The new man is a contradictory composite: 'one who is becoming more self-conscious of what it is to be a man, and one who sees through the farce of masculinity and all the entrappings that accompany it'.

The emergence of the New Man has been as much a reaction to the impact of feminism and changing opportunities for women as it has been a reassessment of masculinity itself. One outcome of feminism has been the characterisation of men in negative ways and attacks on 'macho' notions of masculinity. Alternatively, attributes of narcissism and nurturing have been added to codes of masculinity. Marketers have capitalised on these attributes by emphasising lifestyle marketing rather than simply product marketing. The marketers' version of the New Man placed the male body at the centre of identity and sexuality. Appearance, and therefore narcissism, were central to this construction of masculinity. The New Man was not only aware of fashion but an active consumer in the pursuit of his sense of self.

The early 1980s British advertisement for Pure New Wool has been cited as epitomising new approaches to marketing the New Man . Instead of advertising comfortable cardigans for middle-aged men, the wool marketers developed the 'Beware a Wolf in Sheep's Clothing' campaign which was targeted at younger men who would not read the conventional wool advertisements because wool and fashion were thought effeminate. The advertisers 'developed the idea of the urban animal-a guy on the prowl a loner who had no need of peer approval. It was a strategy to slowly persuade men into a new frame of mind regarding fashion' . The images and text undermined traditional ideas of masculinity and modes of representing masculinity while at the same time establishing new codes and re-establishing the power of the male gaze. In contrast to the usual spectacle of the female body, this advertisement offered viewers the sight of the male body:

> *The model in the advert snarls his unease and disapproval, caught in a feminised image that strips him of his masculine power. His snarl, and the title of the ad, both warn the viewer (woman) that he still retains that animal predatory sexuality that is proof of his manhood. It's an image that confronts the insecurities of a masculine identity in doubt. The model disavows his passivity through his aggressive look, though demonstrating that he still has control over definitions of who he is.*

The advertisement was extremely successful in capturing the new image of a softer masculinity and in establishing reversed codes of voyeurism. A few years later, the advertisers launched another campaign, 'Wool Talks Your Language', which reflected the uptake of the new masculinity. This presented men as 'fashionable, stylish and emotional' and portrayed wool as 'an emotional fabric'. The two-stage campaign not only reflected constructions and representations of changing codes of masculinity, but demonstrated the new attributes required of 1980s masculinity.

Part of this new awareness entailed remodelling men's bodies and their clothes in terms of goods and images, and personal appearance, as well as behaving in 'less aggressive and less stereotyped' ways. The new male fashions were unlikely to be worn by normative men and, indeed, Gentle concluded that the use of the term, the New Man, had more to do with changing roles of women than with changing codes of masculinity. The New Man conflated the emergence of a new male consciousness of being male and living up to the expectations of masculinity with the emergence of erotic fashion for men. Part of this process involved 'the emergence of another "new woman", in as far as these eroticised male garments were training women to sexually objectify men'.

Changing codes of depicting men have been central to the New Man phenomenon. Traditionally, the female gaze was indirect-furtive glances from viewers and averted, demure gazes towards the camera. The male gaze, by contrast, was direct, dominating and castrating. The structure of both gazes has been changing. Although male models still tend to look 'either off or up' or through the camera and spectator, the number of images directed at either male or female viewers and consumers has increased. As the nature of the male gaze has become more complex, conventional viewing relations have changed. The male body has been sexualised by dissection into fetishised objects of desire.

The New Man has prompted the fashion industry to distinguish different male markets in terms of lifestyles composed of attributes of personality, roles and prestigious imitation. Types include: the quiet family man (self-sufficient and family-oriented); the traditionalist (conservative, conventional, ordered); the discontented man (dissatisfied with his lot, suspicious, wanting a change); the ethical highbrow (aesthete, sensitive, ascetic, discriminating); the pleasureoriented man (macho, hedonistic, impulsive); the achiever (forceful, ambitious, status-conscious); the he-man (action man, dominant, thrill-seeker); and the sophisticated man (intellectual, socially aware, cosmopolitan). These types translate into three kinds of clothing groups: non-fashion basics, fashion basics, and high fashion.

Segmentation enables marketers to target particular demographic groups while taking account of lifestyle and patterns of consumer behaviour. Advertisers have found print to be the most effective advertising medium. Moreover, advertising is not restricted to male-oriented magazines. They are 'equally effective in "dual readership" magazines and woman-oriented magazines [such as] *Cosmo*'. Department stores, such as Bloomingdale's, cater for the range of male consumers by establishing different physical sales areas with names like Europa, Peterborough Row, The Traditionalist, The Sportsman, The Polo Man, and Saturday's Generation. Through such strategies, marketers have developed a significant market for men's fashion products. According to Mort, a 'new bricolage of masculinity is the noise coming from the fashion house, the marketplace and the street'.

Throughout the 1980s, media and popular culture have anticipated the emergence of the rejuvenated peacock, a man who is aware of his body not just as a machine but as an object of sexual attraction enhanced by his choice of clothes and ways of wearing them. The New Man rhetoric has accompanied the intensified production of male fashions, and cosmetics. In the 1990s, two new kinds of masculinity were identified: the New Lad and Iron John. While the New Man has aged into a contented family-oriented lifestyle, the new boys are more outgoing. The New Lad acknowledged the attitudes of the New Man but was more interested in a hedonistic lifestyle and male pastimes. Iron John was something of a throwback to the chauvinistic male. According to Carter and Brûlé, the three types could be distinguished in fashion terms. While Iron John dressed in practical, casual, non-designer clothes with boxer shorts for underwear, the New Lad preferred Versace, Montana and Calvin Klein-with Y-fronts underneath. The New Man chose Romeo Gigli, The Gap, Agnes B., and Nicole Farhi, with Paul Smith tropical boxer briefs as underpants. In short, the New Man has spawned variants of masculinity which exhibited distinct fashion statements.

As a result of these changes, men's fashion has become a growth industry. The length of fashion cycles of men's clothes has reduced as seasonal collections have become the norm. While the clothes are still more conservative and less extreme than women's, that is, still based on shirt, jacket, trousers and the suit, much greater variety of cut, colour and fabric has become possible. Male fashion also includes distinct categories of leisurewear, underwear, and specialist fashion wear. To accompany these developments, men's fashion boutiques have challenged the monopoly of gentlemen's outfitters, department stores and chain stores. A variety of composite looks have been achieved by adapting classical looks to contemporary images of youth. Not only are more collections of men's clothes available, but men have entered the modelling industry in significant numbers. The change has been reflected in the fashion magazines which regularly feature advertisements and specials composed of images of masculinity and male body parts.

Designers such as Jean Paul Gaultier, Giorgio Armani, John Galliano, Kenzo, Rei Kawakubo, and Yohji Yamamoto have deliberately pushed the limits of men's fashion by proposing new radical looks. Many have swapped the unisex themes of the 1960s and 1970s for androgyny and cross-dressing, using softer fabrics, and flowing lines, for example, in shirts and trousers.

Meanwhile, women have taken to wearing men's shirts and modified men's suits, as well as 'His Pants for Her' underwear. Designer Romeo Gigli, acknowledging that many women prefer to wear trousers and men's shirts, has explicitly designed clothes for the androgynous couple, who share a wardrobe. At the more extreme end of high fashion, Gaultier has, for example, used 'feminine' fabrics like lace and silk, sexualised leather garments, and experimented with men's skirts. His collections have created controversy because they question and undermine definitions of masculinity by creating clothes that are effeminate. Yet frequently Gaultier's ideas have had an impact on male fashion in subsequent modified versions. His early 1980s skirt, for example, was revived in the early 1990s as the 'skuit' (a mid-calf-length 'skirt' tailored in suit cloth), and promoted not as high fashion, but as a practical and comfortable alternative to trousers. Rather than being an aberrant form of male dress, versions of the skirt have been common historically and cross-culturally (for example, among the ancient Romans, among Arabs, Greek Imperial Guards, the Scottish kilt, sarong, kimono, shepherd's smock, and so on). Religious and military garb has frequently incorporated 'female' items of clothing.

Male models, too, make eye contact with the viewer, adopt sultry expressions, display their best masculine features, and allow their bodies to be dissected by the camera. Garber has shown that dress codes have established the boundaries of self through rules concerning status and gender, and the 'anxieties' associated with them. Calculated cross-dress (transvestism):

> *was located at the juncture of 'class' and 'gender'. To transgress against one set of boundaries was to call into question the inviolability of both, and of the sex of social codes-already demonstrably under attack-by which such boundaries were policed and maintained.*

Thus, codes of clothing conduct detailed the particular circumstances where 'transgressive' dressing was sanctioned, although even these circumstances were invested with ambivalence and anxiety. In western cultures, the popularisation of 'women's' dress for men, via a garment such as the 'skuit', would constitute a significant re-alignment of categories of gender and clothing. It would escalate changing conducts of masculinity, prompted by the relaxation of men's dress codes away from garments associated with authority and formality towards a greater range of outfits denoting informality and leisure.

Changing conventions of men's fashion have entailed re-worked attributes of masculinity that have transformed male bodies into objects of the gaze, of display and decoration. This radically undercuts the Victorian and post-Victorian idea of masculinity as the display of restraint in a disciplined body. The re-writing of male dress codes may have other implications. Finkelstein has argued that the more frivolous, casual look of men, and their overt concern with their bodies and their looks, may reflect the changing status of men. No longer are they the sole representative of social power, or the primary worker dressed in 'business-like' clothes, but many men now share jobs or home duties, are students or, increasingly, are unemployed. Men's dress codes have been modified in accordance with these changed life circumstances. The growing acceptance of 'casual' wear for men has also modified the working wardrobe, with the 'leisure suit' and a range of jackets, slacks and shirts challenging the dominance of the formal suit, business shirt and tie. Once again, a process of 'trickle up' has allowed clothes not previously associated with the workplace and social elites to revise clothing codes for men. Conversely, as women move into careers, professions and high-status arenas, their wardrobes are incorporating aspects of traditional male dress. Even so, the differences between the clothing conduct of the middle classes and wealthy elites does not epitomise the fashion behaviour of other groups. Rules maintaining status and gender distinctions persist. A significant proportion of men and women have resisted overt decoration and display of the male body. The revival of the peacock may be some way off yet.

❑❑❑

9

Fashion Design Sociological Analysis

Introduction

In addition to revealing a small scale and economically wobbly set of activities, more or less a cottage industry though now thoroughly urban and studio based, this book also highlights some of the tensions embedded in these practices. There is a great deal of fluidity as the designers flit from one employment or self-employment option to the next; there is the continuing attempt to project a public image as creative artist while having to develop expertise in business; and there is also the reality of being a one-woman enterprise and relying on some of those skills including knitting and sewing which the art school training suggested should be relegated to low skilled, paid employees. This is summed up clearly in Gillian P.'s comment 'I was knitting away night and day'.

In this chapter the focus is on how the young graduates themselves describe what they are doing, how they envisage it and how they make sense of their own labour processes. I argue that they rely on a double discourse of arts and crafts. These often conflict with each other. The craft element is relegated to the more private vocabularies of the practitioners, while art provides an identity in the public domain. They are nonetheless mutually dependent categories which function together as professional ideologies for fashion design. The discourses of art perform two further and articulating roles. They connect with those relatively new patterns of meaning used in designer retailing which present fashion as art at the point of consumption, and they also feed directly into the broader social process which Jameson has labelled the 'aestheticisation of culture'. The idea that society is somehow becoming more and more cultural is one which is threaded throughout this book. For this reason it is useful at this point to comment more concretely on how this broad social process, which Jameson argues is one of the defining features of the postmodern society, connects with fashion.

As I argued at the time in response to Jameson's seminal article on postmodernism, there was a marvellously panoramic account of the world of images, with one picture, film or advertising image being flimsier and more superficial than the next, and yet there was little sense of where these came from, who produced them and what their training comprised; what sort of educational or other institutional practice supported or grounded this production of a 'postmodern culture' and how attention to these dimensions might provide a different, more expansive account from the gloomy prognosis offered by Jameson. This book is in many ways an attempt to offer in the British context a more sociological and historical analysis of these processes by showing how some of the fashion 'signs on the street' are produced and circulated in particular urban economies. I also try to counter that tendency in the thinking of Bourdieu and Donzelot as well as Jameson, which sees these practices as futile or as merely evidence of social and economic regulation.

For Bourdieu, cultural products are the result of the activities of the lower, or sunken middle classes, the new culture intermediaries, who have stumbled across a relatively undesignated field in which they hope to profit. Advertising, design and marketing all offer opportunities for the 'dream of social flying' and thus, for Bourdieu, a strategy on the part of this class strata for upward mobility. Donzelot, in contrast, implies that the young designers are part of that group of new workers for whom some distant promise of creative reward transforms unendurably long hours into a labour of love!

And, for Jameson, as late capital further tightens its grip on production, its goods are increasingly those which take the form of culture, not invigorating, thought-invoking culture of the modernist imagination but, instead, a sorry stream of tawdry 'second-hand' and recycled images, of which we might conclude fashion imagery is typical and also embodies so many of these uninspiring currents.

However, I suggest that we ought at least to listen to how designers themselves describe the work they do, before dismissing it as self-exploitation. The various forms of work thrown up by the deindustrialising impetus of late capital might well push these young women from pillar to post in the context of the United Kingdom fashion economy, but there is also in this activity a real determination to make work something more than dull, routine and meaningless labour. It is this idea of work being a source of self-actualisation, a means of escaping 'alienation' rather than experiencing it, which is a key issue in this book. The theoretical problem is how to interpret the designers' own accounts of what they are doing, especially in the light of the analysis provided by the Foucauldians which would explain such statements as examples of the subjectivising discourses at work in creating human subjects who are also the subjects of new kinds of work. I argue that such perspectives leave little or no room for the actual manoeuvring around governmental strategies (such as the EAS), which indicate some degree of negotiation on the part of the designers, and which even give rise to a redesignation of the category of 'work' altogether so that it means something quite different from how it was conceived of within the rhetoric of enterprise. It is equally important, however, not to veer towards an account which rests on 'agency' as the voluntarist mechanism by which these redesignations are produced. We have seen quite clearly how enterprise culture frames such activities as a strategy of government, understood loosely as the 'conduct of conduct', yet that alone does not explain the various means by which the designers also make work work for them. As Du Gay acknowledges, the conditions of dislocation which now prevail across the whole society, where so many parts no longer fit in the way they once did, make all the more urgent those practices of government which aim to ensure that we 'govern ourselves' in the right way. Yet we cannot judge the effectiveness of these incitements without examining the way in which they are operationalised, and how they appear in practice.

This book attempts then to steer a middle pathway between structure and agency by providing a concrete description of those practices which constitute the micro-economy of fashion design. This means that it seeks simply to show the extent of both the constraints and the manoeuvring around them. In addition, it raises a number of suggestions for policy. Social theory (from Foucault to Giddens) too easily discards or refutes the possibility of 'small improvements' in the field of the social. But this is a limitation. Sociologists have to be concerned with the world in which we live, and not to consider how the insights of sociology can be used to analyse and improve a field of employment, and livelihoods might also be seen as, if not an abrogation of responsibility, at least a refusal of the challenge to recognise the potential role of sociology actually impacting on the world in any meaningful way. Or, to recast the same argument in more Foucauldian terms, the role of sociological analysis is presumably to produce discourses which feed into and compete with the already existing accounts of how (in this case) fashion is, or how it should be. In this book this policy objective is perhaps more foregrounded than is the case in other more theoretically charged accounts of changes in work and employment precisely because of this intention to demonstrate the potential usefulness of sociology.

Ghost of Matisse gets in the Way'

What then is the purpose of graduates utilising the language of art to explain and interpret what they do? First, it justifies poor turnovers and the way many designers are barely scraping a living by appealing to notions of artistic integrity. As Bourdieu would see it, this 'poor performance' in business confirms the legitimacy of fashion as a practice which possesses high cultural capital through its existence also as an anti-economy. According to this logic it almost pays to be bankrupt in this inverted world where the rules of cultural value rely on an apparent, or initial spurning of the principles of profit. The true artist, as Bourdieu puts it, has an interest in disinterest. Fashion relies on this 'anti-economy' to align itself with fine art and against the marketplace. Second, the adoption of an art language also explains the work to potential consumers. But this is not simply a question of explication or instruction, it is also the start of the representational process more thoroughly pursued by the retailers, when the clothes are there to be seen on the rails. So, in a sense, art language serves both to protect the designers from the logic of the market and to mark their distinctive and differentiating presence in the market. This is clearly expressed by Jasmine S. who was working freelance for a Covent Garden retailer at the time of the interview. She explains how the presentation of the clothes was intended to challenge the customers in the same way as a trip to an art gallery or exhibition might do:

The director of the company was trained as a fine artist and that makes all the difference. It means he knows what I'm talking about and he lets me go off and if I come back not with sketches of clothes but with some quotes and some colours and objects...and some idea of superimposing them together he really appreciates that. For the advertising campaign I have just done, we use no clothes or models at all, only abstract images. We chucked the ideas around. It was a kind of antifashion campaign but the director liked that because he is a fine artist. He understood that what I wanted to get across was the idea of fashion as constructed from debris and from obliteration. How it will be received comes down to the question of who is the J. customer? I would want them to think about it. We shouldn't feel we have to spoonfeed the customers all the time.

This can be seen as a way of flattering consumers by acknowledging their possession of the sophisticated codes of art and culture, thus differentiating them from the average or mass consumer. This form of segmented retailing, or niche marketing, would fit both with Bourdieu's scheme of class inequalities being maintained through taste cultures, and also with Lash and Urry's notion of 'aesthetic reflexivity' which comes into play more broadly across the society as a whole as culture, knowledge and information feature more prominently in the emergent post-industrial society and feed directly into everyday life providing categories for experience and understanding. Bourdieu also explains at length how the middle classes expect images and representations designed for their consumption to require the play of specific codes and competences which are the sign of a middle class upbringing and education. Thus, advertising images of the sort Jasmine describes will be abstract and 'diffi-cult' for the simple reason that this corresponds to the cultural expectations of this class strata in their consumption of high culture. It should not be easy, direct, gratifyingly emotional or sensual since these are the expectations of a lower class of consumers. This differentiating process can also be seen with clarity in the promotional material for the Helen Storey collection at the fashion retailers, Jigsaw: 'Her own woman in a suit yes but shockingly bright; a dress sometimes but gossamer light in chiffon and jersey it could slip away in the blink of an eye but the ghost of Matisse gets in the way.' The liter ary poetic image is further emphasised in the interior design of the Jigsaw shops. Not only are the distinct features of the architect s work described in the press material accompanying the opening of a new branch ('noteworthy details include Nigel Coates' tongue armchairs in brickdust velvet'), but there is also special mention of 'a spectacular specially commissioned wall painting by the artist Stuart Helm'. Fashion design is connected here with architecture and with painting, to create an aesthetically defined 'experience' of fashion shopping and, simultaneously to confirm the existence of fashion design in an art world and to legitimate the class and status of the Jigsaw consumers.

So far, then, it seems that Bourdieu offers us two contradictory ways of understanding the role of art in fashion. First, it provides the necessary distance from the vulgarity of cash and commerce and, second, it acts as a strategy of taste and distinction within the field of cash and commerce. I propose a slightly different scenario. This would see the aesthetic transformation of fashion and consumption as articulating both with a traditional feminine discourse of pleasure and desire, one which Barthes found most clearly manifest in his 1960s study of fashion magazines, and also with the more recent breaking down of the traditional boundaries of high art and low culture which has been taken as one of the distinguishing features of cultural postmodernism. This suggests that there is both something familiar in the contemporary feminine aesthetics of 'art' (the *Vogue* tradition) and also something new (the widening of the audience, readership and market for the fashion as art imagery, the *Elle* reader). This, in turn, indicates an opening out of 'culture', not so much a flattening or deadening effect as claimed by Jameson, but more a feminisation and a popularisation. The consequences of this, for artists and designers still educated in the modernist tradition which venerates the charismatic status of art and the art world, are far-reaching and as yet unresolved, as art work becomes less exceptional and more 'normal' and as the categories of art travel further into the commercial field and into the marketplace for clothes, magazines, food, leisure and lifestyle and the whole arena of consumer culture.

Art Vocabularies in Fashion Design

The availability of the codes of fine art operates for the fashion designers both to insulate them from the failures they might experience in the market and, at the same time, to promote or market themselves as creative practitioners. This is how they distinguish themselves as professionals. It is also a rhetoric of persuasion this is how the fashion designers want to be recognised and because there is a risk this might not happen, they are all the more insistent. Only two of my own respondents struck a note of discord by refusing the pretensions of their peers. For example, one young woman said: 'Quite honestly that stuff about walking through the woods and being inspired I think is nonsense. I work on new shapes and I know a good collection means a slim pair of trousers and a wide pair of trousers' (Marcia R). Another commented: 'I'm one of the sensible girls as distinct from the gay boys. I'm not going to make big announcements every season. And I also happen to think Galliano is a load of overrated pretentious rubbish. I want to make clothes that women enjoy wearing, whatever shape they are' (Gaby T.).

The closer the graduates still were to their time at art school, the more pronounced was their commitment to a fine art based identity. This is best summed up in a statement made to me by a male graduating student interviewed when I returned to college after completing the body of the fieldwork, to get a renewed feel for students graduating ten years after my main group of respondents. This boy said (and his comment also displays all the signs of casual flamboyance adopted by 'the boys' in the hope that their provocative style will get them noticed):

> *In my work I want to explore the deeper meaning of my laziness and link it with imagination. I want to hold onto and work with spontaneity. And I want to engage with eclecticism. I like the idea of a perfect finish but not the work that it involves. By far the most advanced designers are Miyake and Galliano. They are doing what they want to in spite of the need to make money. Nor is their work just about fashion. It's about imagination and projection. Like them, I find two-dimensional work*

exciting. And I like the idea of a crossover between fashion, painting and illustration.

This is one of the best examples of the 'creative self' as a performative strategy which constitutes the graduating designer as artist through the very act of self-description. Everything he says contributes to confirming this identity. The exuberant conflation of fashion with the fine arts serves as a kind of overstatement of intent on the part of the student preparing for his degree show. It also echoes the art school ethos of exploring the boundaries between different art practices. The student clearly wants to challenge the basis of what we mean by fashion and this is summed up in the disregard he shows for finish. He emphatically doesn't care about 'finish' and doesn't want to have to do the sewing and handwork to achieve this polished or professional look. He discounts money in favour of the designer doing what he or she believes in. And he positions the fashion designer firmly within the landscape of the art world. The more shocking his stance and his collection, the better, since shocking or outrageous clothes are not only more likely to attract attention, they also bring the designer closer to the kind of artists who find themselves ridiculed or scorned (though hopefully admired by the significant audience) for wasting the taxpayers' money. And finally, abstract or difficult work on the catwalk is also testimony to the avantgarde aspirations of the designers. Whether or not this approach pays off, it demonstrates very clearly how so many of the designers ideally see themselves, especially in the first year or so after leaving college. The girls may be less sure of themselves and more muted in their hopes and dreams, but the imagery of the creative artist tallies exactly with what they want to achieve. And for some like Celia M., as we shall see, this language is utilised with the same vigour as it is by the boys.

The designers working in the United Kingdom who most clearly personify the fashion designer as practising artist are John Galliano, Vivienne Westwood and, more recently, Hussein Chalayan. Both males are graduates of Central St Martins, Galliano in 1984 and Chalayan ten years later in 1994. Westwood's design education came through the do-it-yourself ethos of the punk movement in the mid-1970s and is reflective of the kind of informal training I described in the introductory chapter as not unusual within the field of British youth subcultures. Despite these similarities the artistic strategies they employ are quite different. Galliano is frequently described as a 'maverick genius' possessing 'outstanding talent' and, as the acknowledged favourite of fashion journalists, has received more coverage than almost all the other well-known United Kingdom fashion designers put together. He 'claims never to have read a book' but, according to Sally Brampton in the *Guardian* 'one need only look at the collection of John Galliano or Vivienne Westwood to appreciate the mastery of fantasy sometimes wantonly perverse and sometimes lyrically beautifully that this culture can produce.' Galliano also fulfils all the qualifying criteria as a struggling artist, sometimes misunderstood but true to his own ideals and talent. One of the graduating students (who has since followed the same rapid pathway to success) described his time working for Galliano as follows:

It was brilliant, I learnt so much from him. He is like a child excited by ideas. He's got no business sense at all. It's all complete naÏvety, the way he works. It's instinct, feeling and imagination. He would ask me out of the blue, what do you think of this? He has such vision and strong themes, like his bias cut, throughout all his work. He's also aware of other influential designers like Westwood and he looks closely at what she is doing.

This comment demonstrates once again those 'technologies of the self' which can now be recognised as producing the fashion design 'subject'. Galliano is childlike, instinctual, ignores the need to make money, possesses 'vision' but has also mastered specific and recognisable techniques, for example, bias cut. Journalists, friends and admirers help to make this space for the creative subject by repeating, often mantra-like, its mythological elements. Galliano's various financial disasters and his time spent sleeping on friends' floors in Paris with no money to buy food, never mind the fabric for his collection, have been told and retold. He has consequently emerged as head designer for the French house of Givenchy (and more recently Dior), as a haute couturist of acclaimed genius Hussein Chalayan 'performs' as an artist even more uncompromisingly than many of his counterparts. He attracted the attention of the fashion press at the Central St Martins degree show in 1994 when his collection was accompanied by a text which told the narrative of its own construction. The story of how the clothes had been buried in earth for some weeks and were then disinterred and shown on the catwalk in this grimy state was then further explained in the context of another story, a fictional meta-narrative written by Chalayan himself. This kind of 'textual fashion' bore all the hallmarks of contemporary mixed-media art. It attracted a lot of attention and put Chalayan on the fashion map almost instantly. As he said to journalist Andrew Tuck:

> *I just happen to symbolise my ideas with clothes. I am a fashion designer technically because my clothes are sold in shops, but on my card it doesn't say 'Hussein Chalayan, fashion designer', just 'Hussein Chalayan'. I think some of the clothes could be hung on a wall and because there are pieces of writing in them perhaps that would remind you of things like an ornament does.*

As part of his prize-winning collection Hussein had yet another piece of narrative printed onto one of his full-length dresses which could then be read down the dress from top to bottom. He explained:

> *I wrote a fictional story which related to the collection and printed it on a dress, the clothes symbolise the story. Parts of the story are sewn into garments, it involved you with how the garment evolved, the garment had a history, as labels, facings, back, pocket.*

Chalayan envisages himself less as a fashion designer and more as an artist working with ideas through the medium of clothes, fashion and textiles. In both the above examples of his work, he is concerned with drawing attention to the material processes of garment construction. He presents himself as an intellectual or theoretical designer: 'Basically I'm very much against the mechanistic world view, this whole idea of mechanising everything and creating formulas and models for things we can't really rationalise. Descartes was someone who created this whole world view'.

Vivienne Westwood also embraces a strongly fine art mode. She does this by returning to the world of classical painting and incorporating elements of dress and costume and other items found in a wide range of works, drawn from over the centuries. Westwood combines these historical references with a number of more constant themes based around contemporary femininity, female sexuality and ideals of beauty. She presents herself with an air of practised eccentricity, which is of course a recognisable and accepted way of being an artist. She affects a combination of British matronliness (a 'dame') with girlish naïvety. This exonerates her from the charge of taking liberties with history. She can delight in the production details of the dresses of Marie Antoinette, for example, without any broader references to their symbolic significance as signs of unacceptable wealth and luxury in the context of the French Revolution. So, despite the radical vision of Westwood in terms of the images she creates of women which break sexual taboos and suggest female strength and power, she actually reactivates the most conservative tradition in the history of costume (which is to extrapolate items of clothing from their social context) and integrates this into her work as an innovative fashion designer. Westwood makes definitive, often disconnected, statements in relation to her work: 'I work from my academic interests, like baroque theatre, for example. The Rococo period offers wonderful drapery'.

Despite this blindness to the political context from which she selects her historical references, fashion journalists heap praise on Britain's most famous woman fashion designer: 'Vivienne Westwood uses fine art and literature as her inspiration rather than poring over the rails of clothes on the high street'. However, like Galliano, when Westwood talks about how she actually works, she becomes a craftswoman. This corresponds with Becker's account of how artists make use of, or draw upon the language of craft when discussing the technical details of their work. So it is quite admissible for Westwood to say, as she did in her recent television series, 'my work is anchored in English tailoring.' Or that creativity comes through technique, or that fashion is 'the manipulation of materials, as it is with painting. Every tiny decision you make, this is technique. You have to work in a craft way or a technical way to be creative. You have to build up the finished result.' At the same time she says: 'students must learn to draw, life drawing builds up judgement and aestheticism'.

All three of these designers conform to the accepted image of the practising artist. Their interviews frequently take the form of statements or proclamations. These comprise a 'poetics' of the work, a commitment to technique and a location of the work in philosophy (Chalayan's Descartes), history (Galliano's Les *Incroyables*) or period (Westwood's *Rococo*). These provide titles, captions and headlines for the shows which are easily appropriated by journalists, and so once again the art dimension is qualified by the pitch for the market and for publicity. This particular 'articulation of elements' has set a standard for that distinctive presentation of work which is now the mark of identity of the United Kingdom fashion designer. For most of the young designers, and for the less well-known designers interviewed for this book, these elements are less flamboyantly combined but they still provide a crucial underpinning for the work by providing an authoritative art-world frame of reference:

> *We are both strongly influenced by the fine art tradition in fashion. Our last collection started off by drawing on two colours combined in the work of Mark Rothko a very distinctive blue and a chocolate brown. For this coming season we have been going back through Paul Klee's paintings and that feeling will come across strongly in the clothes we are planning to make.*

Several of the graduates associated this crossover between art, fashion and also literature with their training. Christine F. commented: 'The emphasis at college was on ideas and history. I did a whole project on the world of Vita Sackville West. I've tried to hold onto the art aspect of fashion in my current work.' This kind of approach was confirmed in an article in the London *Evening Standard* which included a statement from the Dean of Fashion at Central St Martins, Jane Rapley:

> *We deal with concepts and visual metaphors, not one shirt, two jackets, three pairs of trousers. Our students are more likely to say 'I'm really excited about the American heartland'. We've bent over backwards to 'keep our flexibility. It's a gamble sometimes it works, sometimes it doesn't.*

The journalist added: 'Certainly Central St Martins is more serious than it was, but it's still a place where you are more likely to be asked to design around a piece of music than draw up a co-ordinated collection for Principles'.

Fashion design culture needs art to explain its dynamic and its creative drive both to itself and to the outside world. Art acts as a source of legitimation. For this reason the designers eagerly refer to its authority. It provides a means of explaining themselves and their work to the public. Celia M. echoes the romantic tradition of Wordsworth to describe how she works:

> *I am not like most fashion people who think things out in advance. It pours out of me. It's a totally emotional process. I'm a designer with passion and motivation, and I work like that. I like making clothes and dressing up. Sometimes I dream my next collection, I have millions of clothes in my head that I haven't got the time to produce them. It's like painting with the body as a canvas. Every garment in my collection has been on my body.*

And it is precisely this kind of identification which led a spokesperson for the British Fashion Council to comment in August 1993:

> *Living on a shoestring is how most fine artists exist. How many of themmake a decent living? British fashion designers see themselves in the same way. It s a distinctive mentality. They would rather do their ownthing, even if it never sells. It's a complete cottage industry in theUnited Kingdom.*

Craftsmanship and Fashion Design

We have seen how art provides a vocabulary of value and personal confirmation for fashion designers. It also grants them legitimate access to a language which permits a degree of abstraction, not to say obfuscation. In fact, when they talk about how they actually work there is a noticeable shift away from an aesthetic vocabulary towards a more technical or practical one. The values of craftsmanship suddenly appear on the agenda and the more rhetorical flourishes of art temporarily fade away:

> *I work with plain fabrics, never prints. It's a very small collection and very careful. I do viscose jersey, silk trousers and crepes. It 's simple and understated. I go to the fabric shows twice a year and I know my clothes are pricey because I only use expensive fabrics. Tweeds are OK in Britain, but nothing else. You have to buy from France or Italy. We work on a shoestring, no doubt about that. I am committed to my design work and I like to work in a totally creative environment which is what we have made the studio, with the bits of sculpture, the music and so on. The problem is finding a way of doing this kind of work and making a living. I don't know the answer to that one yet.*

Paula's account of her working practice offers a clear insight into 'creative labour' as a combination of artistic endeavour and craft-like skill. Her expertise is evident in the conception of the collection and the knowledge of fabrics, while the studio decorated with its pieces of sculpture and with background music provides a'high art' environment for inspiration and ideas. It also provides the important 'space' which confirms her creative identity.

Yvette M. and Lisa R. lasted only five years in business before being forced to declare themselves bankrupt. They were interviewed twice for this book, once just when they were heading for the media spotlight and then briefly again a few months after they went into receivership. At the time when they were attracting enthusiastic publicity they described their creative labour as follows:

> *We start with a colour and a piece of clothing that we like. With the last collection we began with a seventies pair of trousers and a jacket to go with it. We made them both up in calico as we couldn't afford to make up in real fabric. Then we did the amendments and the changes. For example, with this navy crepe suit we put in a lace-up front in the jacket instead of the buttons, which gives them what is basically a seventies shape but with a new feel to it. We pattern cut ourselves unless it is a jacket, in which case we pay a freelance pattern cutter to do it for us.*

Despite the emphasis on drawing as the basis for innovation and originality in design, and also as the point of connection with the world of fine art, during the interviews the graduates were keener to talk about working with the fabric and the idea than with the drawing and art-work stage. Overall, they were less concerned with being at the drawing board and more interested in seeing the garment emerge as an object in itself. Only one designer mentioned drawing and she quickly moved from there on to talking about the next stage:

> *At the beginning I'm at the drawing board all day and if I end up with three sketches that I like, I'm happy and I feel I've done a good day's work. Then I do a sample on the knitting machine and then I go back and rethink the colours and the texture and it just keeps developing until I've got the right yarns, the right shape and the feel for the whole garment.*

Celia M. who, as we have already seen, most closely conforms to the image of the designer as visual artist, also repudiates the drawing stage, but this time from a position which reconfirms her identity as an artist/sculptor:

> *I work in a very unorthodox way. I cut straight into the fabric as soon as the ideas have formulated. I find that drawing beforehand stunts the natural direction. I follow any interesting mistakes, which somehow determine my whole collection. After having adjusted and readjusted a garment, I then make a pattern by taking the rough sample apart. It is then re-cut and passed onto my machinist to finalise the small finishing details.*

The three women team who work under the English Eccentrics label developed a division of labour as follows:

> *The starting point is Helen Littman's abstracted, lushly coloured, rich prints, mostly on silk but also on heavy cotton. The three women work on colours and themes together but the actual designing of the prints is done by Helen who is exceptionally talented in her field.*

In another interview for the Telegraph magazine, Helen Littman describes how they got started: 'We would print, cut and sew and then try to sell what we made.' The journalist comments that like so many other British designers, English Eccentrics 'began by selling homemade clothes at Camden Lock market in London.' 'We used to carry huge rolls of fabric around on the Tube,' Judy says. 'We would print it ourselves on the concrete floor of this place in Wapping and then smuggle the clothes into a launderette and bake on the dyes in the tumble driers'. The emphasis on craftsmanship in the work of English Eccentrics has been praised throughout the fashion press:

> *It is the beautiful patterns which make the garments of English Eccentrics so distinctive. The clothes themselves are those simple, well-cut classics shirts, tunics, waistcoats which hardly deviate in line from season to season. The silks from which they are made, however, are printed with Helen Littman's designs. These are rococo fantasies peopled with cherubs, dodos, whorls and curlicues of fantastic colours. An outfit by English Eccentrics does not come cheap. The fabric is cut by hand to ensure that the design is centred on the back of each garment. The printing too is done by hand and a screen has to be made for each colour.*

Helen Littman also remembers the influence of the arts and craft tradition on the undergraduate course she did at Camberwell School of Art, and the way this influenced her own practice as a designer and her preference for producing individual handcrafted garments in favour of long runs and higher profit margins: 'There was a craft emphasis, a William Morris feel to the course and it was very good indeed on the technical stuff'.

Engrossed in work, the designers, like those mentioned above, switch their vocabularies to embrace the craft dimension of their practice. They emphasise their involvement right through from the start to the finish of the single garment. They rely on a machinist close at hand and also need the services of a pattern cutter, and it is this small team-based approach which actually provides the framework for 'creative labour'. Indeed, it is this craft element which provides a crucial underpinning for the art work. Becker has described this process in the following terms:

> *Members of art worlds often distinguish between art and craft. They recognise that making art requires technical skills that might be seen as craft skills, but they also typically insist that artists contribute something beyond craft skill to the product, something due to their creative abilities*

and gifts that gives each object or performance a unique or expressive character.

Designers like John Galliano who have reached the heights of fame and success are more able to acknowledge this dimension than others who still need to promote a more inspirational and purely creative image of the designer. Galliano shrugs off the label of artistic genius by claiming that 'It doesn't take into account all the hours of work that go into making something look right. Or the people I have around me who are brilliant'. This also corresponds with Becker's important argument that art is the product of collaboration: 'art is social in being created by networks of people acting together'. Galliano's interest in the fine details of technique, 'we had the spots especially printed down, so when the fabric's cut on the cross, all the spots go round the body and are never interrupted by a seam' forces the journalists to acknowledge that his work is as much about craft as it is about art, 'For it is his craft which most absorbs him, he is one of the greatest technicians working in fashion anywhere today'.

In conclusion, art codes introduce the work of the designers, typically in the form of a 'statement', and function also as promotional devices (in the press releases). Most importantly, they provide an anchor of identity for the graduate designers. This language is strategically deployed as the highest status of the available discourses of self-representation available to graduates who have been through the art school system. It makes the misery of being poor, and the disappointment of not being successful, something that can be turned into a legitimate mythology of being misunderstood. It is also a discourse of hope since the mythology of the struggling artist is that quite suddenly and unexpectedly he or she will find success and recognition. Finally, it is appealing because it corresponds with the images (and fantasies) of creative work which in a post-industrial economy have taken on a new importance. Fashion in this respect has benefited from the new culture of creativity as the aura of art has moved beyond the fine arts to embrace cultural fields previously seen as 'lesser arts'. However, in the dayto-day environment of the studio, a more practical and technical language evolves and this involves knowledge of, and expertise about, fabric and cut and the way a garment will hang and it is also about trial and error and process. Skill and technique come into this as does the need for collaboration and for teamwork. But this all stops short at the point of putting a collection into production. The 'arts and craft' vocabulary, anxious to rid fashion of any connotations of the 'rag trade' and thus secure its own autonomy, conceals the equally important but menial practice of manufacture and production.

Back in the outside world, the art language and the individual image of the designer (with his or her own distinctive design 'signature') is part of the process of marketing and also branding. These come together in the concept of the label. So there is a double movement around the status and meaning of art. On the one hand, it represents integrity and the disavowal of the marketplace, on the other hand, it gives fashion the aura, status and the distinctiveness it needs to set itself apart from the high street and the rag trade, as a kind of niche market. It therefore also functions, with all its pretensions, as a commercial device. The designer as artist retains a value on the freelance or consultancy job market as a name with an image. But the imperative of the market is balanced by the sheer effort of the designers to see their work hung on gallery walls, featured in art magazines such as *Artforum* and acknowledged as an object, piece or collection like an 'installation' or 'performance'. Ally Capellino's new outlet, opened in July 1997, describes itself as having an 'exhibition space' at the far end of the store. This kind of art space is where the fashion designers want to be. They also want to sell clothes and make a living. Celia M. and Hussein Chalayan are 'artists' who happen to be working with fashion and, as we have seen, the scissors and the fabrics are their paint and canvases. This raises the interesting question of whether fashion actually offers a more successful career for the conceptual artist, than the more conventional practices of fine art. In which case the business of fashion takes a legitimately secondary place, while the market and the publicity for this kind of 'art-fashion' is even more extensive and enthusiastic than it is for conventional art, for the simple reason that the supermodels add a further element of visual interest. This scenario suggests an even more fluid mix of the categories of art and craft, high culture and low culture, practice and production.

❑❑❑

10

Nationalising the Fashion Industry

Introduction

Italy very much followed the capitalist model common to other European countries and the USA. It must be remembered, of course, that thanks for the results achieved in all sectors of the Italian economy went in great part to the massive exploitation of low wage laborers, the majority of whom were women and children from rural areas, as dress historian Grazietta Butazzi has noted. The basis of Italy's textile industry, then, did not differ much from that of the US garment industry, which expanded considerably in these decades on the back of the huge immigrant workforce, composed to a great extent of Italians, many of them seamstresses, embroiderers and tailors.

Under fascism, the Italian textile industry took two directions, one traditional, promoting regional handicraft products like lace and embroidery; the other more innovative, giving great attention to the development of the so-called new intelligent fibers like rayon. This latter, in fact, came to embody not only the very stuff of the modern image the regime sought to promote of itself, but also a tangible sign of the nation's economic self-sufficiency. Indeed, the advance in production techniques that had given birth to rayon was to be presented as propaganda for the regime, a task that was assigned to the fashion and specialized magazines of the period, as emerges clearly from the extant ENM documentation on the intelligent fibers.

At the same time, however, as it promoted these breakthroughs in technology as signs of modernity, the regime never neglected to emphasize its foundations in traditions and well-established practices. In the field of textiles, for example, a survey of the ENM documentation reveals how at an ideological level the mix of the new and the traditional was to be the battle cry of the regime's propaganda campaign. I here use the term "propaganda" in the sense of "integration" and not in that of "agitation." According to the classification developed by Philip Cannistraro these are the two modes of propaganda to which the regime had recourse at different times. If propaganda by means of agitation had characterized the first revolutionary phase of fascism, between 1919 and 1922, and aimed at achieving quick short-term results, propaganda by means of integration was typical of the phase in which the regime consolidated its power. This latter type of propaganda sought long-term results and acted in a much more indirect manner. If agitation propaganda can be considered a kind of coercion, integration propaganda is a kind of more subtle non-coercive coercion. It was based, in fact, on commonplaces and myths - those of the virile man, and of woman as Mediterranean mother, a model of round-hipped beauty - that were already firmly in place and well-sedimented in Italian culture and daily practices. These myths and others like them, such as the dynamism of the northern cities and the false use of southern culture, peasants and massaie working with textiles, etc., were presented with a veneer of modernity attached to them and came to represent models on which to base one's sense of a fascist identity. It is in the context of this construction of a fascist popular culture that fashion, along with the press, cinema and newsreels, took on an important role for the regime.

One of the strongest propaganda slogans transmitted by the regime as soon as the ENM was founded in 1932, and which exposed the nationalist intent that lay behind this phase of fascist policy on fashion, was that "the Italian woman must follow Italian fashion." Through some of the Istituto Luce newsreels, one of fascism's favorite media of persuasion, we can track this strand of policy, especially in the coverage the newsreels gave to the National Fashion Exhibitions. The first of these was held in Turin in 1933 and was inaugurated by Elena of Savoy, Queen of Italy. To the fore, in the coverage of this event, even before we see the actual shots of the inauguration, we read in very large letters that *La donna italiana deve seguire la moda italiana. Gusto, eleganza, originalità hanno dimostrato che la iniziativa può e deve avere successo* (The Italian woman must follow Italian fashion. Taste, elegance and originality have demonstrated that this initiative can and must be a success). After this, we see a tracking shot of the art deco building where the exhibition is held and where the queen arrives welcomed by the *gerarchi,* all of them surrounded by a large crowd. Following these opening shots we see a series of scenes that focus on single outfits worn by dummies displayed in shop windows. We, then, see real mannequins, surrounded by linear and modern furniture that complements their style of dress, wearing suits, cocktail and evening gowns, and sports outfits. Parallel to this display of modernity, the camera gives special emphasis to local traditions. As well as a great variety of accessories, lace is given special attention. This was to be a recurrent trend at the subsequent semiannual exhibitions. Local craftsmanship would always be presented and exhibited alongside new models and textiles, underlining the fascist desire to combine tradition with modernity and to stress the economic importance of industry and craftsmanship.

Another Luce newsreel, this time from 1936, shown in the midst of the autarchic phase, covers the National Exhibition of Textile and Clothing in Turin. Here, we first see a medium shot of the motto *Vestire italianamente* (Dress in an Italian manner), written on the building where the exhibition was housed, while in a tracking shot the camera dwells on the word RAYON written, like the slogan, in huge letters. Rayon, in fact, was one of the regime's great successes in the field of textiles and Italians were enjoined to produce and buy clothes made out of this home-produced intelligent fiber. A domestically produced fabric to which could be given a veneer of modernity, rayon came to be identified with national identity and patriotism, as is made clear by the juxtaposition of the shots at the opening of the 1936 newsreel.

With the Ethiopian War and the subsequent sanctions imposed upon Italy by the League of Nations, Mussolini proclaimed the nation's economic autarchy and, in the field of fashion, the quest for home-produced fabrics became keener. For the textile industry and for individual designers and dressmakers this phase can be likened to a smithy of creativity. The nationalistic intent, which had been the prime mover behind the fascist policy to legislate the fashion industry, was now accompanied by the economic necessity to survive the crisis and avoid the danger of political isolation. The move towards autarchy was facilitated by the fact that on account of foreign sanctions Italy had little alternative other than to withdraw into itself in order to survive. But if isolation had a price, it also had unexpected benefits. The imposition of sanctions, in fact, had the immediate effect of increasing the level of research and experimentation in textile and design. We can follow much of what was happening in the fashion industry at this time through the specialist textile periodicals and other fashion magazines. These are testimony, certainly, to fascist propaganda, but at the same time they furnish a great deal of information about the activities and the debate on the promotion of Italian fashion and industry.

But how exactly did the textile industry enact a process of modernization? This is no simple question for a nation like Italy that was not as industrialized as Great Britain or France, countries that since the nineteenth century could count on resources, especially textiles, from their colonies. Moreover, the British textile industry profited from a more stable and centralized government, whereas in Italy the deep north/south gap, as well as problems inherited from a very complex and relatively recent unification, still had a great bearing on industrial development, the textile industry in particular. Issues such as these were addressed in the study conducted in 1937 by Roberto Tremelloni, *L'industria tessile italiana* (The Italian textile industry). Here, Tremelloni pointed out that, despite all its structural problems, the Italian textile industry had achieved steady growth and surprising results. Many companies had created experimental chemical and research laboratories in order to further their studies in new areas, above all in the creation of artificial fibers. Indeed, this branch of the industry, he went on, was at the head of a worldwide technological revolution in the production and consumption of fashion and styles. Artificial fibers were playing an increasingly important role in manufacturing all over the world.

In an article entitled "I tessuti artificiali" (Artificial textiles), published in the monthly review *Vita Tessile*, the author, a certain Lancellotti, referring to the aforementioned statistics, writes of the progress made by the textile industry and the impact it had had on both Italy and the world. He begins, however, with a historical overview. The production of artificial fibers, he states, had begun with a series of unsuccessful experiments in the sixteenth century and continued, still with little success, throughout the following centuries. It was only in the nineteenth century that any real progress was made and Lancellotti goes out of his way to highlight the role played in this by the Italian textile industry, and the results it had subsequently achieved in the relatively short span of time since the end of World War I. In these twenty years, in fact, Italy had become the leading European producer of rayon and second in the world only to the USA.

After taking its initial steps from 1904 onwards, the Italian artificial fiber industry took off in 1919 when the SNIA, which had been founded in 1917 as an Italian-American Shipping Company, was reconfigured as an Industrial and Commercial Shipping Company. Gradually the SNIA acquired control of a number of textile companies and by 1929 it had become one of the major groups in the world production of artificial fibers. Indeed, in the years following World War I, Italian production of artificial fibers increased consistently and in 1929 reached its peak accounting for 16 percent of world production.

In the early 1930s, silk production, which in Italy was an important tradition going back to the Renaissance, and artificial fibers represented the two main profitmaking entries in the national trade balance, the modern fiber and the traditional fabric each playing equally important roles. In this regard, the old Italian tradition of knitwear and stockings had an important role for the fashion industry and its developments in the 1930s. The economic historian Carlo Marco Belfanti affirms in fact that:

> *At the end of WWI expansion in the hosiery branch of knitting was recommended and took on a definitive role with a prime position in the knitwear sector. According to an estimate from 1930, the Italian market consumed around 21 million dozen pairs of socks a year, of which half were for female consumption. In the same period the material chiefly employed was cotton, a fibre from which about 70% of hosiery was*

made, while wool had seen a reduction in its use, as had natural silk. Instead artificial fibres like viscose, acetate and cuproammonia were gaining ground. In the second half of the thirties, the three types of thread that were most widely employed in this branch of hosiery were rayon, bamberg and natural silk.

Belfanti also notes that in this phase, as well as in earlier phases of the evolution of the industry, the presence of an organized network of very small businesses completely eluded the view of government statisticians.

If the propaganda surrounding artificial fibers stressed its modernity, that surrounding silk underlined its time-honoured qualities. *La seta,* the official publication of the *Federazione Nazionale Fascista degli industriali della seta* (National fascist organization of silk producers) published very detailed articles about the history of sericulture in Italian cities, their modes of organization and production. In "I primati degli antichi setaioli bolognesi" (The primacy of the ancient Bolognese silk workers), for example, Cesare Marchesini illustrates the steps taken by the industry from the second half of the thirteenth century onwards when a series of decrees facilitated and boosted the production and quality of silk.

With the autarchic phase, however, a new problem arose that threatened to compromise self-sufficiency in artificial fibers. Cellulose, an integral component for the production of fibers, was, in fact, largely imported, since conifers, from which the substance was extracted, were in short supply in Italy. To overcome this very real obstacle, imports of the product being all but impossible, researchers at the SNIA-Viscosa company arrived at a brilliant solution. They discovered that an annual plant called *canna gentile* that grew naturally in some areas of Italy could replace the kind of cellulose that was produced in the northern European forests. In 1936, the SNIA acquired a field near the small village of Torre di Zuino, later renamed by Mussolini as Torviscosa, and located in the area between Venice and Trieste.

Chemical experiments, which intensified in Italy in the autarchic phase, had meant that since the late nineteenth century artificial fibers and textiles similar to those produced in nature had been developed in both Europe and the USA. It must be said, however, that the success of artificial fibers was above all a result of the drastic cultural changes that had taken and were taking place in Italy and elsewhere in the Western world. On account of the simplification of taste in styles, colors and decoration, the amount of time it took to produce a garment dropped significantly, as did its cost. This conferred an extra attractiveness synthetic fabrics that already had the cachet of being modern. Without doubt, they represented a key element in the democratization of fashion and in its revolutionary charge in terms of large-scale production and consumption. Just as importantly, artificial fibers also meant that countries like Italy and their national industries were no longer dependent on variables like geography, weather or political vicissitudes as they had been for the production of garments using natural textiles such as cotton, linen, silk and wool. Given these advantages, it is clear why the fascist regime acted quickly to control and promote to the full the textile, clothing and fashion industries. The interests and scopes of the regime, however, were not only domestically oriented. As we have already noted, the creation of a "national" style and taste also took on the form of an important political and cultural battle that inevitably intertwined with the sense of identity the nation had of itself both at home and as concerns the perception of Italy from abroad. It should not be forgotten that under fascism Italy still maintained strong economic and commercial ties with the USA and Europe, it being only with the outbreak of World War II that the ties lessened somewhat.

Fascism had an eagle eye for how the rest of Europe and the USA regarded Italy and what the foreign response was to the steps taken by the regime in its domestic policy. Consequently, the regime was always quick to publicize any positive comments it received from its neighbors. In the world of fashion, for example, the regime seemed especially alert to the fact that components of fascist uniforms like the black shirt and the fez had become fashion items in France. In 1935, for example, *France Vogue* published an article on the *bonnet du fascio,* headgear that was very similar to the *fez* worn by members of the fascist militia. *Vogue* suggested wearing the fez with a deep green suit trimmed with astrakhan fur, leaving the jacket open in order to show off the black shirt. This French readaptation of items drawn from fascist uniforms was a sign of the fascination exercised by the aesthetic side of fascism that then gripped, and still today occasionally grips, fashion designers. But more than this, the report on the incorporation of a recognizably fascist iconography into the world of French fashion also underlined the fact that the regime had succeeded in producing a strong international image of itself.

Let us now go back to the most important public steps taken by the regime in the field of textiles. As a result of a national conference held in Forlì from December 11 to 13 1937 on National Textile Fibers, the regime decided to set up the *Ente Tessile Nazionale* (National textile body), to which it delegated the task of promoting and encouraging self-sufficiency - autarchy - in textile production. The main purpose of the *Ente Tessile Nazionale,* whose existence was ratified by a decree of April 1937, was to develop close collaborative ties to the several *Corporazioni dei prodotti tessili e dell'abbigliamento* (Corporations of textile products and clothing) and to coordinate its policy for the production of fibers with the Ministry of Agriculture and Forestry. In addition, but no less importantly, the *Ente Tessile,* like the ENM, had the function of publicizing the use and care of the new textiles. It was during the Forlì conference that the ENM underlined the intimate link between the textile and the garment manufacture industry. The concern here was not only one of a domestic patriotic nature, but was also and above all a concern not to lose contact with the international centers of fashion. Indeed, such contact was overtly stressed and the two industries, according to the regime, were to provide "the creative inventiveness of Italian taste in the style of dress for which truly Italian products were to be used." It goes without saying that state backing of the textile and garment industries was, in the long run and especially in the period after World War II, to become beneficial to both. Legislation regulating fashion under fascism played a key role in the involvement of the State and its ad hoc institutions in the production of clothes. Nevertheless, despite the emphasis on autarchy and things Italian, fashion houses never completely ceased to look for inspiration to Parisian fashion, as the designer Fernanda Gattinoni, who used to work for *Casa Ventura* with branches in Rome and Milan, has recalled. France remained a fixed reference point and Rina Pedrini, for example, one of the best-known pattern makers of the epoch retained an important role in the spread of French fashion in Italy. She, it is said, never missed a Parisian collection and over the years acquired at least 250 models that she reproduced and then sold to dressmakers.

All the same, the regime was tenacious in its legislation designed to encourage the production and consumption of clothes of domestic provenance. A Decree of June 26, 1936, for example, authorized the institution of a certificate of guarantee for clothing and accessories approved by the Ente. A year later, in 1937, a label called *Textorit* came into being as the equivalent certificate of guarantee for textiles. In 1938, the *Corporazione dell'abbigliamento* (Clothing corporation) amended the 1936 law, including sanctions against transgressors, and added another kind of certificate, this time known as the certificate of creation and given only to couture clothing that was particularly outstanding for its originality and *italianità*. Subsequently, a decree of April 20 1939, regulating the blending of imported fibers like cotton and wool, established that 20 percent be the maximum amount that could be blended with natural or non-autarchic fibers. Rayon, silk, hemp, national linen, ramia or *ramì* (china grass), produced in Piedmont and in Libya, broom and all other fibers except cotton were considered autarchic fibers and were to be used for blending in cotton manufacture, whereas for wool manufacture lanital, rayon, rayon-fiocco, ramia (china grass), broom as well as the rabbit and angora rabbit hair that gradually became used on a wide scale were designated as autarchic fibers.

Lanital, described in Meano's dictionary as the most national of fibers and whose licence was acquired by the SNIA-Viscosa, was a synthetic textile obtained from milk casein and invented by an engineer named Ferretti. *Lanital,* or the "mozzarella" fabric that was so difficult to iron and to sew, as Micol Fontana jokingly recalls, was a domestic rival to imported wool and for this reason was greatly celebrated, alongside the technological achievements of the SNIA-Viscosa, in the Futurist Filippo Tommaso Marinetti's *Poema non umano dei tecnicismi* (Non-human poem of technicisms). In the course of 1937, in fact, the production of lanital skyrocketed from the 500 kg per day of the previous year to 7 million.

The Forli conference of 1937 was also the occasion for a huge exhibition of the autarchic textiles and included a competition whose first prize went to a fabric made of a black lanital and viscose embroidered relief. Along these lines, a great deal of effort went into the creation of alternative wools like *cisalfa,* which was a wool invented and put on the market by the Cisa-Viscosa company. Nationalist aims were also apparent in other fields of fashion.

Parallel to experiments in technology, a plan was elaborated to promote the regional production of more traditional textiles. One of the products encouraged in this way was *orbace,* the rough and robust Sardinian wool that was widely used for fascist winter uniforms. An article published by *La Nazione* tells us, in fact:

> *The Party Secretary, choosing* orbace *for the fascist winter uniform, has insisted that it be* orbace *made by Sardinian craftsmen. He has, therefore, gladly brought to our attention that the number of people working in this sector is 3,300, and of these about 1,500 work in the province of Nuoro where production has reached, as of today, 60% of that manufactured on the whole island.*

Still, in a context where tradition and innovation went hand in hand, rayon was considered the fabric *par excellence* of modernity, the "most modern of Italian textiles and the most Italian of modern textiles." The rayon-fiocco, a short rayon fibre, first introduced in 1935 by the SNIA-Viscosa, was a new and more versatile fabric that could be used in a much wider range of fabrics, creating new effects and brilliant colors. Often the judicious balance and mix of natural and artificial fibers offered advantages in the production of the fabric, sometimes even correcting or eliminating the disadvantages of natural fibers. In order to publicize rayon, the regime sponsored a rayon train, with shop windows like a department store, as well as a special truck equipped as a radio-cinema with mounted speakers broadcasting advertising tunes such as "Fili di sole" (Threads of the sun), a reference to the luminosity of the fabric. As well as the image of modernity that it transmitted, there were also more banal economic reasons behind the promotion of rayon. It was seen by the regime, first and foremost, replacement for expensive silk on the home market so that more of the latter could be destined for export and thus boost the national coffers.

In the regime's view, the production of artificial fibers was to complement that of natural fibers in the development of new uses and designs for fashion, accessories, furnishings, etc. This is the case with hemp, which was declared a national autarchic fiber whose high levels of production were singled out for praise in several of the regime's publications. Hemp had never been used to any great extent for clothing, however, on account of its brittleness and unsuitability. Again pressed by the constraints of economic isolation, necessity being the mother of invention, efforts were made, mixing hemp and *fiocco* with other artificial fibers, to reduce the stiffness of the fabric and render it suitable for clothing. It had been, in fact, its toughness and durability that had made it ideal for luggage and accessories. Now that it had been rendered more versatile, the regime ordered an increase in the production of hemp and promoted an impressive campaign aimed at hemp stockpiling. This, in fact, became law with a November 8, 1936 decree, supervised by the *Federcanapa,* the organization in charge of organizing and directing the new sanction. Indeed, hemp held a prominent position in the Italian pavilion at the World Exhibition of Textiles that was held in New York in 1939, where the *Federtessili* exhibited all the Italian textiles then in production, from silk to rayon and including the vast range of hemp and its combinations with artificial fibers such as the *canapafiocco.* Interestingly, this Italian fabric became so successful that a *canapa balilla* appeared in the 1935 Parisian fashion shows.

In a number of articles, the periodical *Fibre Tessili,* a publication whose ideological agenda was so close to the regime's heart that its pages are peppered with reiterations of the fascist slogan of "Impero, razza, autarchia" (Empire, race, autarchy), emphasized the importance of the production of hemp. One of these featured a poster of pictures of several hemp stockpiles accompanied by an English text explaining the advantages for the increase in the quality of the fabric. Moreover, what this poster aimed at showing was the interest Italy had in promoting a better trading relationship with the USA. In fact, the articles spell out the need to bolster this relationship on occasion of the future World Exhibition, another projected feather in the cap of fascist achievements, that was supposed to be held in Rome in 1942, but which was cancelled due to the outbreak of World War II. As a further sign of official sanction, the activities and work of the Federcanapa, as documented in a photographic report that was sent to fascist party headquarters, are highly praised by Secretary Starace in a telegram he sent to the "Presidente Federazioni Consorzi Difesa Canapicoltura" (President of the federation and consortia for the defence of hemp cultivation).

Interestingly, it is not only the economic advantages to the production of hemp that are emphasized in specialist publications such as *Fibre Tessili.* One may be surprised, perhaps, at the seemingly inordinate amount of space that they give over to accounts of the workers' leisure time activities that were organized by the local

Dopolavoro associations, especially those of the workers in the key consortia in Bologna and Rovigo. In several Italian cities and regions in which textiles were produced, the *Dopolavoro* often organized exhibitions in conjunction with the silk and hemp associations. An important part of these exhibitions was the awarding of prizes to those *massaie rurali* and *dopolavoristi* who had distinguished themselves in the workplace. This was little more than a trick, of course, used by the regime to induce workers to think of themselves as protagonists in a great project rather than as exploited members of a subaltern class.

In the field of textiles, attempts were also made to Italianize fashion. As well as the linguistic project of Italianizing the French terms commonly used, the process of disciplining the social body bore on the economic as well as the personal, extending its reach to all branches of culture, sport, leisure and fashion. It is for these reasons that Riccardo Del Giudice, President of the *Confederazione fascista dei lavoratori e del commercio* (Fascist confederation of workers and commerce), writing in the article "Autarchia tessile. Contributo dei lavoratori del commercio" (Textile self-sufficiency. Contribution of trade workers), expressed the belief that all the steps taken by the regime in the field of fashion led to, in his view, the "work of national reeducation and propaganda of *italianità.*" The author gives a list of the most important steps undertaken by the institutions set up by the regime following the Forli' "Convegno delle fibre tessili nazionali e dell'impero" that, as mentioned already, spawned a massive plan to achieve Italy's economic selfsufficiency. He states, in fact, that "we cannot explain to others, still less persuade them, if we do not have a culture suitable to our aim."

Similarly, several local and national exhibitions, like the one held at the Circo Massimo in Rome, the *Mostra del tessile nazionale* (Exhibition of national textiles), one of the biggest, promoted the production of domestic textiles. Inaugurated on November 18, 1937 and kept open until January 31, 1938, the exhibition was organized by Starace and saw the participation of all the associations and institutions connected to the textile industries. In the numerous stands regional handicrafts and autarchic textiles like rayon and lanital were exhibited. On its own stand, the SNIA-Viscosa, as well as showing the stages of production of *lanital,* also organized a fashion show on December 21. Along with "The week of artificial fibers" in January 1938, this was one of the major events of the exhibition. In a populist and folkloric manner, the exhibition also emphasized the work of the *massaie rurali*. Given great prominence by the *Giornale Luce* newsreel, one stand mixed the modern and the traditional by showing a group of women weaving the new artificial yarns on their old-fashioned looms. One newsreel, in particular, produced in the spring of the same year as the Rome exhibition, covers the National Exhibition of Clothing and Textile held in Turin, where the new fibers played a major role. Here, the viewer is immediately introduced to the SNIA pavilion where a group of young women dressed in floral print dresses weave autarchic yarns at their loom. To this, a shot of technicians wearing their white work uniform (such as that worn by medical doctors and scientists) is juxtaposed. The women are framed in the act of offering the visitors a sample of the yarns for them to feel the fiber, while at the same time answering any questions they might have. Even without considering the obvious juxtaposition of the "old" looms of the women and the SNIA technology, this particular newsreel is interesting on account of the iconography of one of its advertisements. In fact, if we focus only on the representation of women, we find a confirmation of the fascist ploy of combining once again tradition - represented by the women who weave, which is a sort of archetypical image of woman-like Penelope - women who are not wearing the folkloric dress typical of the *massaie rurali,* but light and modern dresses made out of the new fabric they are advertising, thus emphasizing their young and slender bodies. Nothing better than these images offers a more vivid illustration of the fascist ideology of incorporating tradition while at the same time striving for modernity.

As we mentioned, as part of the events at the Circo Massimo exhibition, a fashion show was organized, and among its guests of honor were Dino Alfieri, the Minister for Popular Culture and the poet Marinetti who at the conclusion of the event read his "Poesia simultanea della moda italiana" (Simultaneous poem of Italian fashion), an aestheticized celebration of the "arbitrary whimsical and fantastic" character of fashion. As Cinzia Sartini Blum has noted, for Marinetti: "Anything goes, provided it is 'made in Italy' and is 'favorable to woman's feline softness'." We might recall that Futurist writers and artists had been, since the beginning, involved in conceptualizing and redesigning male and female wardrobes. In

1920, Volt, the pseudonym of Vincenzo Fani, wrote the "Futurist Manifesto of Women's Fashion." Here, the author establishes an equivalent relationship between fashion, women and Futurism identified in: "Speed, novelty, courage of creation." Volt stresses the need to reconsider the greyness and conservatism of some current styles. Instead of considering them to be of "good taste," he labels them with "lack of originality, a withering of fantasy." In the final paragraph of the manifesto, Volt underscores that the three-year war period had inevitably led to the lack of materials such as silk and leather. It is for these reasons that, looking forward to the use of new and innovative materials, he proclaims:

> *The reign of silk in the history of female fashion must come to an end just as the reign of marble is now finished in architectural constructions. One hundred new revolutionary materials are rioting in the square, demanding to be admitted into the making of womanly clothes. We fling open wide the doors of the fashion ateliers to paper, cardboard, glass, tinfoil, aluminum, ceramic, rubber, fish skin, burlap, oakum, hemp, gas, growing plants, and living animals. Every woman will be a walking synthesis of the universe.*

Apart from the overt exaggeration of this long list provided by Volt, some of the materials mentioned, such as cardboard, hemp and growing plants, would be used in the production of accessories and clothes in the period of autarchy.

But if the Futurist concern with dress, here illustrated by Volt and Marinetti, was nothing new in the Italy of the 1930s, what was new was the nation's foray into colonial practices. These too were to have repercussions in the field of fashion.

In this respect an exhibition worth mentioning is the *IX Mostra-Mercato di Firenze* (Florence Trade Exhibition) held in the spring of 1939. Of interest here is the attention given to experiments in design and textiles that aimed at the creation of a new fashion for those Italians about to live in the newly acquired colonies of Ethiopia and Libya. To this end, a competition for "abbigliamento e arredamento coloniale" (colonial clothing and furnishings) was organized by the ENM in conjunction with the *Federazione Nazionale Fascista degli Artigiani e le Piccole Industrie* (National fascist federation of craftsmen and small companies). Acting as an indication of the cultural climate surrounding Italy's colonial experience, the coverage given to the exhibition by fashion magazines of the period, like the popular literature of the time, bore witness to the presence of a new imaginary landscape that mingled with existing visions of both fantastic geographical lands and true and proper models of male and female identity. A specific analysis of this very important topic goes beyond the scope of the present study, but it certainly deserves much critical attention. However, what I would like to underline very briefly is the bearing this had on the creation of the fashion discourse and on style.

Prior to the fascist invasion of Ethiopia, liberal Italy under the government of Francesco Crispi had already started colonial expansion. Indeed, Africa, since the second half of the nineteenth century had already entered, as historian Angelo Del Boca has pointed out, Italian homes in the forms of popular newspapers and magazines such as *L'illustrazione italiana, L'esploratore, Il giornale popolare di viaggi* and others. Fashion magazines such as *Lidel* and *Bellezza* contained a variety of articles and references to the colonies and their products. For instance, Mario Scaparro, author of *L'artigianato tripolino,* wrote an article for *Lidel* entitled "Tripolitania" in which he described the exotic landscapes epitomizing the "fascist work" of the colonizers who administered the foreign cities and territories, civilizing them under the western hand. He goes on to describe two faces of Tripoli: the one, the "barbarian city," the other the "Italian city," where he explains that fascist officials sought to preserve its integrity especially as far as local and crafts products were concerned. Pictures of local Libyan craftsmanship illustrate the article handbags, leather mules or "tarlik," with embroidery in parchment. These were all products that were becoming known then in Italy by way of exhibitions of "colonial art," thereby finding their way onto the European market. In the article we also find detailed descriptions of ethnic female clothing, with a picture of a beautiful young woman encapsulating the mythic vision of exotic Arab beauty. Often, however, in this colonial context, the images of feminine models are accompanied by an age-old paternalistic stereotype that sees civilized men offering uncivilized women the gift of culture, good manners and progress. Parallel to this we can also note a subtle Western fascination with an unknown culture - that of the colonies - and the resulting fertile terrain that this offered for literary and ideological representations. The magazine, *Lidel,* for instance, is punctuated with a series of articles on "L'eterno femminino nero" (The eternal black feminine nature) and "La donna abbissina," (The Abyssinian woman), accompanied by pictures of very attractive black women; or reports on *Mudundu,* a documentary shot in Somalia by newsreel journalists who worked for the *La Stampa* newspaper; or of another documentary called *Abissinia* that was edited by the *Istituto coloniale fascista* (Fascist colonial institute). In addition to this, articles on the Italian soldiers' civilizing mission, advertisements for perfumes with mysterious namessuch as *Egizia,* which was produced by the Ducale company in Parma - a city famous for fragrances - aimed to reinforce the power of exotic fascination. For example, in one advertisement for this perfume, we read: "*Egizia* Charm of distant lands, fragrance of exquisite essences " Confirming this new trend towards the exotic, the journalist Coronedi, commenting on the aforementioned exhibition of female colonial clothing in the pages of *Fibre Tessili,* wrote:

> *In the hall of the shiny glass central pavilion one can observe the exhibition of female colonial clothing. Bright white colors predominate, but are filtered by an intense range of tonalities of various nuances, from the warm earth of Siena to pale and fresh yellow straw.* Practicality and elegance, marked by harmonious Italian taste. *A true colonial wardrobe: a theory of particularly elegantly designed trousers made more attractive by the softness of their Meharist appearance Tight sport jackets, hemp safari jackets, and here and there an ample shawl* (sciamma) *with a hood as a reminder of the local costumes.*

It is fascinating to see how the description of the design of these garments and accessories projects the style linking "elegance and ease" that has become the landmark of the so-called "Italian taste." In the central pavilion of the same exhibition dedicated to *Novità, Moda, Tessili,* space was given to interesting experiments in shoes, for which Florence held an old tradition - as well as to textiles made out of straw, which was again a typical Florentine product. In addition, fabrics with sumptuous colors, geometrical prints or, in other cases, prints that take on the form of subtle arabesques recalling the interlace of Sienese fifteenth-century wrought iron were featured. New materials, then, were used creatively to develop new designs in clothing and accessories that mixed traditional Italian historical references with ethnic elements. Besides Ferragamo, Gucci also experimented with the use of new materials such as jute, linen and bamboo for his accessories.

By way of concluding this panoramic view of textiles, I would like to draw attention to the *Rassegna del tessile e dell'abbigliamento autarchico* (Review of textiles and autarchic clothing), organized in Venice in 1941 by the ENM in conjunction with the Textile and Clothing Industries and inaugurated on August 20th in the midst of World War II. In his article on the exhibition published in *Bellezza,* Lucio Ridenti noted that Venice, a city that had hosted important art exhibitions on painting, sculpture, theatre and cinema, had never before welcomed "into its Olympus a goddess who has not yet been officially included among the Muses." However, Venice's debut as host city was made possible by the talent and inspiration of the architect, graphic artist and illustrator Erberto Carboni, whose surrealistic installations gave an artistic twist to the event. Indeed, the exhibition, held at the Palazzo Giustinian, one of the most beautiful buildings overlooking the Grand Canal, was very innovative both in design and installation, as well as for the use of new materials. Carboni designed surrealistic dummies - made by the Rosa company in Milan - made of cellophane, straw and crushed paper and newspaper pages. They were used to exhibit fabrics that were draped over the arms, hips or shoulders of the dummies, or to show off the clothes and accessories produced by various fashion houses and Italian artisans. The subtext of the whole exhibition, which focused on new textiles and their versatility in clothing, accessories and manikins, was to press the case for an official increase in the number of products. In fact, in the space of a year the number of products approved by the *Ente tessile italiano* rose from 300 to 1000. A high point of the Venice exhibition was how the fabrics were spectacularly displayed in the long arms of a surrealistic sculpture on whose wrists drapes of fabric fell as if they were curtains from the ceiling. Here, Carboni enacts a clever reinterpretation and reuse of surrealist artists such as Salvador Dalì, Max Ernst and Magritte, fashioning his fashion spectacle in the suggestive Venetian buildings and landscape. To complement the exhibition in the Palace galleries, more dummies were installed in the Loggia of Palazzo Giustinian overlooking the Chiesa della salute. They were arranged in such a way that they formed a group of three evoking perhaps the three mythological Fates that symbolized the entire exhibition and thus reworking on the classical mythology and sculpture. They are indeed unusual and the reaction they produce is one of both a keen sense of both modern design and of estrangement. Their faces, upper bodies and arms are covered with straw, their arms or hips draped with animal-like print fabric. From this one can also glimpse a hint of ethnicity, while at the same time perceiving a feeling of emptiness and silence. Their faces, especially, are emblematic of the absence of life their bodies exhibit. No attempt is made here to humanize their faces with the presence of recognizable features. The straw, in the illusory effect of the image, effaces their eyes and mouths, giving us the impression that they are almost shuttering off any possibility of speaking or seeing. In looking now at these pictures, one is struck by the juxtaposition of the metaphysics evoked by the dummies and the architecture of the city, while the emptiness of their gaze miming that of statues - evokes an ambiguity and mystery similar to that of a De Chirico painting. Theirs is an unsettling presence, their covered faces hinting perhaps at their refusal to countenance the tragedy of the war then advancing towards them.

Grandi Magazzini and Standardization

Taking as her departure point a publicity hoarding of a Rome-based department store named Zingone, whose slogan read "Zingone veste tutta Roma" (Zingone dresses all of Rome), Irene Brin sarcastically comments on the proliferation of department stores and the sense of "modernity" associated with them:

> *Rinascente, Upim, and Lafayette, and, all over the world, the department stores where at least in appearance you can find everything you need to live (and even to die, as the bigger stores also sold coffins, wreaths and any other funeral accessory) satisfied the noisy sudden and infantile tastes of a generation that believed in mass-produced products, in neurasthenia and in the idea of the fixed price.*

Rather than praising the glittering "phantasmagoria" and the promise of happiness through the dream of goods the department stores offered to people from the rising consumer society, Brin looks sarcastically, and perhaps with a pinch of snobbery, at this jaunty "gift" of modernity. With an elitist eye, she seems to say goodbye to an individualism now undermined by a growing shift in the market towards mass-production. In this light, she goes on to describe how big American department stores were the cause of alienation, loneliness and a sense of anonymity in their female consumers. Of some of these, for example, who shopped in the clothing department of a New York department store, she writes:

They often served themselves, alone without the presence of the assistants, following signposts, numbers, illuminated signs, and almost automatically chose the clothes they wanted to try, once more alone, in front of a mirror, brushing up against each other just like lonely women, lost in their own image, caught in the uncertainty between the emerald green and the cypress green jacket. Housewives flocked to the houseware section, intellectuals to the stationery section, where you could always find wonderful paper. Everyone felt anonymous, very modern and unhappy.

Brin's description gives a less glamorous image to what is seen as the dehumanizing experience of shopping in a big department store. As she notes, Italy, like other Western capitalist countries, recorded a gradual increase in the number of such stores like *La Rinascente,* which was founded in 1917, and a little later, *UPIM,* which was according to its publicity slogan, the "Store that sold at a single price." In 1937, *UPIM* merged with *La Rinascente* to form the *Rinascente-UPIM.* Besides these, smaller scale department stores such as *Zingone,* which specialized in ready-made male suits, were also on the increase. Their existence, despite the stringent economic situation, had a great impact on the organization and production of garment manufacture and consequently their role in the complex process of modernization and standardization of models of consumption was vital. In particular, the emergence of the department store signaled a move towards the production and consumption of ready to wear clothing, rather than the more traditional custom made clothes.

Although other Western capitalist countries experienced similar changes in the production and marketing of ready-to-wear clothing, the situation in interwar Italy was considerably different due to the state of the garment industry itself and the contradictory politics of the ENM, one of whose tasks was that of taking a census of the number of dressmakers' shops and fashion houses then in business in Italy. However, the figure the ENM came up with was, by all accounts, much too low. Skills like sewing and embroidery were, in those days, very common in all social classes, but especially for working class and lower middle class women. The longstanding and variegated traditions that had characterized the Italian peninsula also gave to the nation an incredible patrimony in craftsmanship that many women continued. As we have seen, the richness and immense variety of this patrimony was emphasized by Genoni and considered a plus in the search for a distinct Italian style, which Genoni for one did not see as inferior to French chic. Given this variety, it goes without saying that the quality of the made-to-measure dresses and suits varied a great deal, those garments made by the *sartorie* for the upper classes being of a higher standard than those made by more ordinary dressmakers' and tailors' shops for the middle and lower-middle classes. In addition, there was a high number and different levels of seamstresses. In many families, in fact, it was not uncommon to retain the services of an expensive dressmaker, sometimes called the "good one," who made clothes for special occasions and a less skilled and cheaper one, often the housekeeper for those who could afford one, or alternatively a family member, who made more everyday clothing. In her autobiographical novel, *Lessico famigliare* (Family sayings), Natalia Ginzburg mentions that her family's housekeeper, named Tersilla, was their *sarta di casa* (home dressmaker), but that when her sister Paola married the wealthy industrialist Olivetti she could afford now to have many more dresses, "wisely made by the *sartorie,*" the more expensive dressmakers' shops. The way in which this kind of local economy was organized worked against the spread of mass-produced clothing. There were other reasons too that slowed down the popularity of the department store, not all of which can be explained by Italy's industrial backwardness and lack of organization. The ready-to-wear industry, still in its infancy, came up against the obstacle represented by the common opinion, shared by males and females from across the class spectrum, that, rightly as it turned out, the quality of a made-to-measure garment was higher and conferred on the wearer a greater sense of individuality and distinction. These concerns, which bear on the question of how best to keep up one's *bella figura* in an age of mass-produced clothing, were increased by the fact that mass-produced garments did not fit their wearers in the same way as custommade ones. This was one of the most serious obstacles that the mass-produced clothing industry had to face. Indeed, for the new products to capture a market much more sophisticated techniques needed to be elaborated. However, very real as these concerns were, they did not, over time, prevent the development and spread of either the ready-to-wear industry or the phenomenon of the department store.

A brief overview of the history of the Italian department store and its impact on fashion is now in order, and will give us a better understanding of how the process of standardization went ahead and offer further explanations as to why fascism wished to channel this process and use it to bolster its aim of nationalizing the masses and the social body. The first large-scale department store in Italy was established in Milan by the Bocconi Brothers, Ferdinando and Luigi, in 1865. The store went through several phases of development and expansion and in 1879 it took the name *Aux Ville d'Italie,* but a year later was renamed *Alle città d'Italia.* However, France could boast the first department store, called *Bon Marché:* it was founded by Boucicaut in Paris in 1852. This was followed later by a series of more up-market stores such as *Louvre, Printemps* and *Samaritaine.* Similarly in the USA, several department stores opened in the major urban centers of New York, Boston, Philadelphia, Chicago, Baltimore and Detroit between 1860 and 1880. Although Italy was certainly behind in terms of industry and economy when compared to France and the USA, it is surprising to see that the nation's first department store was established not much later than in the aforementioned countries, on the site of the former Grand Hotel in the heart of Milan. The enterprising Bocconi brothers produced ready-to-wear clothing, but also set up a mailorder catalogue business for the sale throughout Italy of their wide range of articles, from textile to house furnishings to babies' layettes etc. An article about the history of Bocconi's store was published in the in-house magazine *La Famiglia Rinascente-UPIM* in 1939 celebrating the sixtieth anniversary of the store. Here, we find information about the number of people - more than 2000, including those working from home who were employed both on the production and retail sides. We learn, for instance, that garments were made in Milan and Turin and then sent to the several Bocconi branches in Rome, Genoa and Trieste, as well as to those customers purchasing them from the mail catalogue. The innovation brought by the Bocconi brothers, which had been their trademark from the outset, even before they opened their grand emporium in 1879, was to retail ready-to-wear clothing, especially for males. This was quite unusual in the Italy of this time, the suits being made by low paid seamstresses with little eye for very high quality. Yet, despite the many changes in the economy and in society, and due to the inability of the sons who inherited their fathers' store, the Bocconi concern met hard times. In the years before 1917, the date in which *La Rinascente* acquired the Bocconi store, a department store along the lines of the American Woolworth's, appealing to a middle- and lower-middle-class clientele, would probably have guaranteed much more commercial success. Those members of the middle classes with spending power were still far more interested in imitating the model offered by the aristocracy than in embracing the culture of mass-produced goods.

The article about the Bocconi department store that appeared in the *Famiglia Rinascente-UPIM* focuses particularly on two of its achievements: first, how it played its part in the battle for Italian independence from French hegemony in terms of quality and elegance; and second, how it made available for the first time in Italy a wide range of items. The article brings together, on the one hand, the importance of the department store in a modern society and economy and, on the other, the continuity of a national tradition that was recovered and reinforced by stores like the *Rinascente* in the late 1930s. The patriotic intent of this latter, in fact, is evident in the choice of name for the store. It was not by chance that Senator Borletti, the president of the new society, requested that the diva poet Gabriele D'Annunzio, of whom he was a great admirer, come up with ideas for a new name for the former *Alle città d'Italia*. It was D'Annunzio, in fact, who chose the name *Rinascente,* and who was also the author of the motto "Italia nova impressa in ogni foggia" that publicized the newly renamed store.

After several phases of ups and downs in the wake of the economic and political turmoil in the aftermath of World War I and with the advent of fascism, the *Rinascente* was affiliated to the *UPIM* department store. From the mid 1930s onwards, the new conglomerate opened several branches in all the most important Italian cities. *UPIM,* catering to people with lower spending power, soon became a popular shopping venue and when in 1934 the two companies finally merged *UPIM* numbered 25 branches throughout the nation while the Rinascente numbered only 5. It is evident that following the economic crisis of the early 1930s the new trend favoured a kind of store like *UPIM* that reached out to a wider market. This was a trend that was destined to last, as in 1940 the number of *Rinascente* branches was still 5, whereas *UPIM* was now present in 36 Italian cities and employed 6,000 people. Moreover, another department store, called *Standard,* that had been modeled on UPIM, was founded in 1931. Later in 1937, in the middle of the autarchic and xenophobic campaign, as the store was about to open a branch in the heart of Rome, Mussolini himself gave the order to Italianize the name of the store to *Standa.* Other smaller-scale department stores were opened in this period as well, such as the *Zingone* store in Rome, mentioned earlier, which published a biannual sales catalogue featuring various garment sketches for male, female and children's clothing; *Fratelli Romano* which sold high quality fabrics, but who also produced custom-made male suits, had branches in Rome and Naples. The *Rinascente* also published a biannual sales catalogue from which a vast variety of merchandise could be purchased, including women's and men's clothing, to outdoor clothes, sportswear, children's clothing, accessories and stockings. At the same time, it advertised other articles that were not shown, such as sports items, and also explained payment processes and the rewards regular customers were entitled to:

> *The savings book we offer our clients allows you to follow your expenditures in our stores and entitles you to a prize in the form of store products that can be obtained at the end of each year."*

Despite the proliferation of the department stores such as Standa and UPIM, which also opened branches in Libya and Ethiopia, and reached out to a clientele composed of the middle, lower and working classes, like the successful experience of Woolworth's in the USA or Tietz in Germany, the Italian ready-to-wear industry was still significantly slow to take off. This fact was clearly stated in some of the papers published by the ENM in 1940, as we shall see later in the chapter. Although the habit of buying made-to-measure male and female clothing was widespread among Italian consumers, (and even today it has not completely disappeared), department stores such as UPIM and *La Rinascente* created a new demand for ready-made clothing. Further demand was added by the fascist emphasis on military and civil uniforms. In the colonial period following Italy's invasion of Ethiopia, "colonial" clothing for uniforms was produced in order to respond to the differences in climate and lifestyle in the African countries. For instance, a safari jacket for women was included among colonial dress and was to become an item that would be fashionable in both male and female wardrobes.

It is enough to recall, however, that despite this growing demand, the production of ready-to-wear clothes was already one of the major industries in the USA by the mid 1920s.

Cinegiornali on Fashion, Standardization, Stereotypes and Models of Femininity

The *Cinegiornali* represent a great illustration of the emphasis the fascist regime gave both to tradition and to modernity in all its manifestations of ideology, high and popular culture and formation of stereotypes. The *Cinegiornali* that documented the Biannual Exhibition of Fashion and Textile held in Turin always blended local craftsmanship and modern technology especially in the presentation of the autarchic fibers. Turin, however, was not the only city to host fashion exhibitions. Others took place at the evocative Villa D'Este on Lake Como, as well as on more mundane occasions or sports gatherings, such as the Mirafiori horse races we have seen in the film *Contessa di Parma,* in which fashion houses such as Fumach, Ventura, Villa, Biki, Mattè, Montorsi and Mingolini Guggenheim took part.

The Luce newsreels were shown during film intermissions and were used to entertain as well as being a means of propaganda, especially in the autarchic phase. In fact, with the advent of sound films the newsreels' voice-over constantly highlighted the *italianità* of the clothes on display. It is interesting to see in these documentaries the mix of different female types, from the *femme fatale* dressed in an evening gown, to the woman with the reassuring beauty of a mother and housewife, one of the images most strongly valorized by the regime. Along these lines, one newsreel documenting a fashion show held in Rome in the Confindustria Building - we see that it was built in *Anno XVIII* of the fascist era, which means 1940 (1922 + 18) - is particularly emblematic. On the catwalk we see two mannequins who respond to opposite models of femininity: one, the slim idealization of women's form, the other a far more reassuring, house wife like image. It is fascinating to see how these two images of femininity become cultural stereotypes that resurface in a fashion show. Nevertheless, these kinds of stereotype nurtured - as we have seen - the cultural politics of fascism. The same can also be seen in another newsreel, this time about hairstyles. We first see a close up of women in a beauty salon, nervously smoking a cigarette while flipping through fashion magazines. The voice-over entreats the women to find inspiration for their new hairstyles at home, rather than searching for Parisian models since "thanks to autarchy we have shown the door to many exoticisms and have demonstrated that we can do better than others." Once again, the close-ups of the models shown have a very housewifely flavour.

However, as we have noted, exoticism was not completely absent in the media of the 1930s. Following the political alliances between Italy and Germany that culminated with the Pact of Steel of 1939, fascist periodicals, such as Interlandi's *Difesa della razza,* contained references to increased economic, political and cultural relations with Nazi Germany. In this context, emphasis was also given to distinct types of beauty which despite their differences - the Italian, Mediterranean, dark-haired woman and the northern European blond-became both accepted and praised as the perfect models with which women were to identify. In some of the pictures we see how the Germanic blond type is incorporated into the classical Italian type. Indeed, in the vulgar anti-semitic propaganda that appeared after the inception of the racial laws in the late 1930s, certain physical features were highlighted as manifestations of the master race.

If the German influences on Italian culture and sense of self were imposed from above by the regime, the influence exercised by the USA responded to a more genuine demand that came from Italians themselves. Indeed, the USA never ceased to be a strong influence on the Italian imagination by way of films, newsreels and Italian immigrants who kept close contact with their land of origin and supplied their compatriots with information about American styles and fashions. In fact, quite an impressive number of Luce newsreels show fashionable items and styles from the USA, England and France, prior to and even following the period of the sanctions. Some of these are quite entertaining, like the report from New York called "Influenza dell'aereoplano, del dirigibile e dell'automobile nei cappelli delle signore" (The influence of the airplane, the blimp and the automobile in ladies' hats). Hats here take on the design and shape of machines, from cars to submarines, airplanes as well as skyscrapers. Here we find an illustration of the experiments going on in design and how modern objects inspired producers of hats and accessories. This was a fruitful relationship that resulted in many innovative designs, such as the case of Elsa Schiaparelli's surrealistic and parodic experiments in cut, details, accessories and textile.

In another Luce newsreel entitled "Istantanee d'America" (Snapshots from America), we first see three models wearing different styles of hats, then a closeup of each model, the first wearing what is called a *cuffia agreste* (a rustic cap) decorated with embroidered flowers. The model wearing the headgear shows an incredible resemblance to the actress Rita Hayworth (then Rita Casino, before she underwent the cosmetic surgery that attenuated the visible signs of her Hispanic origins so that she would meet Hollywood standards of beauty). In this latter presentation about hats, we can also see female aviators, reinforcing the image of the dynamic woman who is also active in traditionally male spheres.

The *cinegiornali* then, were used to entertain while sending messages about models of femininity in dress and in sport activities and leisure time. The newsreels from abroad, especially from the USA also reinforced the idea that the regime wished to emphasize that Italy was in step with one of the most modern capitalist countries. This was also one of the images emphasized in commercial films such as *I Grandi magazzini.*

I Grandi Magazzini by Mario Camerini as Popular Novel

The film *Grandi Magazzini,* directed by Mario Camerini in 1939, offers an interesting illustration of the process of modernization translated into domestic terms. Set in a department store, *Grandi Magazzini,* a popular sentimental comedy, is the story of the love affair between a sales girl Lauretta (Assia Noris) and a delivery truck driver Bruno (Vittorio De Sica). Cinema in Italy had gradually come to represent an important component in the construction of a national popular culture, which, according to Gramsci, had been completely lacking in Italy, especially when compared to the situation in France and England, where popular novels appealing to a wide readership had existed at least since the nineteenth century. Yet, as Gramsci noted, if the Italian culture industry had never really produced goods that the lower classes could consume this was not due to any lack of demand, but to the way that culture in Italy had always been identified with high rather than popular culture. There certainly was, however, an appetite for popular culture among the Italian masses that had been met by recourse to translations of the popular novels published for the French market. Films like *Grandi magazzini,* and their obvious attraction for the popular classes, found a ready audience. The 1930s, in fact, were a period that saw a gradual broadening of the audience for films, especially women, many of whom became avid moviegoers and eager consumers of fiction and romance.

The culture of consumption and its appeal in a modern city had been, indeed, the subject of *The Ladies' Paradise* by Emile Zola, which is set in a department store. As well as a symbol of the triumph of capitalist society in full bloom, the novel is a very accurate survey of how mechanisms of power, money, gender relations and competition play themselves out in the context of one of the newly established department stores in the Paris of the Second Empire. Zola's novel also allows us to see some very real differences between how Italian and French literature treated the theme of fashion. Italian literature had certainly never ignored fashion, as we have mentioned in the texts of the early modern period. Yet, the form and the tone of these texts remain elitist and inaccessible to a wider audience. The same can be said of texts of later centuries that deal with questions pertinent to fashion, such as Parini's *Il Giorno,* where the protagonist, the *giovin Signore,* is portrayed as a spineless aristocrat who is also a fashion victim; and Giacomo Leopardi's moral essay on fashion and death.

Zola's novel, however, is different and acts as a great example of a nationalpopular literary text able to capture in detail the spirit of Paris under the transformations enacted by Baron Haussmann and the parallel economic changes brought about by the birth of the big department stores, modelled in the novel on the history of the *Bon Marché.*

By its very title, Camerini's film calls attention to the proliferation of department stores in urban Italy and the subsequent birth of new models of consumption and lifestyle. In this way, and not only because it was a commercial success, it can be considered an example of a national-popular text and narrative. This characteristic is, indeed, confirmed by the publication of brochures, articles and *cineromanzi* that accompanied the film release. Indeed, the reference to the *pieghevole* (brochure) for *Grandi Magazzini* confirms how the producers of the film themselves saw the film as a kind of *Romanzo popolare* (Popular novel). In fact, in one of the descriptions of the film stills contained in the brochure we read:

> *This is a film that as well as having all the strengths of refined humour also has a new take on human feelings. Grandi Magazzini* has the delicacy of a 19thcentury novel and the agility of a modern story. *It shows the tumbling of feelings and passions against the background of a large modern store. It is a drama within a comedy, a comedy that touches on the dramatic.*

In addition, several contrasting factors render Camerini's film interesting and worth analyzing for the purposes of the present study. First of all, the film was produced during the most intense phase of development of the department store and during that of the investments made by the regime in mass media, sport, cinema, radio and fashion, means through which it aimed at constructing and spreading a modern image of Italy both domestically and abroad. Although the relationship between Bruno and Lauretta seems to fit the traditional genre of a story with a happy ending, in which good triumphs over evil, and the corruption inside the community where they both work is exposed and punished, they are, nonetheless, credible characters, easy for people to identify with, especially women, who were working in similar environments or for those aspiring to do so. In fact, the issues of the monthly magazine *La Famiglia Rinascente-UPIM,* whose readership was composed of the personnel working in the department stores, detail an impressive number of announcements about the number of marriages between the employees of the store. The message here is clear, of course: namely, that of creating the idea that working for a large department store was like belonging to a family or at least a close-knit community. It is interesting, in fact, to note how the title of the magazine hints at the double meaning of the word *famiglia,* referring both to the affiliation with the *Rinascente-UPIM* and to the paternalistic view according to which employees should consider the company as their family. The magazine goes on to report on the many social activities and gatherings of the store personnel as well as trips made to visit the house of the Duce in Predappio.

The photographs we find in the magazine of salesgirls wearing black satin uniforms with white collar and cuffs are faithfully reproduced in Camerini's film. But among the salesgirls of *Grandi*

Magazzini there is a sharp contrast between two opposite models of young women: on the one hand Lauretta and her roommate Emilia, who maintain until the end their ethical integrity; and, on the other, the ruthless Anna who leads a life well beyond the financial means allowed her by shop girl salary. She leads, in fact, a glamorous life, and in order to do so she has no scruples about collaborating with Bertini, the head of personnel and becomes his accomplice in the fraudulent scheme to steal packages destined for customers from the store. With her extra income, Anna, who adopts diva-like attitudes, can afford a servant and imitate the upper-class lifestyle of the Hollywood actresses she has no doubt seen at the cinema.

Another interesting detail in the configuration of the female characters Lauretta and Emilia establishes the vulnerability of both in moral and economic matters. Emilia, who has left her husband Maurizio, a window dresser, on account of his infidelity, does little to offer a reassuring picture of traditional family values. In fact, at the beginning of the film, when Bertini gives Emilia and Lauretta a ride back home, he is quick to let the young women know what he thinks about Emilia's non-respectable or socially unacceptable marital situation. Since he is attracted to Lauretta, he uses this remark as an expedient in order to underline the vulnerability of the two young women living on their own. At the same time, he offers himself as a form of sneaky protection to Lauretta. Although confined to some of the interstices of the film, *Grandi magazzini,* nevertheless, hints at new models, and the connected problems, of daily life and the relative sexual freedom enjoyed by women living on their own and building their economic and personal independence. It was for the moral issues and class implications such as these that *Grandi Magazzini* did not meet the approval of either the Catholic Church or fascist officials. In fact, Camerini's film, despite its commercial success, occasioned one fascist Minister to say: "If you continue to want to make films like this about young people who eat very little, we'll stop you making them."

In contrast to Lauretta and Emilia, Anna appears to be portrayed as the victim of US-influenced consumerist values. The opposition played out in female types in Camerini's film is similar to that of Roberto Rossellini's masterpiece *Roma, città aperta* (Rome, Open City) by Pina, whose heroism is opposed to the cowardice of Marina, the Nazi collaborator. But differently from Open City, where Pina pays with her life, Lauretta's integrity and honesty, in Camerini's sentimental comedy, are finally rewarded with marriage and with the prize of furnishings for the apartment where she and Bruno are going to settle. In addition, the film brings to the viewers' attention issues that are inherent to the social and personal sphere of women's lives. On the one hand, Lauretta, the victim of the sexual harassment of Bertini, who is always eager to take advantage of any moments of emotional and economic weakness, does manage to fend off his advances; on the other, however, her vulnerability, which is contingent on her modest salary that does not ensure her complete independence, is often laid bare. Lauretta is very much an in-between character, independent enough to share an apartment with Emilia instead of living with her parents, but not independent enough to afford the luxury of the ski outfit she sees on display in the department store where she works. Indeed, there are hints in the film that Emilia needs a second job to make ends meet, as we sometimes see her at a sewing machine working on dresses she is copying from drawings hanging on the wall.

Skiing is an important element in this film and the ski outfit Lauretta craves plays a key role in the narrative. Similarly to *Contessa di Parma,* sport plays a significant role in the development of the plot and its links to fashion and modernity in 1930s Italy are stressed. Skiing was encouraged by the regime and represented an important occasion for socialites, as Blasetti illustrates in setting the final scene of the fashion show at the resort of Sestrières. What Camerini exposes, however, is that skiing is a class-based activity that could be afforded only by a minority. A ski outfit cost, in fact, almost two-thirds of a salesgirl's salary, which was about 300 Lire. Often in magazines, skiing is shown as the chic and trendy sport activity of the moment, offering the chance to imagine romantic escapes and to wear fashionable outfits. In *La Famiglia Rinascente-UPIM,* skiing is even praised as the sport of the intelligent since, unlike other sports practiced in warm weather, skiing can only be practiced in the cold when the prevailing human instinct is to stay indoors.

The chance for a romantic escapade on the ski slopes is certainly in Anna's mind when, within earshot of Lauretta, she invites Bruno to join her for a midnight run at a nearby resort. Jealous at Anna's attempts to steal the man who has been attempting unsuccessfully to court her, Lauretta goes herself to the appointment, borrowing a ski outfit from the store with the intention of returning it the following Monday. Lauretta's romance with Bruno begins, in fact, when she meets him in the mountains where he is expecting Anna. Too tired, however, after an exhausting evening spent on the dance floor, she does not make it to the appointment, and turns out not to be really interested in Bruno at all. In the meantime, Lauretta has had the misfortune to tear the ski outfit she had borrowed and needs extra time to repair it before returning it. At the same time, a scandal erupts in the store around the theft of packages that were not delivered to their destination. Bertini, who will turn out to be the culprit and who has found out about Lauretta's borrowing of the ski outfit, accuses her of being behind these thefts. Bruno is so shocked when he learns of Bertini's suspicions that he breaks off his brief engagement with Lauretta. At the end, however, as can be imagined, Bruno uncovers the truth and exposes Bertini and Anna as the masterminds of the scheme. Justice is done, the guilty are punished and Bruno and Lauretta, naturally, can get married.

Let me conclude with a few remarks about Camerini's representation of class in this film. The contrast that gives structure to the entirety of the film is between the humility of working-class lives and the glamor of the goods on display in the department store and, incidentally, in the store executives' spacious and art deco furnished offices. Any suggestion of fracture within the world of the store is warded off, however, by the good relationship that exists between Lauretta and Bruno and the top executives, something the film dwells on. Bertini, instead, who occupies a middle rank on the social ladder, is shown as a distasteful and corrupt individual out of line with the ethos of the store. We are led, then, toward a sympathetic and benevolent picture of the top executives, who at the end praise Bruno's actions and promise, as a reward, to furnish his and Lauretta's apartment. Middle figures like Bertini and his ally Anna are punished for their dishonesty, the final result being that the hierarchy within the firm is reinforced and unchallenged. In the end, the gesture the film makes towards a concern with class conflicts is diluted and the power relationship that governs interactions between managerial and working classes is untouched. Ultimately, the film seems to suggest, the working classes should be happy with what they have (even if it is only a borrowed ski outfit); or better, happy with what is given to them by the upper classes, rather than desiring to be or assimilate with that class, seduced perhaps by the attractive display and allure exercised by the commodities in the department store. Confirming this, one can note how the couples featured in the film are formed by social equals who share concerns common to people of the same class and who experience the same economic hardship. The story, for instance, would have had a completely different twist had Lauretta married a social superior, like the head of the company, as happens in Zola's novel. Here, the humble Denise - the main character - conquers the heart of her employer and they marry. If Zola's novel, on account of the integrity, ability, strength and good fortune of Denise, can be taken as a kind of female *Bildungsroman,* where the female protagonist embarks on an upward trajectory that enables her to construct her personal and social identity and independence, the narrative of *Grandi Magazzini* traces instead a circular scheme. Denise's independence does little to challenge to the social order and is functional to a capitalist system she makes no attempt to change, only to humanize.

At the end of Camerini's film we are left with two sets of couples: one formed by Bruno and Lauretta; the other by Emilia, who has discovered she is pregnant, and Maurizio, with whom she has reunited. We see them standing outside one of the shop windows that Maurizio has created for the coming Christmas holiday, staring at a doll who dances in a circular fashion like a ballerina in a music box, surrounded by other toys and babies' layettes, a further reference to Emilia's pregnancy. They all admire Maurizio's presentation in the shop window as if they were curious passers-by or potential customers. In these final images, the working classes seem to take part, if only figuratively with their gaze, in the enjoyment of the luxurious commodities that lie well beyond the range of their pockets.

What characterizes Camerini's film is its sharp narrative sensibility and its delicate eye that takes in the new role played by advertising and window dressing in the developing social and cultural space that was the Italy of the 1930s. Shop windows and the art of decoration became important advertising techniques. In fact, Maurizio, a window dresser who also makes dummies, is adamant that his work must be considered art. In the *Ladies' Paradise,* special emphasis is given to the goods on display in the various departments of the grand emporium as a sign of modernity and the changes taking place in retail that were transforming the appearances of cities. Zola, in fact, seems mesmerized by this new world and lingers over long and detailed descriptions of the various techniques used to arrange the goods and display them so that they have maximum attraction for the customers. He dwells on how vibrant silk colors are put on display and on the more mundane but commercially smart practice, known today as "loss leaders," of placing bargains near the entrance to the store in the hope of inducing customers to enter and buy other goods they may not have planned to buy, this time at regular price. Zola's descriptions of the goods, especially those related to fabrics, are highly erotic and stress the power of attraction these commodities have on potential customers (not to mention French novelists).

But, under fascism, shop windows did not only put commodities on display, they also put the regime and the Duce on display, thus reinforcing the cult of Mussolini as well as capitalism.

National Conference on "Clothing and Autarchy," Turin, June 1940

How effective was the fascist legislation on fashion? How did the components forming the world of Italian fashion, the manufacturers of fabrics, accessories and male and female ready-to-wear, designers, etc. respond to the policies and steps taken by the ENM? By way of a conclusion let me turn to some of the material, published by the official ENM organ in April, 1940, that emanated from a planned series of national conferences organized by the *Congresso Nazionale Abbigliamento e Autarchia* (National congress of clothing and autarchy) that were scheduled to be held in Turin in June of 1940. The series of conferences, which included the apparel, fur and accessories, hats, stockings, shoes, gloves and textiles used for furnishing and interior decoration sectors, never took place on account of the outbreak of World War II. However, almost 500 pages of material containing the papers and reports that had already been prepared, but never delivered, by a vast number of people working in the fashion and handicraft industries were sent in advance and have been presented as proofs. This is material of great help in forming an idea of the effects the ENM policies had on the fashion industry.

A constant theme of the papers is the creativity and industriousness of individual clothing and accessory designers, many of whose products, such as shoes, bags, gloves and buttons made out of a new material derived from bark, were exported. In his paper, Salvatore Ferragamo affirmed that even in the midst of the economic sanctions against Italy he had managed, nevertheless, to sell his shoes to all the most important department stores in the USA, Great Britain and France. Ferragamo, in fact, had already been able to establish his landmark designs in the Hollywood market by the 1930s and significantly expanded his business in the following years, but not, it transpires, thanks necessarily to the existence of the ENM. Further testimony along these lines is offered by the aristocrat Gabriella De Bosdari Di Robilant from "GabriellaSport" in Milan. She points out that when she took part in the 1939 New York World Exhibition of Textile, she was approached by the Fox company to make a film of her creations that was shown in 500 American movie theaters. Not surprisingly, following this publicity, her creations were well received and she was contracted to sell her models so that they could be copied abroad with the use of Italian fabric, this being a common practice at that time. However, she complains of the ENM's lack of effectiveness in coordinating campaigns to promote Italian fashion abroad, which was the major brief of theinstitution. In fact, a recurrent problem was one of timing. Collections were presented in the season for which they were intended winter clothes in winter, for example - not allowing enough time for the production and launch of the models outside Italy. In other words, De Bosdari di Robillant, on the one hand, stresses the success and quality of Italian creations while, on the other, she points out that the policies of the ENM lacked sufficient knowledge and understanding of foreign markets, were poorly organized and did little to sustain new ideas and creativity.

Out of other papers came the request, made by several industrialists, for better organization within the garment industry, as well as more specific complaints. Some of those that came to the fore were linked, on the one hand, to the need for better equipment and machines, and on the other, for more skilled workers in order to ensure improvements in the quality and fit of the ready-to-wear garments, both for domestic consumption and export. In this sector, for instance, Austrian and German competition had been keen since they had - Austria especially - acquired great expertise in the field since the beginning of the twentieth century with the creative activities of the *Wiener Werkstaette.*

In April 1940, prior to the Turin conferences, the ENM official bulletin *Rassegna dell'Ente Nazionale della moda* underlined the interests of the *Corporazione dell'abbigliamento*, in developing strategies to promote and develop the mass-produced goods, especially the technology necessary for measuring garments. The article notes how the new model of life in fascist Italy and the demand for clothing that came with it would stimulate solutions to the technical problem with which the industry was beset:

> *But the modern life of the Italian people, with its dynamism, its sports activity, with the inclusion of huge masses of people into the regime's bodies, with the growing adoption of uniforms (young people's organizations, civil servants etc.), will provide for the mass produced industry a great future. One of the most important problems on which depends improvement in mass produced goods is the study of measurements.*

Again in response to what was evidently a deeply felt problem, other papers call for the setting up of a team of specialists hygienists, industrialists, clothing retailers, dummy manufacturers whose task it was to come up with the measurements of the "typical conformation of the individual of the Italic race." During the 1930s, despite problems in organization and backwardness in machines, technology and well-trained technicians, the basis was nonetheless set for the later developments in the Italian ready-to-wear industry of the post-war years. Indeed, some of the companies present at the congress expanded greatly in the post-fascist period and became very successful, most notably the *Facis* company, a male readyto-wear factory that by the outbreak of World War II was the largest manufacturer of men's and boys' suits. *Facis,* an acronym for *Fabbrica abiti confezionati in serie* (Factory for mass-produced clothes), was owned by the Rivetti family who in the 1930s in conjunction with the Levi company formed the powerful GFT group. Both families had traded for some time in textiles, Levi in Turin since 1860, while Rivetti had set up a textile mill near Biella. Alessandro Rivetti, in his paper presented at the Turin conference reported on how industrialists' attempts to export to international markets. He mentions that Sweden, Denmark, Belgium, Switzerland, the Middle East as well as Central and South America and Australia, were rendered impossible by the sanctions imposed upon Italy. In this respect, if the problems posed by technical lacunae regarding the production of massproduced garments held industrialists back, so too did the international political situation that resulted from fascist politics. A further voice in the debate on the production of, this time, male clothing was offered by Francesco Rosso, director of the *Tescosa* company from Turin. His paper, "Lo sviluppo della confezione maschile in serie in Italia," (The development of male mass-produced clothes in Italy) called attention to the term mass-produced, pointing out that in order to evoke a better quality product, it could usefully be changed to *Confezione pronta* (ready clothes, the Italian translation of ready-to-wear). What concerned him was the fear that Italians would respond badly to uniformity. He states, in fact, that in order to appeal to the Italian consumer a successful ready-to-wear garment must not display as high a degree of uniformity as the term mass-produced suggested. Rosso went on to stress the fact that, as a way of resisting overly standardized clothes, Italians have always preferred to add a touch of personal style. Perhaps this is one of the reasons why the variety of styles, quality and color of the fabrics out of which Italian ready-to-wear garments were made set the industry apart from its competitors. Rosso concluded by hoping that the technical problems concerning measurement and execution would soon be overcome as he was convinced the Italian ready-to-wear industry's future would be guaranteed by increasing the quality and fit of the garments it produced.

Umberto Turba from Milan dealt, instead, with the development of women's mass-produced garments. He stated that an interest on the part of industrialists in the production of women's clothing had survived all the stages that the industry had gone through, beginning with its economic development in the 1920s, through the depression of 1928–30, and on to the economic recovery of the autarchic years. Turba noted, in fact, that according to the latest ENM census of 1936, of the 2000 industries producing female and male mass-produced clothes 60 percent were for women's and girls clothes. Furthermore, he adds that, as confirmation of this development, about twenty German ready-to-wear companies were about to come back to the Italian market, facilitated as they were by the Italian and German political alliance.

Further problems emerging from the Turin papers concern the unclear status between high fashion and ready-to-wear, not to mention issues regarding the creation of a national fashion. In this context, the paper by Montano, the head of *Casa Ventura,* one of the most important fashion houses and active in the campaign for the creation of an Italian fashion, is of interest. Montano draws attention to several issues that are relevant for the purposes of this study. He points out, for example, important problems regarding promotional campaigns for Italian fashion. These, of course, were very costly and required thorough knowledge of the foreign market in question. Indeed, Montano notes how Ferragamo stood out among designers as an individual who had been able to market his genial creativity abroad, capitalizing on his prior working experience in the USA. Montano, however, also raised more specific questions. First, he notes that the institution of the certificate of guarantee that had been established by the ENM for the valorization and acknowledgement of Italian garments was ineffective as almost all the fashion houses had received the acknowledgement, thus creating confusion about what exactly was being guaranteed. Following on from this, Montano adds that the new certificate, the *marca d'oro* (Golden seal), which in theory was supposed to overcome the confusion, had only just been implemented, but given out just as widely, making it difficult to evaluate the results. Although Montano praised the fact that fashion had become a national concern and a chapter in State legislation, he complained about the authorities' lack of clear intent and ideas as regards the actual launch of Italian fashion. Indeed, he maintains that the existence of national fashion is contingent not so much on the existence of a domestic market as on the existence of an international one. A national fashion, he says, that is worth its salt cannot be confined for its influences and markets to the closed-in confines of national borders, as it stood in the 1940s. The domestic fashion industry, continued Montano, could not be called a truly national fashion industry because it lacked the necessary strength to project itself abroad. Going back to a point that had been made before him, he stressed the fact that Italy, unlike France, did not have a center that fostered the success of its couture by concentrating all its energies. In other words, Montano's complaint is that in the fashion field Italy was still lacking a cohesive sense of cultural and economic identity that would mark its exports as unique. He says:

> *The reasons why up until today no nation has succeeded in pulling away from that world, artistic, political and industrial center that made Paris the mantle of fashion are well known. In Italy, we do not have a single center where all these qualities could be united under one roof. The characteristics of Rome, Florence, Milan and Turin, all brought*

together, sum up the essential qualities for the formation and launch of fashion. But perhaps it is to be feared, given the speed and facility of communications, the artistic, political and worldly qualities of Rome, the artistic qualities of Florence, the industrial ones of Milan and the traditional ones of Turin, that even separated they cannot form the center that is necessary for the solution of the problem.

According to Montano, then, the marked differences among the Italian cities and their individuality constitute yet another obstacle to the launch of Italian fashion abroad that needed to be overcome in order to achieve what Paris had done for France. Underlying Montano's remarks is his awareness of the difference in the traditions of clothing manufacturing from one Italian region to another and the different consumption habits and tastes that could never be assimilated to a single national model, even in fascist Italy. Nevertheless, if on the one hand Montano was right to highlight the different cultural identities of Italian cities and the entrapment represented by fascist bureaucracy, on the other, he was wrong about his prediction for the future and post-fascist development of Italian fashion. Indeed, the diversity and lack of a centralized Paris-like fashion industry was the enabling condition for the originality and breath of fresh air that Italian fashion brought with it, especially to the American market. Diversity was, in fact, Italy's strength and not its weakness. However, Montano's speech confirms the important point that fascism, despite its state-controlled initiatives and institutions, never homogenized and standardized the cultural and artistic differences that had characterized the history and identity of the Italian peninsula.

Another important strand emerging from the papers presented at the Turin conference is the link between fashion, culture and art, raised in speeches by artists who had expertise in dress design and who had had experience in France, such as Marcello Dudovich. In his paper, he first praises the textile industry for the quality and innovative design it had achieved with the autarchic fabrics, underlining that the original prints for these had been the result of collaboration with artists. Then, however, in more critical key, he goes on to lambaste the overall lack of innovative models, which is the result, he suggests, of the Italian fashion houses' reluctance to follow the lead of the textile companies and collaborate with artists. Moreover, he denounced the lack of effective cooperation between tailors and artists in the creation of new styles, pointing out the paradoxical situation according to which fashion designers in Italy imitated French models that had often been drawn by Italian artists. Dudovich also points out the importance of tailoring the creation of garments to the needs and tastes of Italian women, of their cultures, bodies and lifestyles.

Similar problems and issues emerge in the papers prepared by the artists Ester Sormani and Brunetta Mateldi. Both of them, however, stress that the production of a truly original style is possible on account of the tremendous initiative and creativity of the people working at all levels in the fashion industry. Indeed, it seems at times that the subtext of many of the papers is that of suggesting that ENM policies had had the undesired and undesirable effect of dispersing creative energies rather than focusing them into a united effort. What emerges is the paradoxical situation of the bureaucracy and ineptitude of the ENM, together with the empty nationalistic rhetoric that marked its founding, actually hindering the fashion industry and preventing it from developing and increasing production.

In conclusion, what emerges from a careful analysis of these papers enables us, above all, to pinpoint and appreciate the creativity of those working in the field of Italian fashion under fascism. As a community, they were well aware of the importance of their role in the Italian economy and in the creation and projection of an image and culture associated with the nation. However, apart from the nationalistic rhetoric contained in some of the speeches, the Conference gives good reason to believe that the work of the ENM was neither effective nor timely, nor did it present a clear idea of what Italian fashion was or could be. Indeed, one of the structural and insoluble problems was that fascism tried - through fashion - to package and mold an imposed unified image of the Italian social body, as it had done in other instances. Despite the political stress put on dress, on the many kinds of military and civil uniforms, on the black shirt (the constant trademark of fascism) and on fashion in general, the regime did little to achieve a stronger sense of national identity. There were areas, especially those more isolated and rural ones, where the strong divisions and hierarchy in social class could never be overcome by the populism of Mussolini, where his and the injunctions of the regime in general, delivered in the squares of Italy, fell on deaf ears.

The project of nationalizing fashion failed, I suggest, for two reasons: neither, both workers in the industry nor consumers responded to the regime's diktats and continued to organize themselves independently and according to the time-honored codes of the local economy and of craftsmanship traditions; second, the stasis resulting from rigid model that the regime sought to impose in dress was at loggerheads with the notion of change that is the basic condition in which fashion exists. This is very clearly expressed in the artists' papers Dudovich 's and Sormani's above all - when they say that in order to create new models they constantly need the nourishment of new ideas and inspiration. This implies a movement of openness towards other cultures and artistic experiments and their readaptation to an original design. It goes without saying that here the artists mean that neither the officially sanctioned uniforms nor Italian regional costumes, nor even the Renaissance, could be the only sources of inspiration for fashion and that a culture shuttered in by its nationalistic, totalitarian and autarchic modes was anathema to the creativity and change inherent in fashion.

Fascism saw the great potential fashion had in terms of image, art and what it could contribute to the economy. Opportunistically, the regime used the industry to further its ideological picture of what Italy and Italians should be. However, fascism did little that was really original, since its strategies for fashion grew out of the ferment and creativity, as well as some of the concrete proposals, that had already emerged in pre-fascist Italy. The success of Italian fashion in the fascist years, especially in the design and production of its beautiful fabrics, decorations and accessories, had little to do with the originality of fascist proposals, and everything to do with the creativity of the people working in the fashion industry and with the social, cultural and economic changes that had taken and were taking place all over the world. Italy's relative isolation, its autarchic phase and the tragic war years had the effect of stimulating the imagination of designers to use and combine cheap, previously unused material such as cork, paper, cellophane, straw, etc. for their creations.

Even the emergency conditions imposed by Italy's entry into World War II did little to dull the creativity that Italian designers displayed. In the summer of 1943, for example, the ENM published a special issue of its "Documenti," dedicated to the relationship between fashion and cinema. The issue is a highly sophisticated volume that contains articles on *Cinecittà,* the *Centro sperimentale di cinematografia,* and on the importance of the creation of costumes and fashion for film. Rich in illustrations, the book treats readers to gorgeous black and white and color pictures, as well as swatches of fabrics. One photograph of a black-and-white fabric, inspired by the alphabet and manufactured by the Milan-based Lucchini company, is worth particular mention. The caption accompanying the photograph suggests that the beautiful effect of the fabric and the tight play of the design "can replace those polka dot design textiles, whose uniformity is beginning to be tiresome". Even in the midst of war, although with great difficulty, the fashion industry still managed to manufacture new designs that counteracted what had come to be seen as the boring uniformity of the polka dots fabric. Similarly, in wartime fashion magazines continued to publicize new collections and offer tips on style. In *La famiglia Rinascente-UPIM,* Rina Simonetta urged women not to give up on their concern for the *bella figura* and seek out ways to give their old outfits a fresh look. During the war, due to difficulties in finding and buying fabric, dressmakers and fashion advertisements in magazines such as this encouraged a fashion of transformation, according to which dresses and coats could be worn normally or inside out, several tops could be combined with the same suit, and details such as pockets and accessories could be added.

The lack of material during the war did not seem to stymie the creativity of either designers or consumers. In fact, new styles were produced, using any material that was available, even the fabric of a parachute that had been abandoned in a field, as Giorgio Armani recalls his mother doing in order to sew raincoats. "La vita continua" (Life must go on), this simple motto, which also happens to be the title of the opening article of the ENM volume "Moda e Cinema," symbolizes the resilience of people working in the field of fashion. Even in a country occupied by two foreign armies and in which US forces fought alongside Italian partisans against the Nazis and their Italian allies from Mussolini's puppet regime, the fashion industry and individual designers were never so completely paralyzed by the tragic events as to give up on their profession, their art and their creativity. For example, some couture houses near Milan organized fashion shows in the countryside in places that could be reached only by boats; one of Italy's leading post-war fashion houses, that of the Fontana Sisters, established itself in Rome in 1944, as soon as the Germans had vacated the aristocratic building they had been occupying. Micol Fontana remembers that she acquired the fabric she needed from Jewish retailers who had hidden their goods in their basements in exchange for the potatoes and other vegetables she received from her parents' farm outside Rome. Here, she recalls, they also helped to hide a Jewish refugee.

These are only some of the many examples that show the industriousness, creativity and resilience of the people working in the different branches of fashion and how, despite adverse circumstances, they and their forerunners in the 1920s and 1930s were able to prepare the terrain and premises for the future success of Italian fashion. Although Italian fashion enjoyed international prestige in the period after World War II, it did so because the terrain for its growth had been thoroughly prepared in the previous decades, starting at least with Rosa Genoni who, in the pre-fascist liberal period, laid many of the foundations for the post-war boom. It was this creativity and the nation's long tradition in fine craftsmanship that would bring the success of the "Italian Look." This book has been an attempt to describe and analyze the creativity inherent in the entirety of Italian fashion from the perspective of a key period in Italy's history. This, however, is but one chapter in the long and intricate history of Italian fashion, many of which are yet to be written.

11

Fashioning Women Techniques of Femininity

Introduction

Western culture is obsessed with sex. The topic of women has preoccupied countless philosophers and feminists. The sex-gender distinction is one dimension of this interest. If sex is determined by biology, then gender is learned and acquired as a set of social trainings about how female bodies behave. Mauss observed that 'Nothing is more technical than sexual positions'. As well as techniques of sexual acts underpinned by an array of sexual morals, there is an even more bewildering array of techniques of gender.

It is also possible to distinguish techniques associated with the occupancy of a female body (being female) from techniques that deploy gender as a social strategy (being feminine). While techniques of being female include practices associated with fertility, nurturing and caring, they also include techniques associated with domesticity and the management of everyday life. Techniques of femininity are related to these (and obviously there is a fine line between the two) but are characterised by techniques of display and projection of the female body. This chapter explores some of the relationships between these two sets of techniques, especially where the two are in tension or conflict. Fashion systems-and techniques of dress and decoration more generally manifest techniques of gender specific to any cultural formation. Western fashion became preoccupied with techniques of femininity as 'the woman question' gained ascendancy from the eighteenth century onward:

> *Devotion to fashion in dress was adduced as a natural weakness of women, something they could not help. This view was strengthened in the nineteenth century, when masculine and feminine clothing became so much more different in fabric, trim, and construction. Elegant men's clothing during this time was actually no less complex, demanding, and uncomfortable, but it tended to be more subdued and abstract in the way it looked. Women's clothing was extremely expressive, almost literary, and very deliberately decorative and noticeable.*

The emphasis on techniques of display was double-edged. On the one hand, these techniques were geared to articulating appropriate forms of conduct and facilitating social intercourse. On the other, signs of display had to be intelligible to the observer and a credible reflection of the social position and location of the wearer. Techniques of display were shorthand for moral qualities. Women, in particular, were at risk of being damned by their garb. Depictions of women's fashions were frequently tinged with moral condemnation as in the following description of the women in the new colony of Sydney in 1811: the European women in the settlement spare no expense in ornamenting their persons, and in dress, each seems to vie with the other in extravagance. The costliness of the exterior is meant as a mark of superiority; but confers very little grace, and much less virtue, on its wearer, when speaking of the dashing belles who generally frequent the Rocks.

The ways in which bodies are fashioned through clothes, make-up and demeanour constitute identity, sexuality and social position. In other words, clothed bodies are tools of self-management.

The peculiar inflection of western fashion stems from the philosophical oppositions between subject/object and male/female. Women are constrained by representational codes which position them as passive vehicles of display and the object of the look. In turn, the look is structured by the normative male gaze, as objects of desire and repositories of pleasure. Fashion has been singled out as a domain of representation and practice in which exploitative relations are central. Because femininity is defined in terms of how the female body is perceived and represented, 'a woman's character and status are frequently judged by her appearance'. The body 'is the site on which feminine cultural ideals can be literally manufactured' 'Paintings, advertisements, pornography, and fashion are all practices which produce particular ways of seeing the feminine body'.

According to Sawchuk, the link between fashion and femaleness has three sources: explanations of capitalism that equate men with production and women with consumption art history that associates the development of western art with the portraiture of the female nude and psychoanalytic accounts of the gaze as gender-coded. These preoccupations construct a reductionist framework of explaining fashion: 'as a reflection of the social onto the body, fashion as the repression of the natural body; fashion simply as a commodity to be resisted; fashion as substitute for the missing phallus'. In other words, women 'are sold their image in the form of commodities'.

From this standpoint, fashion constitutes an effective and pervasive means through which women become objects of the gaze and of male sexual desire. If women are confined to the role of display, and 'measured' by the standards of achieving desirable 'looks', they are caught up in a vicious circle:

> *Women's love of clothes, cosmetics, jewellery, their obsession with style and fashion, reinforces the myth that we are narcissistic and materialistic. In turn, this reinforces capitalism, which depends upon this obsession with our bodies for the marketing of new products.*

Sawchuk questions the essentialist basis of the equation between economics and gender. She argues that it is both 'repressive and homogeneous in its effects', as well as depending on a transparent relationship between representations and texts upon readers and viewers. Instead, western fashion should be seen as culturally and historically specific. Western consumer fashion was shaped by the legacy of Christian morality and Victorian respectability. Changing circumstances have changed the parameters of western fashion. A significant number of commentators have revised the ways in which gender should be conceived in techniques of representation and cultural production.

Some of this work has specifically addressed the subject of women and fashion. Common to this work is the argument that gender identity is a multi-faceted process that implicates not only sexual desire but a range of learnings, orientations, identifications and sexual knowledges. These are gained from a variety of sources in processes of prestigious imitation. Sources of knowledge of gender techniques include overtly instructional 'manuals' (such as etiquette guides and women's magazines), role models (prestigious or influential women) and specific techniques of the body. This chapter explores some of these feminine trainings.

Instructing Femininity

Overt forms of instruction about techniques of being female and feminine havesss been shaped by changing ideas about gender. Since the eighteenth century, techniques of femininity have been organised around body techniques, interactive modalities and mental dispositions through which 'feminine' attributes are displayed. Weibel relates this to the 'vast separation in male and female roles that came in with the Industrial Revolution'.

The development of the class system as an outcome of economic growth and restructuring, coincided with changing perceptions of gender. With it came 'the increasing identification of a particular class, the bourgeoisie, with the attributes of a particular gender, the feminine, newly defined wholly in terms of a domestic and private sphere'. Women were the visible correlate of the economic and social standing of their menfolk. Becoming feminine was a 'task' of learning about the attributes of femininity, 'a task wholly identified with the world of leisure, and a task that can be a pleasure, not a labour'.

The convergence of class with gender, and the association of femininity with 'leisures and ornament', were central to the production of advice for women on how to be feminine. Advice came in the form of admonitions on moral conduct, steps to realising feminine 'nature', information about clothing conduct and fashion, deportment and social etiquette, as well as guides to fertility, family and domestic management. The intertwining of personal and social identity were central to European notions of femininity.

The politics of the body were elided with domestic, social and public politics. During the eighteenth century, the publication of magazines specifically addressed to women took up these concerns. While magazines such as *The Tatler* appealed to the social snobbery of the upper echelons, new magazines appealed to wider audiences. They were akin to training manuals for the masses. Dominated by 'domestic' magazines, they concentrated on 'the struggle to achieve marital happiness and perceived "women's issues" as determined solely with regard to this single "career"'.

The format of these magazines set the tone for subsequent publications. Ballaster *et al.* cited the *Lady's Magazine* as the forerunner of modern women's magazines:

> *Every feature common to the twentieth-century form we know so well appears at one time or another in its pages; the agony aunt, occasional news reporting with a 'woman's' slant, features on famous women (past and present), cookery recipes, sewing patterns, medical advice, readers' letters, regular contributors. Like the modern women's magazine the* Lady's Magazine *was not constructed to be read from beginning to end, but rather according to the reader's interests and priorities.*

The popularity of women's magazines grew enormously. Early magazines stressed the qualities of virtue and morality that were associated with femininity. Later, the Victorian ideal shaped the format of magazines including sections offering tips on household management, dressmaking, essay competitions, fiction, literary criticism, gardening, hygiene and healthcare, and 'courtship' advice. Other magazines focused on beauty, dress, and taste.

The late nineteenth century witnessed an explosion of women's magazines which reflected major changes in economic circumstances, social mobility and mass production. Between 1870 and 1900, fifty new titles appeared in Britain and women became 'consumers of magazines on a scale unimaginable a century earlier'. Advertising and consumerism had a growing importance in addressing women in their role as housewives (as opposed to house managers). Several titles, including Isabella Beeton's *Englishwoman's Domestic Magazine,* established in the 1850s, 'set the pattern for middle- and workingclass women's magazines for the next fifty years'.

There was a tension between the promotion of beauty aids and new fashion trends and attention to domestic chores and problems, childrearing and personal concerns. While some women advocated emancipation, employment and independence, others wanted to be 'a quite unillustrious, more or less hampered and dependent wife and mother', as one correspondent put it. Ballaster *et al.* suggest that domestic ideology 'was neither monolithic nor static; indeed, it was deeply contradictory'. Women's magazines were consumed by women readers with very different circumstances of existence.

Gradually, magazines began to identify specific readerships by structuring their appeal and content:

> *the relatively expensive (sixpenny) weekly ladies' paper aimed at the upperclass woman; the good-quality middle-class domestic magazine, which cost up to sixpence per month; and the penny weeklies aimed at the or working-class woman.*

The differentiation of the readership of women's magazines reflected changes in definitions of femininity from the eighteenth to nineteenth centuries. Gone were the moral and religious emphases on women's 'nature' and duty, being replaced by an emphasis on women's labour and achievements. The new woman was defined primarily as a 'homemaker' undertaking practical (household management), economic (managing the household finances) and moral (reproduction, caring and nurturing). Magazines reflected this orientation toward domestic activities by reiterating the work of the household as the organising principle of women's lives. This was increasingly 'balanced' by the insertion of specials on fashion and beauty:

> *On the one hand, woman's role was to be beautiful, dressed in clothes which expressed the social status of her husband or father and her own desirability. But the domestic role demanded that her sexuality could only be expressed through maternity.*

Thus the magazines offered contradictory and competing roles for readers, sometimes resolved by the insertion of a paper pattern enabling the reader to labour to produce the desired fashionable mode. In this way, the magazine could be both a 'work manual' and 'purveyor of pleasure'. By the late nineteenth century, yet another model of femininity could be identified, that of consumer. With the growth of advertising, the manufacture of beauty products and the use of visuals in magazines, the definition of woman became bound up with appearance and dress, which 'depended in turn on her spending power and discrimination as a consumer'. Whether women had the opportunity, or could afford, to indulge in conspicuous consumption, women's magazines-be they 'ladies', homemaker, or escapist penny papers for working women-all played on the contradictions and tensions between different roles and orientations for women.

Nonetheless, Ballaster stressed that 'womanliness was ever the site of competing definitions based on generation, class, status and wealth'. Although these concerns have persisted to set the agenda of women's magazines, subsequent shifts in the definition of femininity can be found. Thus, while the genre of the women's magazine has remained constant, its specific appeals and addresses have varied.

Another strong indicator of the source of feminine trainings came in the huge demand for etiquette guides. Women's roles were specifically associated with etiquette as the 'preservers of morality and arbiters of taste'. A distinction was made between public and private etiquette, with the lion's share being associated with the domestic sphere and the private home. Etiquette consisted of manners, rules of social intercourse, knowledge of what counted as 'taste', rules of dress, and an appreciation of social hierarchies. Victorian notions of femininity were interspliced with codes of etiquette.

As the changing conditions of women's lives accelerated through the 1920s, 1930s and 1940s, so the contradictions and conflicts multiplied. In the home, women increasingly 'did' for themselves. The highly visible role of (middleclass) women as the 'social' face of family life which developed in the nineteenth century declined. A woman was now seen 'as guardian of her family's health and happiness rather than of its social place'. This change was reflected in the changing foci of the contents of household management and etiquette guides. Advice was now offered on social etiquette, household help, beauty, self-improvement and fashion. Women's bodies (rather than moral qualities) became the currency through which success could be achieved in these diverse spheres. Clothes and body silhouettes were the visible markers of style.

Yet, despite the long history of women's magazines, their significance as technical guides has only recently been acknowledged. Despite their long-term success and enormous readerships, women's magazines were not defined as an industry until after World War II. This belated recognition was initiated by advertisers who realised the potential benefits of appealing to this special consumer group. Academic interest in the content of the women's magazines has developed even more recently. These studies have centred on how women's magazines create 'a world of woman: woman to woman', and on the images of women that they offer. Most studies have noted the lack of fit between the ideals of femininity and the practical conduct of women.

During the twentieth century, the established formats of women's magazines have persisted. On the one hand, they offer advice, information and instruction specifically for women (practical techniques of being female), while on the other hand, they offer images of femininity, fashion and beauty (techniques of desire and femininity). During the 1920s and 1930s, the number of women's magazines mushroomed and experimented with new formats. Generally, the newcomers addressed middle- and lower-middle-class women rather than the leisured wealthy class. For example, the British magazine *Woman* sought to 'entertain you with vivid, vital stories and touching every side of life and human interest' as well as giving 'you practical help and inspiration concerning your home'. By contrast, *Good Housekeeping,* launched in 1922, extolled 'homemaking as a full-time job with its own kind of professionalism in a double process of encouraging high standards of household management and providing work-manuals of basic skills'.

The functions of magazines became more explicitly demarcated between service (especially concerned with housework as domestic science), fashion and beauty, lifestyle and consumerism, and self-improvement. This was the forerunner of niche marketing. Different consumer groups were being distinguished by their attributes.

Meanwhile, 'a new and all-pervasive preoccupation with sex' emerged in the twenties. At first, magazines were circumspect, but gradually sex became the centrepiece of the rhetoric and visual presentation of women's magazines. The frivolity of the 1920s turned to an obsession with consumerism in the 1930s, concerns that were muted during wartime. Instead, women were mobilised first to support the war effort and later to actively contribute to it. Although women were still primarily managing home and family, they were also offered new options and occupations as a consequence of the war. The change was short-lived. Magazines of the 1950s returned to pre-war concerns of family and consumerism:

> *The bride replaced the working woman. She was used to sell soap, stockings, soap powders, aspirin and tea. By the 1950s her 'dewy loveliness' was also selling crockery, lingerie and linen. As a newly-wed she supervised a modern home equipped with the latest devices of electric servants, which make her 'a home-manager instead of a home slave'.*

Advertising came to dominate the magazines in ways which disturbed the editors and moral guardians. Advertisers used 'the sexual sell', playing on emotions and fantasies calculated to focus attention on their domestic role, reinforce home values, and perpetuate the belief that success as a woman, wife and mother, could be purchased for the price of a jar of cold cream, a bottle of cough syrup or a packet of instant cake-mix.

The tension between the advocacy of techniques of beauty and self-presentation versus techniques of homemaking were sharpened with the development of mass produced cosmetics and consumer fashion:

> *'Make-up' became not only respectable but essential for feminine beauty. Cosmetic advertisements and advice on their use in advertorials thus brought together consumption and the representation of women as object of the gaze, linking both to the work of femininity.*

Despite the emphasis on 'the look' of femininity, magazines continued to advocate a 'maternal, nurturative role' for women as supportive and resourceful counterparts to men, while women who sought other roles were portrayed as 'selfish, or fractious'.

Two changes occurred. On the one hand, the influence of advertisers increased to the point where they determined the look, focus and success of magazines. On the other, in response to new ideas of consumer sovereignty and the opportunity for consumers to make choices between products, magazines became less dogmatic and more interactive. They were training women to be consumers by encouraging readers to contribute and participate in the pages of the magazine-for example, through letter pages, diverse advice columns, reader makeovers, and fashion features. Domesticity and new social problems dominated the content. Magazines offered discrete sections which corresponded to the different departments of women's lives, and offered advice to improve the management of these arenas. Homemaking was structured as a blend of work and leisure and a happy home as the product of hard work:

> *the home is simultaneously* just *an arena of leisure for women, and one of leisure and* work, *where 'work' is justified as such (even when we might not think of it as work-the work of beauty) by resort to the masculine concepts of work-efficiency, planning, etc.*

The strategies of magazines became more precise as techniques of market research were borrowed from the advertisers and used to characterise the profile, lifecycle and consumer patterns of readers. Readerships were distinguished in terms of ideal types such as the housewife, the young married woman, the teenager, the fashion sophisticate, and the 'with it generation'. Although a range of new titles appeared, including *She, Nova, Cosmopolitan, Options* and *Elle,* 'none of these magazines took the world of paid work as the ground for an alternative definition of the feminine'.

Nonetheless, magazines were changing as was their appeal. For example, in 1965, Helen Gurley Brown used her magazine, *Cosmopolitan,* to transform girls from 'timid mouseburgers', constrained by the 'gender gap' in romance and the 'glass ceiling' at the office to the glossy, confident Cosmo Girl. The Cosmo Girl was proactive-not only concerned with finding a man, but forging a career, living an independent life, and acquiring consumer goods. In keeping with the tradition of earlier magazines, the transformation was the outcome of self-improvement, of setting goals and fighting to attain them. Unusually, *Cosmopolitan* endorsed feminism and (hetero)sexual enjoyment at the same time, as well as taking a stand on a number of controversial issues. Betty Friedan commented that she: was very grateful for the support of Helen Gurley Brown in our early battles for equality. I enjoyed having that sexy Cosmopolitan Girl say that she loved her sports car and her new Chanel suit, but any man who wanted to attract her had to be for the ERA.

Attempts were made to engage with new agendas for women and to reflect the 'inexorable movement towards greater independence, responsibility and social mobility for women'. While *Cosmopolitan* tackled 'the tangled relations of work and pleasure' through sexuality, other new magazines, such as *Nova,* tried to develop a formula that addressed women as intelligent and responsible readers. *Nova* was a complex and provocative magazine with an editorial policy 'predicated on the shared disillusion of a generation turning its back on the shining brave new world'. One of its most memorable features was its use of 'punchy, graphic and unabashedly sexy photographs'. The magazine eventually failed though it remains one of the most radical experiments in women's magazines. While its less radical contemporary *Cosmopolitan* has surived, so too has the explicitly feminist magazine *Spare Rib,* perhaps surprisingly. These deviations did not stop either the persistence of the homeand-family orientation of the majority of women's magazines, nor halt the declining circulation of women's magazines as a whole.

The 1970s and 1980s saw some shakeouts in the market as new titles appealing to the 'new woman' jostled with the evergreen service magazines. While distancing themselves from explicitly feminist publications, the most innovative titles have been aimed at 'women who are not readers of women's magazines', that is, to women who do actively dislike the 'service' and domestic emphasis of traditional women's magazines, but who want magazines that address the circumstances and interests of working women who also value their home lives. The idea of gender-specific appeals has also been questioned in relation to the perpetuation of the separate 'Women's Page' in newspapers.

On the whole, however, most women's magazines still concentrate on offering advice about femininity and providing entertainment for women. Nonetheless, women's magazines construct a 'privileged space, or world, within which to construct and explore the female self. C. White described women's magazines as constituting an arena of femininity:

> *Turning the first page of a mass weekly is like entering a women's club-a woman knows she is on 'home ground' in more senses than one. This is her territory, her profession; she knows the rules and she shares the implicit goals and values. Here she finds warmth, friendship and identification, as well as a little harmless escapism. There is colour, humour and vitality to raise her spirits, and often a money-saving offer to give a fillip to her wardrobe. Over the years a special relationship can grow up between readers and their magazines, a strong bond compounded of trust, loyalty-and habit.*

Critics have argued that women's magazines portray a shallow range of role models for women as well as relying on the sexual sell as the basis of advertising and guides to personal presentation. Millum concluded that women's magazines in the 1960s and 1970s offered women just four roles: hostess, mannequin, self-involved narcissist, or wife and mother. According to Millum, the limited range of roles offered by advertising acts as a social regulator that preserves the status quo by moulding women's points of view and legitimating the lack of choice for women:

The roles offered, the life-patterns indicated, the stances offered, are all consistent in their occurrence and their form, and it must be remembered, cumulative. Not only this, but the magazines themselves in most cases support the advertising in the maintenance of these roles. The reification of the female, loss of individual independence, introversion, the retreat into the womb of the home, woman as the natural half of humanity, guardian of the past and the future, the emphasis on sexual attraction, competitiveness all these occur again and again, the same roles are proffered again and again, consistently and cumulatively.

Despite the persistence of these themes, the range of women's magazines and changing patterns of circulation and readership suggest that women consume and use magazines in complex ways. Magazines of the 1980s and 1990s are organised around diversity and choice as the basis of customised techniques of femininity. This approach accords with the general popularity of the 'psy' complex in contemporary western culture. Women's magazines offer readers a smorgasbord of identifications, practical skills, objects of desire, and competing sources of prestigious imitation. The revised techniques of femininity supplant the choice between domesticity versus self-presentation with a tension between work and family in a lifestyle characterised by activity and independence. By casting women in this proactive model, women's magazines construct women's culture around individuality and achievement rather than around conformity and duty. Even Betty Friedan, the well-known American feminist, has endorsed the 'new look' women's magazines:

> *Actually the world depicted in women's magazines today is much more progressive than it was 25 years ago. There is a much greater diversity of women in those pages-black, Asian, and Hispanic. And the very advice they give out implies autonomy, independence, and a lack of complete credulity or passivity on the reader's part. There's a complex richness to women's culture today that is a beautiful mix of feminism and femininity.*

Even so, the new femininity is still complex and contradictory, posing work against home, conservatism against progressiveness, and habit versus change. The different sections of women's magazines not only place these oppositions side by side, but invite selective reading strategies. Women 'dip into' bits and pieces of magazines explicitly engaging with the 'severely contradictory, if not incoherent, discourses of femininity simultaneously'. Not only are readers selective and inconsistent in their reading patterns, they are also sceptical-even cynical-about what they eagerly consume.

Women read magazines as 'small treats' as illicit pleasures, and as 'time out' from hectic schedules. According to Winship, the revival of crafts and homemaking in the 1980s is not a nostalgic hankering for simpler pasts, but sublime 'surrogacy for practices that might construct another self; another place for women'. It is a way in which women can reconcile multiple demands by fantasising about leisure while at the same time vicariously asserting "'independence", which currently means doing it all: child and husband care, paid work'. The appeal of the image of home cooking, arts and crafts, and home sewing (even if readers are too busy to actually make something) is precisely the way in which work is constructed as leisure. It also reflects the widespread popularity of DIY (doit-yourself) within the home because it seems to 'undo' mass consumption-and the dependence on supermarkets, department stores, seasonal sales and the like. Recipes, instructions, patterns and surveys also constitute practical competances and knowledges associated with femininity. The reason why many topics recur in women's magazines relates to the role of providing popular education about cultural mores. In that way, women's magazines are akin to oral cultures, where the circulation of 'potted' versions of certain topics is a way of reproducing skills and knowledges across generations and different cultural groups.

Designing Women

A woman then, *to attract a man,* should:

- Be easy on the eyes;
- Be happy and self-confident;
- Be feminine, tender, kind, and thoughtful;
- Be poised;
- Be dependent;
- Be well-groomed.

While we may have moved a long way from the etiquette of the *ancien regime,* in which dress 'was clearly invested with a precise socio-political role of selfconfirmation for some and subordination for others, fixing each in his place by signalling the position of each', clothing still articulates the attributes of the person. In western culture, these have been organised by the priorities accorded to aesthetics, sex and class under capitalism:

The practical function of clothing being inseparable from its aesthetic function, itself inseparable from its sexual function (modesty or enticement) or social function (prestige and distinction) this commercialism may over-stress some of them for the better dissimulation of others that are not as admissible, opportune or persuasive.

The emphasis on sexuality has been especially prominent in the consumer fashion system. Changes in style and line of cut systematically relate to changing mores of sexuality such as the prominence of specific sexual and sensual bodily features. According to Perrot, 'there is a periodicity of place and appearance of the erogenous zones or those that are sexually stimulating, in which clothing is necessarily and profoundly involved'. Because western culture has been so preoccupied with the 'problem' of femininity, women's fashions have responded frequently to discourses about sex.

Through processes of prestigious imitation, young girls construct a social persona from techniques of femininity including body trainings, codes of dress and decoration and mental techniques (acquired through imitation of friends, siblings, relatives, popular role models, magazines and television). Social and sexual identity is lodged in the way the body is worn. Gender-especially femininity-is worn through clothes. But although clothes allude to persons as sexual beings, they do not automatically denote sexuality. This is most clear in the case of children's clothes. Although girls and boys are dressed differently according to sex, they are not expected to behave in a 'sex-typed' manner.

The separation between sex, gender and sexuality runs through codes of dress and decoration in complex ways. Furthermore, understandings of these distinctions are not necessarily shared by women and men. For example, some evidence suggests that the model of the 'male gaze' as the basis of codes of looking and ways of seeing may be just one arrangement. In terms of dress behaviour, there may be multiple understandings of allusions to sexuality. Despite the rhetoric that women dress to please men, other evidence suggests that women primarily dress to please other women. Further, there is no clear pattern as to whose 'eyes' women view other women through.

Moreover, men and women have very different ideas as to what constitutes a fashionable look. For example, the Australian magazine *Cleo* invited men to rate various clothes, assuming that the 'sexy' looks would rate best. In fact everyday looks (casual top and skirt or jeans) were preferred while the 'way out' high fashion looks scored poorly. These results suggested that the fashion behaviour and circulating techniques of interpreting dress and decoration are complex and variable.

One of the features of western consumer fashion has been the rise of fashion designers as authoritative sources of advice about clothes-and by extension related techniques of femininity. Often, they have been likened to dictators making pronouncements on what's in and out and what's feminine and what's not. Their rise to influence began in the 1920s and has lasted, despite the declining popularity of couture fashion and the expansion of mass-produced fashion.

The reason for their success stems from their role in defining body-habitus relations through the line and cut of clothes. Individual designers are typically celebrated for introducing a new cut or a new look as a sign of their creative genius and ability to impose their will. But, as well as promoting modish fashions, designers have also extolled an extreme version of a fashionable lifestyle characterised by leisure, pleasure, elitism and conspicuous consumption. The most successful designers-usually men-have become arbiters of taste and social etiquette. As American designer, Oscar de la Renta, reflected:

> *In the old days fashion designers-seamstresses really-made and sold only dresses;* today we sell a lifestyle to the whole world. *We have moved into more and more areas of influence, and this has made a huge difference to how we are perceived. It has made the career more socially acceptable. And I think in the end all social structures come to depend on power and influence. And, of course, on the influence and power that money brings.*

While the world of designer fashion (couture) is big business and extremely competitive, its influence on everyday consumer fashion is perhaps overstated. Although couture design is regarded as the apex of the fashion world, in practice it is geared towards a small, rich clientele. The large design houses in Paris have only about 3,000 customers of whom less than 700 are regulars. Of these, about 250 are American and 250 are European (made up of French, Germans, Italians, and 'half a dozen' British); of the remainder, ninety are from the Gulf countries, fifty from South America, and thirty from the Far East. Americans account for about two-thirds of world sales, suggesting that Parisian design has a greater impact on fashion in the New World than in Europe. While this group is cultivated and monitored as select guests at the seasonal shows of each designer, their fashion choices do not necessarily influence fashion trends. In fact, only about 'fifteen to eighteen women' are regarded as trendsetters. If they take up a new fashion idea, the design is often popularised and modified for mass production and everyday consumption. In general, however, Paris couture is an exclusive club associated with a small section of the fashion industry. It seems plausible to question the amount of influence ascribed to either the designers or regular clients. But in pandering to their preoccupations and prejudices, designers recycle historical themes, icons of femininity and fantasies. Coleridge observed that:

> *The long pedigree of couture is taken seriously by couture customers and permanently bolstered by designers. Historicism has, of course, a certain currency in ready-to-wear too, but allusions tend to be general, to a puritan collar, or a pioneer petticoat. In couture a collection is inspired, they tell us, by Madame de Pompadour, the Duchess of Windsor, the Marchesa Casati, the Duchesse de Guermantes. The allusions are specific. In a quite calculated way, by evoking Madame de Pompadour in a $15,000 bias-cut silk satin evening dress, the designer is selling not only an evening dress but, by association, a stake in the eighteenth century itself. Aligned in this way, its price is hiked into a different league of expectation. The revival of the* haute couture *has been achieved by marketing hand-built clothes as a sure-fire cultural talisman.*

Designer fashion markets dreams, lifestyles and fantasies for a tiny elite for short-term pleasures. While researching his book, *The Fashion Conspiracy,* Coleridge visited a Kuwaiti dry-cleaner shop which specialised in handling high fashion clothes. The back of the shop was filled with almost 300 unclaimed designer gowns, worth about $400,000. Some of the clothes had been there four or five years but were unlikely to ever be collected because the customers 'no longer like to wear that outfit' or have bought the new season's fashions. This 'elephants' graveyard' of abandoned couture underscored the 'pointlessness' of fashion as the failed amulets were rejected in favour of new ones. The clothes acted as technical props for high fashion women but could never live up to the expectations held of them.

While this 'dilemma' confronts few women in such an extreme form, many women are influenced by general trends in fashion and follow-albeit at a distance-the activities of the fashion industry. The relationship between couture (elite designers and consumers) and everyday fashion (high street designers and consumers) is complex. In both cases, it is mediated by fashion magazines but everyday fashion is also influenced by the system of 'looks' generated by high street designers, endorsed by the editors of fashion magazines and the buyers for large department stores and fashion boutiques. When Coleridge asked Grace Mirabella, former editor of American *Vogue,* where the power in the fashion triangle (designers, buyers or magazines) lay, she isolated magazines:

> *Which is not to say that individual designers don't make important statements. Or that store buyers aren't the first on their block. But finally, finally the magazines dictate what's at the top. We don't design clothes, but we can be very selective in our reporting. The insistence by us on a certain ease and modernity has been decisive, and we try to resist moving away from that.*

The role of the fashion editor is to follow the new 'shapes' offered at seasonal collections, select the ones that will be influential, devise a thematic 'story' to unify a selection of clothes, photograph them on location, then present them as a coherent fashion feature. Magazines like *Vogue* must also give their readers the kind of images and looks with which they can identify.

Although national editions of *Vogue* and *Elle* cater for specific tastes, in general the fashion industry makes a distinction between European and American looks. In fashion photographs, the difference is that "American" means the model jumping in the air on a sidewalk, grinning energetically from behind a shillelagh of blonde hair. "European" means more restrained, serious and artistic'. The tension between American and European 'looks' goes back to the shifting power relations within the fashion industry in the 1920s and 1930s, when American customers began to patronise the Paris designers while alternative fashion systems were developing to meet the specific needs of the large American market. For a long time, the position of Paris was maintained through sheer snobbery. The European look was touted as more sophisticated and French women promoted as role models for Americans.

This divide was perpetuated ruthlessly. Yaeger Kaplan has commented on the taste wars between French and American culture in the wake of World War II. She cites a writer in *Life* magazine who promoted 'The French Look' in a feature accompanied by photographs of a 'typical' pair of legs (short and slim), (small) bust in a brassière, and a hand (featuring large and expensive jewellery). The photographs were presented in 'a crude form of pseudoanthropological race cataloguing'. The French women were defined as '"sexier" than their American counterparts', making the most of their 'natural attributes' and generously employing 'artificial aids' where necessary. Beauty was something to be worked at and achieved, the product of labour and technical interventions as much as natural body attributes. The article implied that American women should smarten up their looks for the returning GIs by adapting elements from their French sisters. In this context, the photographs were designed to be used in the way store catalogues could be, by coding the language of fashion in visual terms and breaking it down into consumer items. This visual packaging of women was, Yaeger Kaplan suggests, a forerunner of 'industrialised surrealism or postwar "consumer cubism"'. Codes of dress and decoration were accompanied by aesthetic codes and labour rituals.

High street designers are thus in the business of meeting the requirements of the magazine editors, the store buyers, fashion photographers and advertisers, and the practical circumstances of high street consumers. Although they follow the couture trends, their own collections are shaped by more pragmatic concerns. Above all, fashions must be wearable and suit lifestyles that involve active doing (work) rather than being (leisure). Consequently, successful high street designers must be attuned to the patterns of everyday life and stylistic trends among ordinary consumers. According to Sahlins:

> *we think of designers as plucking their ideas out of thin air. But the fashion expert does not make his collection out of whole cloth; like Lévi-Strauss's famous bricoleur, he uses bits and pieces with an embedded significance from a previous existence to create an object that works, which is to say that sells which is also to say that objectively synthesizes a relation between cultural categories, for in that lies its saleability.*

The challenge for designers is to gain the support of key fashion leaders, in particular fashion editors and department store buyers. Designers must compromise between showing something daring and new while at the same time ensuring that it is wearable (at least in a modified form) and recognisable (draws on previous fashion styles).

Thus, there is always a tension between the promise of fashion and the lived experience. While fashion and advertising are invested with transformative properties which promise to revolutionise body-space relations, the practice of fashion is limited by practical concerns. Everyday consumers constantly negotiate fashion fantasies within the conditions of everyday life. The adoption of new styles entails a compromise between designer innovations and wearability. Because of this, the majority of fashion consumers are extremely selective and reject fashions that are inappropriate to their lifestyles.

In this process, the tension between techniques of being female and techniques of femininity is a major imperative in the transformation of ideas of clothes into systems of everyday fashion. It is perhaps surprising, then, that the vast majority of famous designers have been men. Despite the involvement of women in fashion design since the early days, the impact of women designers has fluctuated and few have become household names-the exceptions include Chanel, Schiaparelli, Vionnet, Vivienne Westwood and Donna Karan. But as Steele argues, the reasons for the male dominance of fashion relate to widely held prejudices and to power structures within the fashion industry. Men are often regarded as more creative than women, and as designing more 'flattering' clothes for women. Because 'women dress to please men', women prefer male designers who do not impose their 'personal design restrictions on their product'. Other reasons put forward to explain this male dominance included the belief that male designers are misogynists who come up with styles that ridicule women yet appeal to the masochistic streak in women. It is also demonstrably easier for male designers to get support and financial backing.

Although the number and success of women designers has been increasing in recent years, it could be argued that they have had a far-reaching impact on everyday fashion and gradual changes in styles and comfort of clothes. Women designers are often more concerned with how clothes can be worn rather than solely with the aesthetic dimensions of design. One woman designer commented that:

> *A woman creates clothes that correspond to her. There is an* identification-*whereas men who create clothes* sublimate *the women that they dress. It is, perhaps, for that reason that the clothes made by*

> *women are less spectacular, because we know the needs of other women, the defects that one wants to conceal and the advantages that one wants to show. Today women designers are the equal of men designers, although they do not create clothes in the same way-sublimation for the men, identification for the women.*

As western fashion has escalated in size and scope, its concerns have accommodated the demands of contemporary women consumers. The idea of clothes as the packaging of inner feminine qualities has been supplanted by a concern with clothes as the technical props for active living. One reflection of this has been the development of fashions for working women, a market niche that has been especially attractive to women designers. In other words, the technical demands made on clothes have changed in accordance with new circumstances in which clothes are necessary accoutrements.

In the process of extending the fashion system to everyday consumers, guides to fashion and style have been appended to other sources of feminine instruction: through etiquette manuals; fashion, teen and women's magazines; role models including pop stars, television characters and royalty; as well as friends and relatives. The process of prestigious imitation has been combined with technical advice. One example of this heady blend was offered in a book entitled *The Princess of Wales Fashion Handbook*. This book was ostensibly about how the Princess of Wales acquired a sense of 'style' and built up a wardrobe, make-up and set of 'looks'. The book also took her 'look' and used it as a role model for ordinary women. In other words, the book used the fantasy of the Princess as the basis of a modern 'etiquette' manual. It is just one of many such books and an example of the sub-genre of manuals based on an iconic role model (such as an actress or model).

James's book primarily addressed young working women who had not yet cultivated a sense of style, developed a multi-purpose wardrobe or learned the behavioural rituals associated with special occasions. The theme of the book was that 'your clothes talk for you, and it is important that the first impression is good'. As an instructional manual, the book used examples from Diana to teach readers how to wear their bodies and to give their bodies a language appropriate to their circumstances.

Style was defined as a combination of simplicity (understatement), practicality, and suitability (appropriate to the occasion). As well as sections on grooming, health and make-up, the book adapted the Princess's clothes for ordinary readers. Although Diana's clothes were hardly suitable for everyday wear, James took specific examples and adapted the 'look' for a basic wardrobe. This included coats, winter casuals (leisure and sporting coordinates), everyday wear (skirts and tops), holiday wear, suits, 'classic' dresses, evening wear, wedding dresses, and maternity wear. These clothes identified the key departments of women's lives. Each example was illustrated by taking one of Diana's outfits and adapting her 'look' for other body shapes.

Diana's thin (model-like) body was endorsed as the ideal body shape. Clothes that suited this canonical body would not suit other bodies so the outfits were adapted for four 'flawed' body shapes: hourglass; pear-shaped; short-waisted; and top-heavy. The adaptations involved disguising the body flaw. For shortwaisted people, clothes should be shaped in order to take the emphasis away from the waist (for example, using longer line jackets, tubular shapes or dropped waistlines). Top-heavy types should use wrap-over, asymmetrical tops and jackets in plain colours. In addition, 'off-centre buttoning is good for big-busted women because it takes the eye away from the centre of the bustline'

Ballgowns and traditional evening dresses are very flattering to this shape. Always make sure that you have a definite waistline; this, together with a fine elasticated neckline, will show you at your best. A deep sash or cummerbund is ideal, and can even be tied in a bow to give a touch of extra femininity.

On the other hand, straight-cut dresses belted at the waist 'would look awful-a sack of potatoes tied around the middle'. Pear-shaped bodies are the most problematic. One should avoid clothes that emphasise the waist because it' will only call attention to your problem'. Instead, emphasis should be given to the top with skirts and pants designed to minimise the bulk of the hips. Moreover:

There is no way of making a style that is too body-hugging look good on someone with big hips. At the other extreme, a large 'sack' shape will only make you look frumpy and bigger. The best way to get over the problem is to go for a striking top half that will combine well with a softer skirt to give you an overall slimmer appearance

The theme of these adaptations was not only that everyday body shapes did not conform to the ideals of the fashionable body, but that misshapen bodies should be regarded as 'problems' to be rectified or disguised. The language of the makeovers was accordingly instructional, authoritative and critical. Readers (ordinary women with ordinary bodies) could not achieve the Princess's perfect look, just an approximation to it depending on the severity of their body faults.

James also stressed the importance of dressing for the occasion. In a break from earlier style guides, this book emphasised the need to create a working wardrobe. This was illustrated by advice for choosing clothes which were suitable for job interviews which James described as 'one of those occasions when your clothes talk for you':

> *The clothes you wear will depend largely on the type of job you are applying for and the impression you wish to make. The right outfit for someone applying to work in a trendy boutique would be entirely wrong for the girl who is being interviewed for a job with a bank. However, some rules apply, whatever the situation. Always try to be yourself, and dress comfortably. If you are uncomfortable, you will lack confidence in your clothes and it will show. Looking smart doesn't mean looking dull and try to dress to a standard that you can maintain should you get the job.*

The tone of this fashion handbook indicates the fluid and dynamic relations between body and habitus inflected through clothing, behaviour, personal demeanour, and occasion. The style conveyed by choice of clothes articulates the contours of our habitus. Whether calculated or habitual, wearers construct themselves through clothes. As Angela Carter observed:

> *Clothes are the visible woman-the detachable skin which expresses inner aspirations, dreams and fantasies; they are the signs of our status to ourselves and to other people. Nevertheless, we are never fully in control of our appearances. There are movements in the wearing of clothes-movements not completely dictated by the fashion industry.*

The idea that clothes constitute a language and means of communication has been central to the proliferation of the fashion industry and its promotion through women's magazines and by sanctioned role models. The identity and social position that are established through dress codes include the ascription of femininity. Women are fashioned by the desire to re-form or mould the body itself. The reconstruction of body shape is part of the acquisition of a particular range of body techniques, concerning posture, and specialised body movements. Reshaping the body itself is merely another technique.

Managing the Feminine Body

The intelligible body includes our scientific, philosophical, and aesthetic representations of the body-our cultural *conceptions* of the body, norms of beauty, models of health, and so forth. But the same representations may also be seen as forming a set *of practical* rules and regulations through which the living body is 'trained, shaped, obeys, responds', becoming, in short, a socially adapted and 'useful body'.

The intelligible body and the useful body are two arenas of the same discourse; they often mirror and support each other. But the two bodies may also contradict and mock each other.

The desire to manage the body is the key to producing the social body. It is, of course, culturally specific. Bartky has considered fashion and beauty practices as modes of *body disciplines* concerned with: body size and shape; gesture, posture and movement; and producing the body as an ornamented surface. She argues that these practices produce selfregulating female subjects through the demonstration of control over the physical body. Although body disciplines are not unique to western culture, the obsession with the physical body as a visible index of moral qualities is specific. Prior to the nineteenth century, dieting and fasting had been associated with the development of the self. Moreover, these qualities had been identified with the select few who were deemed capable of attaining self-mastery and moderation:

> *In the late nineteenth century, by contrast, the practices of body management begin to be middle-class preoccupations, and concern with diet becomes attached to the pursuit of an idealized physical weight or shape; it becomes a project in service of 'body' rather than 'soul'. Fat, not appetite or desire, is the declared enemy, and people begin to measure their dietary achievements by the numbers on the scale rather than the level of their mastery of impulse and excess. The bourgeois 'tyrany of slenderness' had begun its ascendancy (particularly over women), and with it the development of numerous technologies-diet, exercise, and, later on, chemicals and surgery-aimed at a purely physical transformation.*

Body management became a means of 'normalising' the body in the process of reproducing gender relations and power relations more generally. Through processes of self-monitoring and self-regulation of the body, multiple demands and conflicts placed upon it could be accommodated. Bordo hypothesises that the 'preoccupation with the "internal" management of the body (i.e., management of its desires) is produced by instabilities in the "macroregulation" of desire within the system of the social body'. Bodies have become the 'site of struggle' over politics generated elsewhere but conducted through body techniques.

Concern with body management is also gender coded within western culture. Bordo argues that dieting and eating disorders are ways in which women can simultaneously express protest and retreat against prevailing definitions of gender and techniques of femininity. By controlling the intake and physical form of the body, women exhibit mastery over the body and their habitus. Moreover, they demonstrate 'male' qualities of 'detachment, selfcontainment, self-mastery, control' that are perceived to offer 'freedom (from a domestic destiny) and empowerment in the public arena'. Such displays undo associations of femininity with excess, over-indulgence and lack of control. The threat of femininity (and its manifestation in a 'womanly' body) is neutralised.

According to Bordo, women with eating disorders are merely the extreme version of the widespread desire for 'a slender body' prompted by the opposition in consumer culture between discipline and excess. Indeed, she suggests that eating disorders characterise the modern western 'self:

> *bulimia emerges as a characteristic modern personality construction, precisely and explicitly expressing the extreme development of the hunger for unrestrained consumption (exhibited in the bulimic's uncontrollable food-binges) existing in unstable tension alongside the requirement that we sober up, 'clean up our act', get back in firm control (the necessity for purge-exhibited in the bulimic's vomiting, compulsive exercising, and laxative purges).*

As the conditions of women's lives alter with higher formal education, incorporation in the workforce, assumption of careers, greater mobility, and voracious consumption of images of ideal bodies, the incidence of eating disorders has increased. They are a correlate of body techniques associated with the changing roles and definitions of self.

The incidence of bulimia nervosa (one to two per 100 women) and anorexia nervosa (one per 1,000 women) of western women suggests a social pathology. A recent survey of readers of the popular Australian magazine, *Cleo,* suggested that almost 15 per cent of 20-

to 24-year-old respondents were anorexic or bulimic; 11 per cent and 19 per cent of 25- to 30-year-olds were anorexic or bulimic respectively; as were 18 per cent and 14 per cent of 31- to 40-year-olds. These results correlated with respondents' extreme concern about their body image, self esteem and ability to cope with stress. Respondents over-estimated their own body size and identified over-thin models as their ideal body shape. Almost all women said they disliked something about their bodies, most commonly citing their thighs (71 per cent), bottom (58 per cent), stomach (56 per cent), hips (40 per cent), legs (32 per cent), breasts (22 per cent), and upper arms (17 per cent). These results endorsed the view that dieting is 'the peculiar consequence of a culture fascinated by individual competition, dietary management, the narcissistic body and the presentational self. In an article concerning 'the elastic body image', Myers and Biocca suggest that objective body shape is significantly greater than the internalised ideal body which, in turn, exceeds the socially represented ideal body:

> *As one's internalized ideal gets further away from one's objective body shape, the individual may experience a kind of self-loathing that exaggerates the perceived 'deformity' of one's objective body shape. This is supported by the observation that anorexics and bulimics, individuals who pathologically pursue an extreme internalized ideal, experience the greatest body image distortion. But body image distortion appears in normal populations as well, especially young females.*

Lynch argues that the mismatch between the slender ideal of role models and the fleshy attributes of ordinary women contribute to a 'lived tension of disembodiment' in the inability to fulfil the ideal. Increasingly, analysis of anorexia has been linked to feelings of powerlessness. But what begins as a refusal to be part of the power structure becomes a form of power and control in the behaviour itself: *not* eating becomes the locus of power and focus of attention in the anorexic's life:

> *The anorexic avoids the shameful world of eating, while simultaneously achieving personal power and a sense of moral superiority through the emaciated body. Their attempts at disembodiment through negation become the symbol of their moral empowerment.*

This argument fits into Elias's claims for the existence of a shame frontier and moral codes as the basis of European cultural behaviour. The physical components of the condition are subordinate to its moral dimensions. The anorexic is prompted by the inability to cope as an adult woman (not the ideal shape, unable to communicate, compete and achieve) and appears to become powerful through the condition:

The classic anorexic is the master (the gender-specificity of 'to master' is another complexity) of disguise and deception, only acting as if she had no appetite, while being fascinated by food.

While 'looking good' (attractive to the opposite sex and able to compete with other women) may be one of the factors leading to anorexic behaviour, Turner notes that, in fact, the condition leads to sexual and social unavailability, and ultimately to exclusion. Anorexia functions as a moral, ascetic defiance of contemporary culture. The complexity of the issue suggests that it would be misleading to over-emphasize the influence of specific role models in its incidence. But it does confirm Caputi's suggestion that a woman's body becomes her 'enemy and obsession for life'.

In a similar vein, Bordo compares the habits of dieters with those of bodybuilders engaged in 'the quest for firm bodily margins'. Although body-building appears to 'have the very opposite structure from anorexia...building the body up, not whittling it down', many body-builders 'talk about their bodies in ways that are disquietingly resonant with typical anorexic themes'. As a technique, body-building entails self-denial, purity, pain, a sense of the body as alien, and of mastery:

Most strikingly, there is the same emphasis on control, *on feeling one's life to be fundamentally out of control, and on the feeling of accomplishment derived from total mastery of the body... The technology of dictating to nature one's own chosen design for the body is at the centre of the bodybuilder's mania, as it is for the anorexic.*

The recent popularity of aerobics and fitness-as adjuncts to the diet industry-are generalised manifestations of these approaches to body management. Firm bodies, muscles and 'working out' have been redefined as 'a symbol of correct *attitude;* it means that one "cares" about oneself and how one appears to others, suggesting willpower, energy, control over infantile impulses, the ability to "make something" of oneself. In short, the feminine body is the site of severe conflict and prodigious labour. Body management constitutes a bewildering array of techniques aimed at realising the *intelligible* and *useful* body that can cope with the practical circumstances of one's habitus.

□□□

12

Fashion Image and Fashion Journalism

Introduction

The fashion media does indeed function as a pillar of support for the industry. Had it not been for the appearance of *The Face* magazine in 1980 and *i-D* in the same year, British *Elle* magazine in 1985, and the British edition of *Marie Claire* in 1988, the boom in United Kingdom designer fashion through the 1980s and into the 1990s could hardly have happened. However, the magazines did not provide this support in an unconditional, unmediated or uncomplicated way. The fashion media 'represents' fashion and in so doing adds its own gloss, its own frame of meaning to the fashion items which serve as its raw material. The support it offers, and the role it plays, are limited by the various traditions and conventions which have defined fashion journalism as a specialist field, shaping what can be said, and in what kind of format. And so the initial and most significant difficulty faced in exploring the relations between these two sectors is that the fashion media exists within a set of institutions and organisations whose working practices are entirely different from those of fashion design. We are entering the world of journalism as soon as we step foot inside the offices of *Marie Claire* magazine, or *Elle*, or the *Guardian* newspaper. It is the professional codes of journalism which dictate the way in which fashion is packaged and presented on their various pages. The fashicn media is therefore as separate and as autonomous from the world of design as the fashion departments in the art schools are from the working lives of the designers. We are talking about an entirely different institutional environment.

The work of the editors and journalists as well as the other creative practitioners including photographers and stylists, is driven by a different set of logics from that of the fashion designers. These are the logics of creative and editorial reputation, circulation figures, competition from rival publications and advertising revenue. These considerations play a key role in influencing the way in which fashion appears within these different media. But one of the significant features of fashion journalism is that it is set apart from other forms of journalism. The fashion media finds itself more closely linked with the fashion industry than would be the case in other journalistic fields. The low status of fashion writing within the hierarchical field of print journalism pushes those who work in fashion closer together. The writers, photographers, fashion assistants and contributing editors share the same 'fashion world' as the designers, the company directors, the press officers and publicity personnel. This is a narrow, even closed, world which perceives itself to be trivialised and associated with a kind of stupidity, for example, Linda Grant in the *Guardian* 15 April 1997 writes, 'the brain of a supermodel isn't much, and so it was that Naomi Campbell came late to understanding that the fashion industry is in the business of selling and that what sells are blonde haired, blue eyed girls'. Likewise, in the aftermath of the murder of Gianni Versace another journalist wrote in the *Guardian*, 'Why all the bother, sceptics ask, over a preening victim of fashion, who belongs to the fashion press, not to Fleet Street?'. As a result, fashion journalism does not have the security and confidence of other media worlds. Tunstall argues that because specialist fields in journalism associated with consumer-based activities are advertising-revenue led, they inevitably have a closer relationship with the industry which manufactures and promotes the product, since this is both the source of 'news' and of revenue. Fashion, because of its feminine status, is something of a special case in this respect. It has a presence in both the women's magazine market and in the daily press. Where the readership for the women's magazines can be assumed to be interested in fashion, there is less of an emphasis on fashion having to prove itself. But in the daily press, where the staff journalists are predominantly male, even in the context of appearing within the remit of the 'women's page', fashion is more unsure of its status. This often produces a shrill, often overblown, language so that the reader is reminded once too often of the creative genius of John Galliano or Vivienne Westwood, triggering a counter-reaction exactly like that expressed in the wake of Versace's death in the *Daily Telegraph,* where a headline ran 'Was Versace Really A Genius?' and the journalist added, 'Nothing wrong with being vulgar. Versace had a very good idea. It's just that it seems odd to treat it as high art'.

The limitations of the role played by the media in supporting the fashion sector stems from the conservatism and timidity of fashion journalism and its genres. This in turn is the product of the ethos of 'keeping the advertisers and the readers happy' which is particularly strong in the magazines. In practice, references to 'the readers' are typically a means of gatekeeping or controlling the flow of copy so that the advertisers are indeed kept happy in the knowledge that their product is being seen by huge numbers of the right kind of people. This knowledge of the readership gained, according to the editors through polls and market research, is actually a useful fiction, a means by which the power of the editor is deployed. It is a crucial part of his or her professional language. It is also one of the means by which all editorial decisions are justified 'Our readers wouldn't like it' is a familiar response. But resistance to change couched in these terms produces a strangely old fashioned and unchanging feel to the fashion writing and reporting in magazines. The reliance on 'tried and tested' formulae pushes fashion out on a limb in an otherwise rapidly changing and innovative media world.

The images might be designed to shock, but the text remains culturally reassuring. On these pages fashion reporting and writing conform to a pattern wherein no real offence is ever spoken and no rules appear to be broken. The 'shock of the new' remains carefully contained within the legitimate avant-gardism of fashion photography (for example, the 'dirty realism' of grunge) and the fashion media regulates itself with a system of informal censorship. Of all forms of the consumer culture, fashion seems to be the least open to self scrutiny and political debate. This is because the editors deem that fashion must steer well clear of politics, and fashion journalists are expected to go along with this. With *Vouge* acting more or less as a universal benchmark of quality, fashion-as-politics is only conceivable as a catchy idea for a 'fashion story'.

Fashion reportage is almost the same now in the 1990s as it was in 1967 when Barthes it was turned his attention to fashion writing and found on the pages of the French fashion magazines a kind of rhetoric which was always anxious to reassure the young female reader that there was nothing out there in the world that was anything other than pleasurable or at least enjoyable. Barthes wrote 'Fashion's bon ton, which forbids it to offer anything aesthetically or morally displeasing, no doubt unites here with maternal language: it is the language of a mother who "preserves" her daughter from all contact with evil'. The world existed to give these young women excuses for luxury holidays and romantic reveries ('a weekend in the country', 'visiting his chateau', 'a Bermuda break'). What Barthes described, still more or less prevails today with the provision of an occasional ironic, postmodern gloss on such stories. The rules on fashion reportage, the conventions which define the field of fashion representation, also set the fashion world apart from the rest of the media by virtue of this very conservatism. It seems that the overwhelming emphasis on images, indicating that the magazines are primarily 'to-be-looked-at', somehow relegates the role of text to accessory, to banal commentary, to a poetics of mood, to simple information, caption, headline, 'statement', or else it conforms to the tradition of superlatives in fashion writing. Even the more radical youth culture-oriented magazines such as *The Face* and *i-D* abide by these rules to an extent. Although they have pioneered new styles of fashion photography which sometimes suggest that the world is not such a pleasant place, (for example, fashion as a poverty aesthetic as promoted by *The Face* and *i-D* in the early 1990s) this remains a visual genre with an artistic signature. It is 'just' a style. And, as Dick Hebdige has forcibly argued in relation to The Face, where everything is on the surface, laid out as a style, there can be no place for serious discussion, there are only superficial skirmishes or 'style wars'. An article about manufacturing for Hussein Chalayan, or about graduates working for free? Forget it. In this context sociological analysis or political debate are either simply not the 'house style' or are 1970s' 'retro' phenomena and thus a bit of a joke.

There are some important points of difference between the smaller, more independent press and the large circulation glossies. *i-D* retains a focus on ordinary young, black and working-class, men and women as the source of most fashion ideas. In interview the fashion editor, Edward Enningful, argued that fashion designers look to the magazine for their inspiration: 'Designers use the magazine as a reference. It's a question of what's up, what's going on? It's a visual thing'. By claiming that fashion ideas come from youth cultures, *i-D* provides a more open and accessible version of fashion culture, certainly a counter to the *haute couture* approach. But this, too, has its limits if we also take into account what cannot be said or shown in *i-D* and what is ruled out by its own editorial commitment to promoting fashion and style while ignoring completely its existence as a place of work and a space of livelihoods. *The Face* also offers an important forum for cultural and creative workers from a whole range of fields to have their work seen and commented on. *The Face* unproblematically sets fashion design alongside painting, sculpture, music and cinema without subjecting it to the old high and low culture divide. This might be seen as one of the redeeming features of its postmodern ethos, to break down that distinction. But these magazines also draw their own boundaries which exclude any detailed or serious discussion of the social processes or economic relations which underpin fashion as a cultural activity. Instead they construct style and fashion as insider knowledge, possessed by young, urban taste makers whose seemingly innate sense of 'what's going on' sets them apart from the masses and puts them in the lead in terms of what Thornton argues is a kind of 'subcultural capital'. This insight and expertise is then recorded, re-worked and translated into the language of the magazine as a series of distinctive taste cultures by the editors, art directors, photographers and stylists. The problem then is that as these firm up as genres of reportage which in turn become a set feature of the style magazines, the apparent openness of this media in fact becomes more closed.

Why has the fashion media developed in this way? To begin to answer this question we need to know how it works, including who does which job, and how key decisions are reached. This is a more difficult task than might be imagined. Just as we have seen an extraordinary amount of job mobility within the field of fashion design, with many designers doing two jobs at once, so also when we look towards the fashion media we are confronted with occupational fluidity which makes it difficult, if not impossible, to actually define and specify different jobs and the people who do them. This is partly because fashion journalism and many of its associated activities, in particular fashion publicity, has grown enormously throughout the 1980s. Until then, there were a limited number of outlets. The quality newspapers each had a fashion editor and a weekly slot, usually a single page, and apart from this there were only the fashion and women's magazines. But since the 1980s the scale of coverage given to fashion has expanded into television and across all the new magazine publications, as well as commanding more space on the daily newspapers. Fashion has become a subject of interest to a much wider section of the population. This can be seen most clearly in the family magazine programmes on daytime television. Not only do the programmes have daily fashion reports, they also have the immensely popular fashion make-overs where couples of all ages come forward to have themselves restyled from head to foot by a team of experts.

This attention to fashion is part of the general expansion of the media and, more broadly, of visual culture and it also connects with the new attention to personal image and style led by the fashion retailers throughout the 1980s. A key dilemma for the fashion industry is that while millions enjoy looking at these images on the page or on the screen, there is no direct relation between looking and actually consuming. The availability of cheaper full colour print technology, the celebrity value of the fashion 'supermodels' and the sales appeal of having a glamorous model on the front page of all the newspapers has given fashion a more prominent position as a cultural phenomenon. One consequence of this is that a lot more people are employed in producing these fashion images and in writing about fashion. As in other similar areas of recent expansion (pop videos, for example), specific jobs often emerge in the process of somebody doing one job and seeing gaps and opportunities existing in related areas which have as yet no formal title. This indeterminacy, which Tunstall and Elliott both argue are characteristics common to media occupations in general, gives rise to both high degrees of labour mobility and to the creation of new job titles almost overnight. For example, a fashion manageress at a key department store will meet with buyers, fashion agents, designers and merchandisers, as well as with the fashion press, on an almost daily basis. With this kind of experience and with such a wide range of contacts, a shift into being a fashion agent, doing fashion public relations and sales, or even setting up an agency for photographers, models, stylists and others, is not at all an unusual step to take. In effect these are media jobs, especially when we consider how reliant journalists now are on pre-written press release material for their own copy. Two respondents in this present study followed this kind of pathway. One young woman, Naihala Lasharie, started as a sales assistant at Harvey Nichols. She moved to a well-known fashion public relations company, worked for nothing for a few months and was then put on the payroll. After a year she began to build up her own list of clients. Now working for herself, her clients included the Italian label, Alberta Ferretti. As she says: 'Mrs Ferretti was a good story. I got full page coverage for her in *Vouge, Elle* and The *Independent*.' Naihala then moved full time to promote the cult shoe designer Patrick Cox (whose Wannabe loafers became an international brand) and looked after the shops, sales and public relations. At the time of the interview Naihala had left Patrick Cox to set up once again on her own in public relations and sales with twelve clients, her own office and a small staff.

Paul Davies also began his career in the mid-1980s in sales:

> *After two years at Harvey Nichols as senior sales assistant where I was liaising with buyers, merchandisers, floor controllers and suppliers, and then a further two years at Jones with responsibility for visual merchandising, I set up a Press Office for the group which at that time had five stores on the Kings Road and at Covent Garden. After that I went out on my own with the Z Agency for models, hair and make-up artists, stylists and photographers. I was primarily a photographers' agent which involved trips to Germany to introduce the photographic side to the fashion magazines in Munich, and the same thing elsewhere.*

A third respondent, Marysia Woroniecka, was, at the time of this interview, London's best-known fashion PR. She, too, had created her job on the basis of experience in retail and getting to know key people:

I started aged eighteen working in retail. Then I moved into wholesaling 'own collections' which I presented to the fashion editors. I went to parties and got to know more of the fashion people and then went to work in an advertising agency which I hated. From there I went to Jean Bennett PR who had ten clients and I had lots of freedom and learnt about the whole fashion business. By the age of twenty two I had my own company. There were fewer fashion magazines then, and a different kind of fashion press. It was a lot more limited. One of my jobs.was advising clients (that is, the designers) which editors to contact and try and get to come to the shows, even what clothes to highlight. So I was also advising them on their collections. I knew what the media would go for. The bubble burst at the end of the 1980s. There was a different, much more demanding fashion media and the designers often couldn't come up with the quality or the finish. You could have 800 people turn up for a show, but if the quality of the product wasn't up to scratch, it could all become a complete disaster. The publicity could be top notch, but that still couldn't solve the production problems which the designers at the time all seemed to have. It was costing me more to have them on my books so I eventually had to lose them and concentrate on my two main clients, Benetton and Jigsaw.

As well as indicating the limits to the kind of support given to designer clients by their press and publicity agent, while also acknowledging the weaknesses in production, both of the above comments not only tell us something about the flexibility of the career structures opened up with the expansion of fashion culture and the growth of the fashion media through the 1980s, they also describe a high degree of integration and overlap between different sectors of the industry. Individuals can move from being shop assistants to setting up their own media companies within the space of less than three years. Marysia Woroniecka, has now, at the time of writing, moved to New York and works as a fashion journalist setting up web site magazines.

Harriet Quick, who at the time of the interview was fashion editor for the *Guardian*, described her career moves as follows:

I have worked for five years as a journalist, after completing the one year postgraduate course at City University. I started in design journalism first, on the World of Interiors *magazine for six months. Then I went to* Fashion Weekly *as menswear editor. I was there for two years. In 1992 I was freelance and won the Jackie Moore Award in the* Vogue *writing competition. I went back to* Fashion Weekly *which was superb training for the whole fashion industry, and while I was there I was also freelancing for* Elle *and* Vogue*, and also doing some designer interviews*

> *for* i-D. *I started doing some bits for Louise Chunn who was then fashion editor at the* Guardian *and then I took over from her when she left to go to* Vogue.

This demonstrates both the high degree of mobility within a specialist field such as fashion journalism, and also describes ways of working which Philip Elliott has argued are standard practice in media journalism, for example, doing several jobs at once, and doing low pay or no pay work as a means of getting, and remaining, known (Harriet would have worked unpaid for *i-D*). Again, this is not unique to fashion but is, argues Elliott, a way for journalists to maintain a more creative profile or of having some outlet for writing pieces which would not find a home within the more commercial sector. More specifically, the degree of to ing and fro ing between journalism and public relations encourages a kind of professional dialogue which makes it difficult for those involved to draw hard and fast lines around where reporting finishes and advertising begins, a task made even more difficult with the rise of lucrative, sponsored advertising features which have come to be known as 'advertorials'.

It is the rise of the stylist which is the most significant development for the way in which fashion design finds itself represented in the media. The stylist operates within the space between the design work itself and the creation of a broader environment or setting for that work. He or she does this by bringing those items into a particular and 'styled' relationship with other pieces of clothing. Located midway between assistant to the fashion editor and photographer s assistant, styling became a recognised job as these various assistants (often with an art school training in fine art or photography) began to realise their own creative input into the fashion pages and the freelance potential of their work. They planned and then put the whole image on the page together, including the combination of clothes (usually from a range of different designers) the look of the model, including hair and make up, the props needed for the narrative or non-narrative setting, the lighting and the overall 'look' of the image or series of images. Starting off as assistants who ran errands and went out scouring the second-hand markets for props, the stylists were increasingly given more of a free hand by imaginative editors (such as Sally Brampton at *Elle*) and soon a number of them began to develop a distinctive 'style' of 'styling', to the point that other editors could put a name to a page without looking at the credits. From this a new creative occupation was born. The stylist's services were suddenly in demand across the fashion media, but also and more lucratively they were brought in to 'style' individual pop stars (like Kylie Minogue, for example) and to work on pop promotional videos and advertisements. This career developed out of the smaller independent magazines like *The Face* and *i-D* which were at the forefront of what came to be known as the 'designer decade'. Spurning the need for advertising revenue the editors allowed the stylists to experiment with fashion on the page. When it was launched in 1985, *Elle* magazine also relied on the work of key stylists such as Melanie Ward and Debbie Mason to give its fashion a look which was quite distinctive and different from *Vogue,* its main competitor. However, it was *The Face* and *i-D* which helped to create the stylist as a new strata of media professionals. People such as Judy Blame, Venetia Scott, Melanie Ward and Anna Cockburn all worked for nothing for these magazines, but it paid off in the longer term since the readership included art directors from international companies, advertising account managers and key people from the music industry. The magazines therefore provided an ideal venue for this kind of 'art work' and also helped to create these new jobs in the media industries.

Anna Cockburn described in interview how she became a stylist:

I did two years of fine art at Central St Martins, but I knew I wasn't going to paint. I was much more interested in making images, so I left and worked as an assistant to a fashion photographer, knowing nothing much about fashion. For six months it was a bit of a nightmare. Then I got a job at Joseph (the designer fashion retailer) and it was interesting to me because of the contact with customers. I became more conscious of clothes and the personal thing of helping the customer to choose. At that stage I didn't know what a stylist was. But I wanted a change and heard there was possibly some work at *Harpers and Queen,* assistant to the fashion editor, and I got the job. During this time I was also working in a pub during the evening to pay my bills. At *Harpers* I found myself with six pages and whether it was a collection I saw, a film or a dream, or a painting, it was the idea that was important. The stylist and the photographer can both be mavericks and it works. I got promoted to Junior Fashion Editor in 1988/9 and then the recession hit and it all became more commercial, you were forced to be less creative. I went to *Elle* and I was on Best Buys with cheaper clothes and of course I tried to make it good with the best photographers, but there was a lot of pressure and I didn't really settle down. I then spent a year in America on various projects, came back as contributing fashion editor at *Vogue*. It was a bit disappointing because everything had to be agreed and approved, from the models to the photographers it was all done at the level of 'house style'. Since then I have been completely freelance. The agent, Camilla Lowther, calls me up and says there is a job here or there. At the same time, right through this whole period I have worked for *The Face* and *i-D* who don't pay but it is exposure and it's advertising for people like myself and the photographers who I've worked with for them. I ring them up when I have an idea of something I'd like to do for them. It always costs me, but it's worth it for the freedom, the exposure and the space. They are also generous with the credits which are more visible and bold.

This comment is worth quoting at length for the detail it provides on this emergent occupational category of the stylist and the insight it offers on a number of themes which are directly relevant to this and the following chapter. These are, first, the idea of 'making images' as creative work; second, the opportunity of movement in this field from working as a shop assistant to being a fashion editor on a glossy magazine; third, the way in which creativity conflicts more directly with commerce in the magazine environment when the industry goes into a recession; and, finally, the extraordinary working schedule of this young woman who has, throughout the entire period of paid work, also done unpaid work for the style press in order to keep her own creative profile visible. It has been suggested that this kind of pattern of working is by no means unusual in media occupations. But the move towards working on a permanent, freelance basis is much more marked in the 1990s than it was in the 1970s. Not only are the culture industries more crowded than before, with the growth of the service sector and the impact of privatisation and deregulation, but the expansion in self-employment and freelance working has been enormous. This is a way of 'capital' unburdening itself of responsibility for 'workers'. In a high unemployment labour market the very idea of working for no pay or on spec becomes more acceptable as young people are increasingly desperate to get their foot in the door.

It is not, I think, coincidental that the final destination of the fashion designers who participated in this study was to work in an entirely freelance capacity. With the same drift in fashion journalism we can reasonably ask, how sustainable are these micro-economies, these self-employed careers? How long, for example, can somebody like Anna Cockburn carry on at this level of activity? What would happen to her career and her personal livelihood if she was ill for even a short period, or if she took time off to have a child? Is she a valuable asset because of her talent or is this as crowded and as competitive as the other media occupations? The growth in this kind of work has been more than matched by the number of young people keen to work in the fashion media. It is an area of work brimming over with graduates from universities and art schools including prospective writers, photographers, graphic designers, and art directors, to the extent that the Prime Minister himself, writing in the *Guardian*, claimed there to be over 300,000 people now employed in Britain in the design sector. As Anna Cockburn's career indicates, most of the work in this field is of a freelance character. This is highly advantageous to the employers. It also creates more competition and almost certainly results in the undercutting of set rates of pay. Even the biggest circulation magazines like *Marie Claire* now operate with a tiny full-time staff and a whole range of different kinds of contracts for different kinds of work, for example, contributing fashion editor, associate editor, contributing features editor, and so on.

This freelance culture produces new social relations in work. A stylist commissioned to put a series of pages together needs to know that she can pull in the photographer and the models and also get hold of the clothes she needs, all to a tight deadline. The informal team-work and even sub-contracting which comes into being around this new freelance economy has been barely documented in academic writing or in the media. Often it emerges from friendship groups which go back to art school or university, or a stylist will develop a 'feel' for working with a particular photographer and they in turn might have contacts with a couple of models and a new fashion design graduate and they will all pull their resources together and do a number of 'tests' (a fashion story) which they will then present 'on spec' to magazines such as *The Face* or *i-D*. A number of international careers have been launched on this basis (the model

Kate Moss teamed up with 'model-turned-photographer' Corinne Day for *Vogue* in 1993, having already done a number of trial shots or 'tests' for *i-D*). The magazines and newspapers are inundated with these presentations of work and many have now adopted a commission only policy. Harriet Quick of the *Guardian* reported receiving up to five portfolios per week. Recognition of the value of exposure has also given rise to new glossy publications like *Dazed and Confused* and *Don't Tell* It (again non-paying) setting up in competition with *The Face* and *i-D*. The entire copy for these magazines is in effect 'donated' in the hope that it will be seen by big budget magazine editors and advertising companies looking to recruit new talent.

Keeping track of the economics of this kind of work is difficult, if not impossible. Only by interviewing individual participants in the field can we develop any sense of how it functions and what kind of living these people actually make. To be able to get some picture of the kind of division of labour which exists in fashion journalism what is needed is a thorough documentation of the field. It seems however, that the only practical methodology is indeed the individual interview. People move about so quickly and there are so many short term contracts or part-time jobs that it is difficult to keep abreast of these changes. It is not at all unusual, indeed it is increasingly the norm, for a fashion editor to be employed for just three days a week in order to put her pages together on a major monthly fashion magazine or even a daily newspaper, leaving the rest of the week 'free' to freelance elsewhere (though not on a similar title) as a way of making up a full-time wage. At the same time, full-time magazine staff also freelance or 'moonlight' for other slots, particularly on television or radio. A highly paid fulltime fashion editor may also be filing copy for a foreign newspaper or working with a new cable channel or consulting for a design company. Editors regularly move on. Some, like Glenda Bailey of *Marie Claire*, move to take up lucrative posts in New York while others, like Sally Brampton, go on to combine teaching fashion journalism with freelance writing. Nor is it uncommon for well-known fashion editors to work for the big fashion companies such as Armani, usually in the press and publicity departments. Crossing the boundaries in this world is also common. For example, the German designer, Jil Sander, employed Anna Cockburn to add her distinctive 'styling' talents to Sander's original collection. This involved designing the catwalk show (make-up, set, logo, lights, music, etc) and then also styling the models with the clothes for a series of advertisements and an in-house brochure. This shows how, in the world of the image industries, fashion design recognises the need for additional skills in the transition from three dimensional fashion to the one dimensional page, or from the art of fashion to the art work of the page.

Fashion is not the only field to have so many ill-defined jobs and such high degrees of job mobility. This is a mark of the creative sector as a whole although the nearest comparison is the music industry where, as Negus has argued, the creative ethos produces occupational fluidity unheard of elsewhere. Artists can move into production, even a shift into journalism is not uncommon, while journalists are often aspiring musicians waiting for a break. In the fashion world it is uncommon but not altogether exceptional for designers to move into journalism (Helen Storey has recently made such a move). And while several editors or journalists may have started out with ambitions to be a designer (Glenda Bailey, editor of British *Marie Claire* from 1988-95, studied fashion design before moving into journalism) most of the journalists have simply combined an interest in fashion and style with writing and reporting. However, like the music industry, this is a small and close-knit community where everybody seems to know everybody else. It is also a precarious world in terms of both jobs and income and this means that individuals are continually thinking and projecting into the future for contacts, new work or consultancies or similar offers. As we have seen, there is also a high degree of mobility between press office work and journalism and together these factors produce a culture of consensus in the magazines and the fashion press. It is simply not worth upsetting those who occupy positions of power. Journalists quickly learn the rules of the game and this means knowing what kind of story not to offer.

The relatively closed world of fashion makes it more difficult to untangle the relationship between fashion design and the fashion media. We are not able to simply place the designers in one corner and the editors and journalists in the other. There is so much mediation between the two (through public relations departments, press offices and agents) that the very idea of looking at how the fashion media 'represents' fashion design is immediately more complicated than it might seem. Each separate magazine, newspaper or television programme has its own particular 'house style', its own image of itself and of its audience or readership. Different media favour different kinds of fashion. We therefore need to tackle a further set of relations between actual, rather than imagined, readers and consumers and their fashion preferences (fantasy or otherwise) in order to chart the connection between editorial policy and the choice of clothes featured on the pages.

There are hard and fast rules which govern the field of fashion journalism and magazine production and which set it apart from other areas. I have already argued that these have remained in place over a longer period of time than might be expected. The conservatism which characterises fashion journalism is also the product of its marginal and feminine status. It has managed to safeguard its own tradition, one which perceives itself to be quite separate from the world of mainstream journalism. There is, for example, a reliance upon a set of conventions, and a generic structure, for dealing with fashion which date back to the 1920s heyday of *Vogue* magazine and its commitment to fashion as art and as luxury consumption for upper-middle-class women. This is the dominant tradition of fashion journalism. Despite the various popularising forms of fashion media (like the BBC's *The Clothes Show*) the *Vogue* model retains a strong influence over the practitioners. The old élitist image of fashion lingers among the professionals, in particular in their respect for the litany of Vogue editors whose snobbishness and tyrannical ways of working are mythologised as part of fashion history. Figures such as Diana Vreeland, one of the most influential of *Vogue* editors for over thirty years, and currently Suzy Menkes of the International Herald Tribune, embody this fiercesome, flamboyant and immensely respected image on the basis of their knowledge of fashion and their writing about it. Students are encouraged to emulate their style of writing, with its eagle eye for detail combined with sweeping judgements and dramatic proclamations as in the famous statement by Freeland, 'Pink is the navy blue of India'. Because these editors see fashion as an extension of high culture, a branch of the fine arts which has been neglected, while at the same time being part of a luxury consumer culture, the last thing in the world they are going to draw attention to is pay and conditions. They might express concern when designers go out of business, or they might ocassionally write about the economic state of the industry as a whole (although this is unusual), but they do not see this as in any way a priority. Their typical response is that this is not what readers want to hear about 'It's not a *Marie Claire* story.' Instead the editors deal in a world of fashion images and fashion fantasies, and fashion imagery as part of the wider popular culture works at the level of fantasy or enjoyment. The emphasis on looking, with function and information being reduced to the merest hint of a new seasonal look, means that editors can indulge all their own fantasies and show clothes which are well beyond the financial reach of the readership. The logic of the fashion image on the page is not primarily to stimulate immediate consumption the reader need not feel any obligation to buy, this is not a selling strategy, nor is it an advertisement instead it is a journalistic strategy. For example, in one issue of the *Guardian* the clothes by the designer Alberta Ferretti shown on the three page spread included a chiffon dress at £1,010, a kimono coat at £1,467 and a chiffon skirt at £601. This article comprised a profile of the woman and her work and described her success in business and her high-tech factory in northern Italy. Ferretti's clothes are extraordinarily expensive and so the point of running such a feature is to say something to the readers about Ferretti as somebody they ought to know about, and to show the work so that it evokes a certain mood or fantasy about beauty, wealth and 'lifestyle', as well as about female sexuality. The abstract and sexually evocative way in which the pictures are shot (in one picture the model is absent-mindedly touching herself, as though aroused simply by what she is wearing) appeal to the features of taste and distinction by which particular readers are addressed as a means of confirming their class, status and cultural capital. Readers of the *Guardian* are expected not to be shocked precisely because these are clothes which carry an art value. They are 'pieces' to be admired. This determines how they are presented on the page and how they are to be written about. As long as the editor is confident that the *Guardian* readers will not be put off by such a feature (although a few might write to complain about the prices as in this case, 'I mean £1,010 for a tarted up bit of net curtain as I say, disgusting and obscene' the *Guardian Weekend* 12 April 1997) and that they will consume the images at the level of art, fantasy and enjoyment, then she can be satisfied that she has made the right choice. The fashion copy creates both a particular kind of readership and flatters it with its good taste. Harriet Quick explained her editorial strategy at the *Guardian* in the following terms:

With the weekend supplement we are in the fortunate position of being able to be adventurous. There is a good deal of forward thinking, a mix of literature, art, music, culture. Newspapers are obviously different from magazines, we don't have to be cutting edge and we take fewer risks visually. We have to make fashion communicable and accessible. The writing has to balance detail with the visual side, information with the conceptual angle.

This comment locates fashion within a triple framework of the arts and culture, lifestyle and leisure interests and, as we have seen, less directly with consumer culture. With such a broad remit it might be expected that other issues which relate more to the fashion industry as a whole, such as sales, turnover, export and import, might also be covered. But this is very rarely the case. There are as fixed a set of genres of fashion writing as there are of fashion imagery. These do not include the business or economics of fashion, or its existence as a sector of employment. While newspapers like the *Guardian* will run the occasional story on the success of Marks & Spencer, or a profile on a key retailer such as Jigsaw or Whistles, there is little serious attention given to how clothes are produced and exactly who consumes them. Fashion journalism and fashion photography are unique in the field of mass communications. The fashion pages show clothes available for consumption and list the stockists or they talk about designers and retailers and report on the new collections, but these pages do not have to sell the clothes.

Because they are neither advertisements nor reviews in the traditional sense, nor simply consumer information, they occupy a vague and indeterminate visual space. It is precisely this that licenses the move into the field of fantasy and sexuality. The photographers and stylists welcome the creative freedom provided on the fashion pages. For them it is a unique opportunity to show off their talent. The magazine page functions like the gallery wall. For the editors and the creative teams the art work of the page takes precedence over the clothes that are being featured. Sometimes they can barely be seen or they fade into the background. Edward Enningful, fashion editor of *i-D* described the fashion pages in the following terms: 'The magazine itself is art. The main thing about the work here is that it is creative. *i-D* isn't fashion, it's ahead of fashion.' Sheryl Garrett, editor of *The Face* took this even further when she said that the art directors sometimes commissioned designers to create specific fashion pieces to go with the pages:

> *Fashion-wise we are pushing back the barriers, it's not a question of simply presenting clothes. Often we commission clothes to be designed to go with the overall art idea. It's more of an art direction approach to fashion. And, because of this, the best fashion photographers and stylists will work for us for free.* The Face *is a career ladder, a huge opportunity for creative professionals to get attention and to show their work.*

What these statements show is that the style magazines promote their own art work and their own overall look or image. They are much less concerned about showing the work of designers. Fashion fits into the vision of the editors, photographers and the stylists but it does not define what they do. So in this sense even the style press, so committed to fashion, cannot be said to be supporting it or promoting it in any direct and unmediated way. The art work is the means by which the style press 'advertises' its own creative talent, offering valuable exposure for photographers, stylists and also models. Sheryl Garrett said in interview that if one of the supermodels wants to change her image, or liven up a slightly flagging reputation, she will offer to do a cover shot and fashion spread with her favourite creative team at *The Face,* again for no fee. There is in this transaction, wherein virtually no money passes through anybody's hands, a multiple trade-off between the model and her image, the magazine and its status and identity as being at the leading edge of fashion, the photographer who takes the picture and, finally, the person who designs the clothes which the model is wearing. Indeed everybody is in it for 'image'.

The style press encourage their freelance creative teams to produce images which break boundaries and attract a lot of attention. Sheryl Garrett described how this happened with a fashion spread in The Face which featured models splattered in blood: 'Most of the magazines followed up Tarantino images with the men in suits, they played around with that. What we did was the blood issue, the fashion with blood story.' Controversial images like these also mean publicity for the photographers and stylists and for the magazine itself. It is by giving the creative teams a free hand with the fashion pages that the work ends up being shown in exhibitions and gaining the approval of the art critics. If newspapers like the *Guardian* provide readers with cultural capital through their fashion coverage, and thus also 'cultivate' the readership, the style press participates in a similar process through its embodiment and distribution of 'subcultural capital'. But unlike art magazines and journals, magazines such as *The Face* or *i-D* which are by no means simply visual publications and do carry written text do not, however, run any serious or critical commentaries on the sort of work they promote and feature on their own pages. As Hebdige points out, there is only the catchy tide, the witty caption, or the ironic few lines of commentary. This precludes the possibility of dialogue or critique or even judgement. As Hebdige says, it simply puts everything on the surface.

The art directors and graphic designers also relegate fashion to second place in this visual field. The photographers and stylists see this as their space and do with it as they pleasethey compose the page and have no obligation to fashion designers, they merely use their work where it suits. It could be argued that it is none the less by this means that fashion has achieved the status it has craved, it is turned into an aesthetic image *because* there is no text, no reviews and thus no procedures or criteria for judgement (as there is in film criticism or music). Fashion remains a 'spread' and its values are simply stated or asserted. There is no substantial and accompanying discourse which debates questions of value or which casts judgement on the basis of agreed criteria. A number of reputations get made by this means, photographers end up having their work exhibited in art galleries and designers become household names. Nobody requires that the fashion journalists defend or even explain the basis of their judgements. It seems to be enough that the work which is shown, and the image itself, are recognised as important. Of course, Bourdieu would argue that this is the traditional means by which the 'creator is created'. Cultural outsiders are excluded from understanding how such decisions are arrived at, precisely as a strategy of power and as a means of protecting already existing cultural hierarchies. In such a context it hardly matters that the old divide between high art and popular culture has been broken down because, even in this more flattened world where fashion is treated as art, it is still subject to these traditional patterns of representation.

In addition to this process of aesthetic transformation, the fashion item itself need hardly exist as an object for sale in the shops because its existence is more concrete, more assured and much more widely seen on the page. The style press and other magazines have contributed to the visibility and popularity of fashion culture, but the truly postmodern dilemma for the fashion designers is that fashion has a more substantial and a more popular existence as an image on the page than it has as a set of clothes on the rail. As an economy of images operating in the field of magazine and newspaper publishing it works effectively the pictures on the front pages sell more copies while the economy of fashion, the dresses themselves rather than the images of the dresses on the page, tells a different story altogether.

The fashion pages are also increasingly art or exhibition spaces. The same photographers work for the glossy, more commercial magazines as for *The Face* and *i-D* and they bring similar values to both, even if they are forced to make some compromises with their own creativity for *Marie Claire, Elle* or even *Vogue* (although *Vogue* has always championed strong art direction). Whether these are narrative features where the pictures tell a story and create a particular visual effect, or whether the emphasis is on the relation of text to image as news or information, the aim is to create an aesthetic effect. A fashion feature centres around the visual image and it is this surplus of visuality, 'spreading' out all over the pages, which has attracted the critical attention of feminist cultural theorists who have seen these spaces also as sites for fantasy and female visual pleasure. This is important, usually psychoanalytically informed work. But its exclusive focus on the fashion spectacle reinforces the wider cultural emphasis on the image. The sexual politics of the page produce a kind of sociological amnesia as if nobody was employed to produce the pages or to create the clothes.

Power of the Editors

I have argued that fashion journalism is a peculiarly unchanging kind of practice. The forms or 'slots' for fashion coverage are narrow and restricted. Fashion stories tend to fit one of the following types: first, the designer or company profile or interview; second, the reports from the collections; third, the fashion spread or 'centrefold'; fourth, the consumer-oriented feature (for example, *Marie Claire's* influential '100 Best Buys'); and, fifth, the single item feature (the 'new' fitted silk shirt). These genres regulate the flow of fashion knowledge and also create a relatively self-contained world of image where text is a subordinate feature. It is on this basis that fashion meanings are constructed. It was *Vogue* magazine which in the early years of the century established these rules of fashion reporting. Other magazines followed suit and also provided advertisers with the wider readership they required. The key figures in this world were the fashion editors, both feared and adulated, with dominating personalities who ruled the world of fashion and were also patrons to both the designers and the photographers. The history of fashion magazines is full of such legendary characters. The spectacular figure of Diana Vreeland, dramatically configured in old age with raven black hair cut into a bob and scarlet lipstick, and contributor to and editor of American *Vogue* from 1940-71, was the most influential of these figures and fashion editors since then have almost inevitably acknowledged the importance of her editorial style and sought to emulate the avant garde aspects of this style in their own practice. In particular, they have inherited the *Vogue* rhetoric which simply asserts the overwhelming importance of fashion as an unquestionable truth and, with this, women's love of luxury as the embodiment of femininity. As Billen has recently said: '*Vogue* delivers such an elevated version of an already elevated lifestyle.

This image of the fashion editor as a powerful and influential figure, an icon of glamour and a patron of the arts, continues to influence the practice of fashion journalism today. The emphasis on status and hierarchy is important as the editors have to fight to be taken seriously outside their own territory. Women s magazines and glossy fashion magazines have always been quite separate from the broader field of journalism. As a place of employment this is a woman's world, in the same way that fashion education in the art schools has also been dominated by a series of strong and influential women. And, for all these reasons, women's magazine journalism, including fashion journalism, occupies a much lower status than many other forms of journalism. Most male journalists consider it lightweight, trivial, entertainment, domestic and consumer-based and, as a result, it is hard for journalists working in this area to move outwards into other fields, particularly news or feature writing for the press or for television. This induces a sense of isolation and inferiority which makes the fashion world all the more brittle and defensive, more self-contained and concerned with its own status and importance than might otherwise be the case. It is not surprising that everybody knows everybody else and although there is a high degree of labour mobility it is very much within the same field. Lacking the broad cultural capital of the Oxbridge-educated journalist, few fashion journalists ever find themselves moving across different specialisms on a newspaper as staff journalists are still expected to do. No fashion editor ever moves to a general editorship in the press or television, and it is rare for a beauty editor to move away from her field. While many of the journalists who write features for the new men's magazines also cross over into the wider media (Tony Parsons is a critic for *The Late Review* on BBC2, for example), this is primarily because what makes the men s magazine market different is the coverage of a wider range of material than their female counterparts. Sports, politics, music, even literature, all command more space in *FHM, GQ* and *Arena* than they do in *Marie Claire, Elle* or *Vogue*. 'But we are fashion' is how the editors would respond to this point. Yet because they are too concerned with fashion images and too little concerned with the fashion industry, it is actually qualified support that the fashion editors provide for the fashion industry. What they do is much narrower. They set the agendas for the look that will be promoted each season. They go to the shows and sift through all the work shown on the catwalk and presented to them in the smaller studios to decide which designers to feature and which looks to promote. This conforms with the gatekeeping role of editors across the different forms of media. They have the power to select one story and veto others. In fashion the editors play a hands-on role. Glenda Bailey, editor of *Marie Claire,* said in interview that she always had the final say on the fashion pages because, as she put it, they were so central to the image of the magazine as a whole:

We sit round after the collections, with the team, and have an ideas session. We've already done our predictions and our own forecasting. That's where the training comes in. We have this sense of what the designers are going to be doing and usually we're right. Good fashion fits with the way society is going, and that s what we also pick up on. It's my decision in the end. I have to take that responsibility and thank goodness it's worked so well. We do our own research through the magazine twice a year and ask the readers to give comments on every article, including all the fashion features, and there is often no surprise I find that my theories are the same as what the research shows.

Glenda Bailey also described her commitment to showing the work of British designers:

> *The great thing about Britain and the art schools is that they do encourage eccentricity and individuality. It's all so connected with youth culture and working-class life and the greyness of Manchester and that kind of thing. It's also because we encourage people to fight against things. In my first year at Kingston, John Richmond and Helen Storey were my-hero and heroine. They fought against all the rules and discipline.*

These are the terms in which the editors express their support for British fashion. It's a championing role and one which also emphasises, as Glenda Bailey does here, the 'eccentricity' of the British designers. But this merely confirms the image of the designers who must be bad at business if they are good at design. We have already seen how one editor arranged for a stockist to take a few items from the collection of Yvette M. and Lisa R. so that she could feature them in her magazine. If an editor really believes in an up and coming designer she will often go to great lengths to help them gain a foothold in the industry. This can also extend to the role of 'patron'. It is widely recognised that for all the right reasons the exeditor of British *Vogue,* Anna Wintour, acted in this role on behalf of John Galliano. She took him to parties and introduced him to businessmen who might be potential 'backers', she advised him and supported him as a friend and gave him space in *Vogue*. Inevitably this helped him gain the post he now holds as chief designer for Dior in Paris.

This kind of support then sets a whole set of gendered relations in motion where Galliano becomes the editors' favourite and, as we have already seen, gets more coverage than all the other United Kingdom designers put together. This form of patronage is quite unique to fashion and is very much the product of it being an enclosed, culturally anxious and virtually self-regulating world where notions of objectivity and impartiality do not have the same impact as they do elsewhere in journalism. Indeed, because they adhere to traditional 'high culture' values the editors would possibly see this role as patron of the arts as a kind of philanthropy, a way of helping the poor, starving artist to achieve the success which he deserves. This is another sign of how old fashioned and conservative fashion editors are. This role of patron is, in fact, far removed from the way in which contemporary artists define their own role. Most of them would angrily reject the idea of patron as a throwback to the eighteenth century. Anna Wintour's patronage of John Galliano reveals the extent to which fashion imagines itself to be following the rules of high culture, while in fact it is quite out of touch with the contemporary politics of art. While this might work as a kind of camp comedy, a means by which fashion gently pokes fun at itself, this is also one of the ways by which the mostly gay 'fashion boys' find themselves the darlings of the editors and journalists. In the emotionally charged world of the catwalk shows, the passionate relations between the gay, male designers and their female journalist followers (recently parodied in BBC television s *Absolutely Fabulous*) finds the female designers squeezed out of this particular fashion circuit.

Bourdieu provides an interesting account of this positioning of critics and commentators close to the artist. He argues that as a cultural practice develops, its commentators position themselves more and more closely with the creative figures at the centre, in this case the designers. The writing and reporting is often produced more for them than it is for the readers or for the public, while at the same time this activity in effect writes the creator into being, almost bringing him or her to life. As he puts it, they 'create the creators'. By this means, the critics also feel as if they can share something of the aura of the artist they have earned their place in the sun and they can bask in the warm light. In this respect 'the discourse about the work is not mere accompaniment, but a stage in the production of the work'. Bourdieu also says 'Words, names, schools...are so important only because they make things'. This process clearly happens in the world of fashion where a few key figures can shape the career of an equally tiny number of designers to begin a snowball effect, so that within some period of time the artist, designer or whoever it is at the centre, becomes a household name. This is exactly what happened with John Galliano, less so with Westwood and McQueen, but still enough to make this threesome now representative of the summation of British talent. My point here is that although Bourdieu is right and this process occurs across the artistic field, the art critic does painting and fine art the service of writing seriously about it. The analysis and commentary, directed as it may be at the artist, performs a role in producing criticism. This is an altogether different activity from being a fashion editor/patron and simply enthusing about or publicising certain designers.

If we take into account this individualising process which produces the designers as simultaneously eccentric artists and also part of the celebrity world of popular culture, we can see the dangers as fashion becomes more and more reliant upon media hype and whatever is new or up and coming, including the designers themselves. As Sally Brampton said in June 1994, unusually for an editor, 'the irresponsible thing is that the fashion press has a voracious appetite for novelty.' This means that the editors and journalists have priorities which appear to promote United Kingdom fashion but which in fact also contribute to its problems. The instant negation of the recent past ('say goodbye to this summer s chiffon frills and move into something much sharper'), the forgetfulness about last year's successful designers, as well as the increasing pace of fashion coverage set by the global media which means that the designers themselves have to run to keep up, are not necessarily good news for the stars of last year or the previous year, nor is it much help to the designers who cannot afford to put on a show or to pay a good public relations company. Like the music industry, a good deal of journalism is increasingly PR driven. Just as the record company will jet out a planeful of journalists to Los Angeles to meet Meat Loaf, wining and dining them in the process in the expectation of a good review, the big fashion companies have huge budgets for the launch of a new line or even simply a new collection. The opening of a 'flagship' store will result in editors and journalists being inundated with invites and the promise of interviews. Indeed, it is just this kind of promotion (including a glittering party) which resulted in the feature described earlier on Alberta Ferretti. The article coincided with the opening of a new and exclusive store on Sloane Street in London.

The smallness of the world I have just described and the feeling of being marginalised from other fields lessens the possibility of a more open and critical form of journalism. Where a new book or film, or a new record or play can be panned by the critics, it is very different in fashion. It is not unusual for editors who have published even mildly critical reports about a new collection (along the lines of

'Lacroix was disappointing') to find themselves barred from entrance and deprived of an invitation the following season. The shows are where the editors do their groundwork and they have to be able to see these one-off events. If filing poor copy means that they won't be invited back, this at least influences what they say. The designers can get away with it because, after all, they are 'artists' and they can be as temperamental as they like. This reliance upon keeping 'in' with the designers means that editors back down from covering even a news item which might cast the designer in a poor light. I was told by the fashion editor of a daily broadsheet that it would be 'more than my job is worth' to cover a story which suggested that one of the leading American designers was using cheap, exploited labour to manufacture her clothes, even though this story came from reliable sources and had already surfaced in the American press. The response was similar when I suggested a story myself about what happens when United Kingdom designers are forced out of business. The reason given for the first issue was that this editor might at some point in the future need to do an interview with the American designer and would not want to find herself refused and, for the second issue of designers going out of business, she did not want to be seen giving poor publicity to the British fashion industry!

There are other factors which shape the nature of fashion coverage. The growth of the star system and its connections with the wider world of show business and entertainment means that editors focus more on international fashion and on *haute couture* because it is where the good stories (including expensive press packs, luxury lunches, flagship opening parties) are. Their commitment to promoting British fashion needs then to be set alongside the competition from the big brand names such as Calvin Klein, Donna Karan and the Italian designers, all of whom can afford the kind of publicity stunts and perks which are beyond the wildest dreams of any single British designer. As this trend begins to set the pace for fashion coverage, and as the haute couture collections begin to show at different times across the year (rather than on the traditional seasonal basis) the British designers find themselves squeezed into the London Fashion Week or into the low seasons or quiet times for the fashion press (for example, mid-summer or mid-winter). The increasing prominence of the brand names also has the effect of isolating and marginalising the United Kingdom designers.

International designer clothes might well be beyond the reach of most consumers but they also provide images which will surface on the high street soon after the shows. There is no longer the long wait for the high street versions to eventually arrive in shops as high street retailers can now make use of high technology batch production, or simply the proximity of the local labour market, to rapidly produce cheaper copies so that what is on the catwalk one week can be in Miss Selfridge a few weeks later. The fashion media play a role in orchestrating this connection through their high profile reports on all the shows. In- house designers at Kookai, Warehouse or French Connection only have to read the papers to see what they should be concentrating on over the next few weeks. With all the power and resources of international *haute couture* on the one hand, and the high street on the other, the British designers begin to look less exciting. They cannot command the same kind of attention unless they themselves have moved into this international fashion circuit. The cottage industry of United Kingdom design finds itself in competition with multinational companies and huge corporations such as Donna Karan and Calvin Klein. The small scale designers fade away from the spotlight and the catwalk, and it is the European houses (all subsidiaries of giant corporations) which hand pick one or two people a year to provide a frisson of celebrity; for example, Stella McCartney s move to Chloé in Paris to replace Karl Lagerfeld, 16 April 1997; novelty (McQueen at Givenchy) or glamour and eccentricity.

Summary

The relation between fashion design and the fashion media is one of dislocation and unevenness. The media might be a pillar of support but this does not mean that the gossamer slips and the silky summer dresses won't slide to a crumpled heap on the ground every so often. This is not the fault of the fashion media it is after all an image industry and for the editors the priority is not the designers but their own consumers, the readers who buy the magazines. While the editors claim that their readers are the type of people who want to buy the clothes found on their pages, they are not really thinking about actual sales. These clothes play a symbolic role in the fantasies and aspirations of the reader. The fashion pages are fantasy spaces through which the reader is free to wander, but there is nothing there that pushes her in the direction of the shops. Instead, the images and the meanings attributed to them, produce taste groups within the over-arching concept of the readership. The taste groups are also produced for the benefit of the advertisers. So, as Sean Nixon writing on the growth of the new men's magazines argues, the fashion magazines serve a double function of providing advertisers with the right kind of visual and textual environment for their products (in the case of the fashion magazines, a luxury, 'glossy' environment, rather like an upmarket department store) and they also create for the advertisers a'shaped up' group of consumers. Nixon shows how effective this has been in the promotion of a range of male products including jeans and male toiletries.

However, this model does not have the same direct applicability when we look at the women's fashion media and fashion design. There is no one-to-one relationship because the fashion spreads are not advertisements and the designers cannot afford to advertise themselves. Even with a good public relations company, when and where the designers clothes get featured is something of a hit and miss affair. Neither is there any guarantee that coverage will generate sales, especially if the item can barely be seen. In short, this is not how women's magazines work. Fashion on the page is there to be looked at and a whole range of activities intervene before this process of looking leads to the concrete act of purchasing. There is no necessary relation between the play of pleasure, tension and anxiety in looking and the very different social relations of consumption.

The fashion magazines and the fashion press operate within an economy of looking. They also produce distinct cultural values which feed directly into the formation of taste groups for the broader consumer culture. The editors provide the advertisers with an appropriate visual environment within which they can insert their own copy. So the visual pleasures of the fashion pages are actually used indirectly to sell other products such as perfume, make up, shoes, bags, in fact all the goods whose market size allows them to pay for expensive advertising space. And, once again, the fashion industry, particularly the small, independent British fashion design industry comes off worse. As far as fashion is concerned it is difFicult to avoid coming to a Baudrillardian conclusion about the economy of the image replacing and even negating the economy of the actual product . But the apparent imbalance which exists between the success of British fashion as an image industry, and fashion design as a straggling, crisisridden sector, can also be explained in more sociological terms. There are two interlocking economic circuits in operation in this field, one belongs to the ever expanding world of the image and of visual culture, to which vast numbers of people have access at relatively little cost, while the other belongs to the world of making things and selling them within a highly competitive market, where small producers (that is, the designers) find it almost impossible to sell their clothes cheap enough to attract a wider section of the market (because of the power of the big retailers and the numerous agents in the fashion chain who each take their cut). The balance is tilted in favour of the fashion media which is not just a publicity machine for the designers (a selective one at that) but also, in effect, a market in its own right, a first port of call for up-and-coming designers. This picture is complicated further by the role of the image industries as a *de facto* market for the designers, anxious to establish a name for themselves independent of, or prior to sales.

However, with all these advantages the fashion media remain none the less unadventurous and trapped in a format which came into being when fashion was an exclusively female and 'society', or upper-class, interest. The history of Vogue magazine reveals a lineage of *grande dame* editors most of whom were unashamedly élitist in their desire to create a luxury magazine for well-to-do readers. These editors did a great deal to bring fashion design into prominence as an art. They achieved this partly by treating key fashion designers as creative geniuses; they also provided the space in which fashion photography was able to establish itself and this, too, was celebrated as a branch of modern art. Since then this tradition has been taken as the canon of fashion journalism. The editor of *Vogue* magazine occupies the best seat at all the shows and her power and influence are undisputed. Because fashion feels itself to occupy an inferior place in high culture and also in the world of serious journalism, and because it does not really want to be associated with mass culture, (in just the same way as it does it utmost to dissociate itself from mass production), this creates an inward-looking and culturally isolated group of fashion media professionals who seem to belong to a time when politics did not intrude upon the world of fashion and when fashion people had no need to dirty their hands with what went on in the outside world. There are residues of this kind of thinking across the fashion media, in particular an insistence on the irrelevance of social or political issues. This is expressed in different ways according to the different media. For example, while I am sure that Sheryl Garrett, the editor of *The Face,* would recognise the importance of sexual politics in fashion, (including those which involve work and employment), and while Edward Enningful of *i-D* as a young Ghanaian living in Britain, would, like Garrett, want to bring to bear some elements of contemporary political reality on the magazines, these can only be conceived of as gestures of style and they can never take the form of a social analysis. Everything within these magazines has to be translated into a kind of secret, insider knowledge about what is 'cool' and 'hip' to which only they, as editors and journalists, have access and which they can then sell to the big companies in exchange for valuable advertising revenue by providing them with knowledge of 'the street' and of black youth culture and urban life.

In the more mainstream women's fashion magazines there is an even stronger reliance upon tradition. Fashion writing is informative or celebratory, it is never critical, only mildly ironical. Nowhere does it ever touch upon some of the most important dynamics in contemporary British fashion which hinge around fashion as a place of work and as a space of livelihoods. The editors and journalists rarely break ranks and produce more engaged and challenging writing on this subject.

This, in turn, keeps them isolated and away from those policy makers and politicians who are anxious to see the fashion industry become more stable and more profitable and give a better return on the investment made in education and training. The fashion media thus secures the marginalised, trivial image of fashion as though it cannot be bothered to take itself seriously or to consider its own conditions of existence. The excuse is invariably that this kind of material frightens both readers and advertisers. Yet, as women and girls become more highly educated and as the fashion sector is increasingly recognised as an important part of the national economy, this seems like an increasingly ill-considered stance. It only serves to keep fashion journalism in the ghetto of femininity, whilst in almost every other sector of public life femininity and gender issues are increasingly coming to occupy the political centre stage.

BIBLIOGRAPHY

ANGUS, I. (1989), 'Circumscribing Postmodern Culture', in I. Angus and S. Jhally (eds), *Cultural Politics in Contemporary America,* London: Routledge.

AYNSLEY, J. (1993), *Nationalism and Internationalism: Design in the Twentieth Century,* London, V&A.

BAILEY, R. (1992) 'Clothes Encounters of the Gynecological Kind: Medical Mandates and Maternity Modes', in R. Barnes and J. B. Eicher (eds), *Dress and Gender: Making amd Meaning.* Oxford: Berg.

BALLARD, B. (1960), *In my Fashion,* London, Seeker and Warburg.

BARANSKI, Z.G. and LUMLEY, R. (eds) (1990), Culture *and Conflict in* Post-War *Italy: Essays on Mass* and *Popular Culture,* London, Macmillan.

BECKER, J. and KHIPPING, F. (eds) (1986), *Power in Europe: Great Britain, France, Italy, and Germany in a Postwar World 1945–50,* Berlin and New York, De Gruyter.

BELL, Q. (1976), *On Human Finery,* rev. edn., London, Hogarth.

CAMPBELL, C. (1995), 'The sociology of consumption', in Miller, D. (ed.), *Acknowledging Consumption,* London: Routledge.

CAMPBELL, C. (1996), 'The meaning of objects and the meaning of actions', *Journal of Material Culture,* 1 (1): 93–105.

CARLYLE, T. (1888), *Sartor Resartus,* London, Chapman and Hall.

DALY, M. C. (1999), 'Ah, A Real Kalabari Woman!: Reflexivity and the Conceptualization of Appearance', *Fashion Theory* 3 (3): 343–61.

DALY, M. C. (1984), *Kalabari Female Appearance and the Tradition of Iria,* Unpublished Ph.D. dissertation, Minneapolis: University of Minnesota.

DALY, M. C., EICHER, J.B., and EREKOSIMA, T.V. (1986, May), 'Male and Female Artistry in Kalabari Dress', *African Arts 19* (3): 48–51, 83.

DE LA HAYE, A. (ed.) (1997), *The Cutting Edge: 50 Years of British Fashion 1947 1997*, London, V&A.

EICHER, J.B. and EREKOSIMA, T.V. (1987), 'Kalabari Funerals: Celebration and Display', *African Arts 21* (1): 38–45, 87.

EICHER, J.B. and EREKOSIMA, T.V. (1992), 'Textile, Trade and Masquerade among the Kalabari of Nigeria', 9th Triennial Symposium of African Arts, 21–25 April, Iowa City, IA.

EICHER,J.B. (1981), 'Influences of Changing Resources on Clothing, Textiles and the Quality of Life: Dressing for Reality, Fun, and Fantasy', *Combined Proceedings, Association of Clothing Professors of Textiles and Clothing*: 36–41.

FINKELSTEIN, J. (1991), *The Fashioned Self,* Cambridge, Polity.

FLUGEL, J.C. (1950), *The Psychology of Clothes,* London, Hogarth.

FONTANA, M. (1991), *Specchio a Tre Luci,* Turin, NuovaEri.

FORGACS, D. (1990), *Culture in the Industrial Era 1880–1980: Cultural Industries, Politics and the Public,* Manchester, Manchester University Press.

GANDEE, C. (November 1999) '1960s: photographer David Bailey revisits Swinging London', *Vogue*: 540.

GARBER, M. (1992), *Vested Interests: Cross-Dressing and Cultural Anxiety,* London, Penguin Books.

GASTEL, M. (1995), *50 Anni di Moda Italiana: Breve Storia del Pret-a-Porter,* Milan, Domino/ Avallardi.

GINSBORG, P. (1990), *A History of Contemporary Italy: Society and Politics 1943 88,* London, Penguin.

GIORDAN! ARAGNO, B. (ed.) (1988), *Moda Italia: Creativita e Tecnologia alia Sistema della Moda Italiana,* Milan, Domus.

GRAHAM, PAULA (1995), 'Girl's camp? The politics of parody', in Wilton, T. (ed.), *Immortal Invisible: Lesbians and the moving image,* London: Routledge

GRAMSCI, A. (1971), *Sections from the Prison Notebooks,* London, Lawrence and

GROSS, M. (1995), *Model: The Ugly Business of Beautiful Women,* New York: William Morrow, 1995.

GROSZ, E. (1995), *Space, Time and Perversion,* New York: Routledge.

GUNDLE, S. (1996), 'The Arericanisation of Daily Life: Television and Consumerism in Italy in the 1950s', *Italian Culture and Society,* 2.

HANDLIN, O. (1959), *Immigration as a Factor in American History,* New Jersey, Prentice Hall.

HARPER, J. (1986), *America and the Reconstruction of Italy 1945–8,* Cambridge, Cambridge University Press.

HARRISON, M. (1991), *Appearances: Fashion Photography Since 1945,* New York: Rizzolli.

HARRISON, M. (1994), *Outside Fashion: Style and Subversion,* New York: Howard Greenberg Gallery.

HARRISON, M. (1999), *David Bailey: The Birth of Cool: 1957–1969,* New York: Viking Studio.

HEIDEGGER, M. (1971),'The Origin of the Work of Art' in *Poetry, Language, Thought,* trans. Hofstadter, A., New York, Harper Row.

HOBSBAUM, E.J. (1990), *Nation and Nationalism since 1780: Programme, Myth, and Reality,* Cambridge, Cambridge University Press (second edition).

HOGAN, M. (1987), *The Marshall Plan: America, Britain and the Reconstruction of Western Europe, 1947–1952,* Cambridge, Cambridge University Press.

JACKSON, L. (1998), *The Sixties: Decade of Design Revolution,* London: Phaidon.

KODA, H., MARTIN, R. and SINDERBRAND, L. (eds) (1987), *Three Women: Madeleine Vionnet, Claire McCardell and Rei Kawakubo,* New York, FIT.

LAVER, J. (1966), *Dress* 2nd ed., London, John Murray.

LEBOURHIS, K., RLoci, S. and Settiirbrini, L. (1996), *Emilio Pucci: Looking at Fashion,* Florence, Skira.

LEOPOLD, E. (1993), 'The Manufacture of the Fashion System', in J. Ash, E. Wilson (eds), *Chic Thrills: A Fashion Reader,* Berkeley, CA: University of California Press; 101–17.

LIATRA PONTI, L. (1990), *GLo Ponti: the Ccrcplete Work 1923–1978*, London, Thames and Hudson.

MASSONI, LUIGI, (ed.) (1986), *ffede in Italy*, Milan, Mondadori.

MEIKLE, J. (1979), *Twentieth Century Limited: Industrial Design in America, 1925 39*, Philadelphia, Terrple.

RADICE, B. (1993), *Ettore Sottsass: a Critical Biography*, London, Thames and Hudson.

RENNOLDS MILIANK, C. (1989), *New York Fashion: the Evolution of American Style*, New York, Abrams.

RICCI, S. (ed.) (1995), *Salvatore Ferragamo: the Art of the Shoe*, Milan, Mondadori.

VERGANI, G. (1992), *la Sala Bianca: the Birth of Italian Fashion*, Milan, Electa.

WALKER, J. (1989), *Design History and the History of Design*, London, Pluto.

Index

D

E